CREATIVE HOMEOWNER®

ULTIMATE GUIDE TO

Fences, Arbors, and Trellises

PLAN ▪ DESIGN ▪ BUILD

CREATIVE HOMEOWNER® Upper Saddle River, New Jersey

64355
ULTIMATE

ULTIMATE GUIDE TO FENCES, ARBORS, AND TRELLISES

MANAGING EDITOR	Fran Donegan
GRAPHIC DESIGNER	Kathryn Wityk
WRITER AND TECHNICAL ASSISTANCE	Steve Willson
TRELLIS AND ARBOR PROJECTS	Bill Hylton
PLANT TEXT	Miranda Smith
PHOTO RESEARCHER	Robyn Poplasky
JUNIOR EDITOR	Jennifer Calvert
INDEXER	Schroeder Indexing Services
COVER DESIGN	Kathryn Wityk
ILLUSTRATIONS	Glee Barre, Michael Gellatly, Frank Rohrbach
FRONT COVER PHOTOGRAPHY	Brian Vanden Brink
BACK COVER PHOTOGRAPHY	(top) Walter Chandoha; (bottom left and right) Freeze Frame Studios; (center) Donna Chiarelli

CREATIVE HOMEOWNER

VICE PRESIDENT AND PUBLISHER	Timothy O. Bakke
PRODUCTION DIRECTOR	Kimberly H. Vivas
ART DIRECTOR	David Geer
MANAGING EDITOR	Fran J. Donegan

Current Printing (last digit)
10 9 8 7 6 5 4 3 2 1

Ultimate Guide to Fences, Arbors, and Trellises
Library of Congress Control Number: 2007933859
ISBN-10: 1-58011-390-7
ISBN-13: 978-1-58011-390-8

CREATIVE HOMEOWNER®
A Division of Federal Marketing Corp.
24 Park Way
Upper Saddle River, NJ 07458
www.creativehomeowner.com

METRIC EQUIVALENTS

Length
1 inch	25.4mm
1 foot	0.3048m
1 yard	0.9144m
1 mile	1.61km

Area
1 square inch	645mm²
1 square foot	0.0929m²
1 square yard	0.8361m²
1 acre	4046.86m²
1 square mile	2.59km²

Volume
1 cubic inch	16.3870cm³
1 cubic foot	0.03m³
1 cubic yard	0.77m³

Common Lumber Equivalents
Sizes: Metric cross sections are so close to their U.S. sizes, as noted below, that for most purposes they may be considered equivalents.

Dimensional lumber	1 x 2	19 x 38mm
	1 x 4	19 x 89mm
	2 x 2	38 x 38mm
	2 x 4	38 x 89mm
	2 x 6	38 x 140mm
	2 x 8	38 x 184mm
	2 x 10	38 x 235mm
	2 x 12	38 x 286mm
Sheet sizes	4 x 8 ft.	1200 x 2400mm
	4 x 10 ft.	1200 x 3000mm
Sheet thicknesses	¼ in.	6mm
	⅜ in.	9mm
	½ in.	12mm
	¾ in.	19 mm
Stud/joist spacing	16 in. o.c.	400mm o.c.
	24 in. o.c.	600mm o.c.

Capacity
1 fluid ounce	29.57mL
1 pint	473.18mL
1 quart	0.95L
1 gallon	3.79L

Weight
1 ounce	28.35g
1 pound	0.45kg

Temperature
Fahrenheit = Celsius x 1.8 + 32
Celsius = Fahrenheit - 32 x ⁵⁄₉

Nail Size & Length
Penny Size	Nail Length
2d	1"
3d	1¼"
4d	1½"
5d	1¾"
6d	2"
7d	2¼"
8d	2½"
9d	2¾"
10d	3"
12d	3¼"
16d	3½"

safety

Although the methods in this book have been reviewed for safety, it is not possible to overstate the importance of using the safest methods you can. What follows are reminders—some do's and don'ts of work safety—to use along with your common sense.

- Always use caution, care, and good judgment when following the procedures described in this book.
- Always be sure that the electrical setup is safe, that no circuit is overloaded, and that all power tools and outlets are properly grounded. Do not use power tools in wet locations.
- Always read container labels on paints, solvents, and other products; provide ventilation; and observe all other warnings.
- Always read the manufacturer's instructions for using a tool, especially the warnings.
- Use hold-downs and push sticks whenever possible when working on a table saw. Avoid working short pieces if you can.
- Always remove the key from any drill chuck (portable or press) before starting the drill.
- Always pay deliberate attention to how a tool works so that you can avoid being injured.
- Always know the limitations of your tools. Do not try to force them to do what they were not designed to do.
- Always make sure that any adjustment is locked before proceeding. For example, always check the rip fence on a table saw or the bevel adjustment on a portable saw before starting to work.
- Always clamp small pieces to a bench or other work surface when using a power tool.
- Always wear the appropriate rubber gloves or work gloves when handling chemicals, moving or stacking lumber, working with concrete, or doing heavy construction.
- Always wear a disposable face mask when you create dust by sawing or sanding. Use a special filtering respirator when working with toxic substances and solvents.
- Always wear eye protection, especially when using power tools or striking metal on metal or concrete; a chip can fly off, for example, when chiseling concrete.
- Never work while wearing loose clothing, open cuffs, or jewelry; tie back long hair.
- Always be aware that there is seldom enough time for your body's reflexes to save you from injury from a power tool in a dangerous situation; everything happens too fast. Be alert!
- Always keep your hands away from the business ends of blades, cutters, and bits.
- Always hold a circular saw firmly, usually with both hands.
- Always use a drill with an auxiliary handle to control the torque when using large-size bits.
- Always check your local building codes when planning new construction. The codes are intended to protect public safety and should be observed to the letter.
- Never work with power tools when you are tired or when under the influence of alcohol or drugs.
- Never cut tiny pieces of wood or pipe using a power saw. When you need a small piece, saw it from a securely clamped longer piece.
- Never change a saw blade or a drill or router bit unless the power cord is unplugged. Do not depend on the switch being off. You might accidentally hit it.
- Never work in insufficient lighting.
- Never work with dull tools. Have them sharpened, or learn how to sharpen them yourself.
- Never use a power tool on a workpiece—large or small—that is not firmly supported.
- Never saw a workpiece that spans a large distance between horses without close support on each side of the cut; the piece can bend, closing on and jamming the blade, causing saw kickback.
- When sawing, never support a workpiece from underneath with your leg or other part of your body.
- Never carry sharp or pointed tools, such as utility knives, awls, or chisels, in your pocket. If you want to carry any of these tools, use a special-purpose tool belt that has leather pockets and holders.

contents

INTRODUCTION

vertical landscaping

When planning a new landscape, or if you simply want to improve the look of your yard, don't forget the vertical elements—the fences, arbors, and trellises—that add structure to the overall design. *Ultimate Guide to Fences, Arbors, and Trellises* takes you through the process of designing, placing, and building those components. You will find them to be handy for enclosing spaces, serving as a base for plants, and as focal points in your yard.

FENCES AND GATES

Fences started out as strictly utilitarian structures designed to either keep people and animals out of a space or to keep them from wandering away. While many of today's fences provide the same functions, most modern fences are built for their looks as well. The *Ultimate Guide to Fences, Arbors, and Trellises* covers all types of fences and gates. Beginning with site design and the tools and materials you will need to build professional-quality fences, the book shows how to design and construct a number of popular fences, including traditional wood picket, split-rail, chain-link, and metal fences. There are also sections on lattice-top, privacy, and maintenance-free vinyl fences. In addition to step-by-step photographs and informative illustrations to lead you through the building process, a number of photographs of existing fences provide inspiration for making a new fence or gate part of your landscape.

Distinctive designs, right and opposite, turn fences, arbors, and trellises into focal points.

ARBORS AND TRELLISES

For a real design boost, consider adding a new arbor or trellis to your landscape. These structures are not only focal points in their own right, but they function as bases for climbing vines and other plants. Chapter 14, beginning on page 258, provides information for selecting the best plants for trellises and arbors.

But before you start picking plants, look at the distinctive projects in chapters 12 and 13, pages 160 and 218 respectively. These cover everything from a simple fan trellis that is a staple of traditional gardens to contemporary custom designs that will make your landscape stand out. The projects offer something for all skill levels, from easy-to-build wall trellises to more challenging trellises and arbors that incorporate benches, exotic woods, and distinctive details.

GUIDE TO SKILL LEVEL

 Easy. Even for beginners.

 Challenging. Can be done by beginners who have the patience and willingness to learn.

 Difficult. Can be handled by most experienced do-it-yourselfers who have mastered basic construction skills. Consider consulting a specialist.

1 site planning

Building any structure on your property will change the appearance of what surrounds it. This is especially true of major projects like a fence, an arbor, or a trellis. Because of this it makes good sense to do plenty of advance planning. Your local building department will demand some of this prior to issuing a building permit. But even if you live in an area where a permit is not required, planning ahead will help protect the value of your property. In fact, if you do a good job, these landscape components can actually increase the value of your home by more than the cost of building them. Remember to choose a design that is in keeping with the architecture of your house and the feel of your neighborhood. And make sure you know where any underground utilities are before beginning work.

DESIGN OPTIONS

Before you start digging fence holes, bear in mind that building codes and zoning ordinances do not always favor a homeowner's desire for privacy, at least not when it comes to outdoor spaces.

In many areas there are rules about building any permanent structure close to your property line and about height restrictions on a fence no matter where you build it. Some areas (mainly in zones with old or historic buildings) even have restrictions on what materials and colors you can use.

There are exceptions to every rule. But the official version, called a variance, can be a drawn-out and difficult process. You may have to submit multiple copies of your plans to the building department or planning board, post notices, and attend public meetings where neighbors can object to your fence design or location.

If you're looking for privacy or protection from street noise, you could opt for a dense line of trees and shrubs. An interlocking line of foliage does a good job of screening out sights and sounds. But unless you spend thousands for mature plantings, you'll have to wait years for the natural fence to fill in.

Filling between Posts

Solid walls can create outdoor rooms nearly as private as the ones inside. You can make them out of bricks or blocks and face them in stucco or stone. But their great weight requires a masonry foundation, which means heavy-duty excavation and concrete work before you start on the wall.

It's much easier to build a screening fence anchored by 4x4 posts every 6 to 8 feet. The posts can support rails and a series of boards, slats, lattice, or pickets to form either a partial screen or a full screen that shields an outdoor space.

The covering on the basic fence frame is the most adjustable part of the design. You can select different types of wood and different widths, set the boards at angles, and increase or decrease the spacing between boards. Each change has a different effect on the overall appearance of the fence and on the amount of wind protection, shade, and privacy.

Even if you have a particular type of wood and fence pattern in mind, take the time to clamp a few boards in place to be sure that the spacing gives you the desired degree of privacy.

Fence Fillers

Once you have erected and braced the basic structural grid of posts and rails, you can add a variety of screening fillers. There are so many options that it's best to experiment. For example, you could tack vertical slats between the top and bottom connectors or horizontal slats between posts.

The screening boards could be set plumb or diagonal and very close together for the most privacy or farther

 LAYOUT

To visualize your fence plan, measure out from the house or nearby lot boundaries to establish straight lines.

You can mark the layout with chalk or use a long extension cord that you can adjust to mark different plans.

WIND

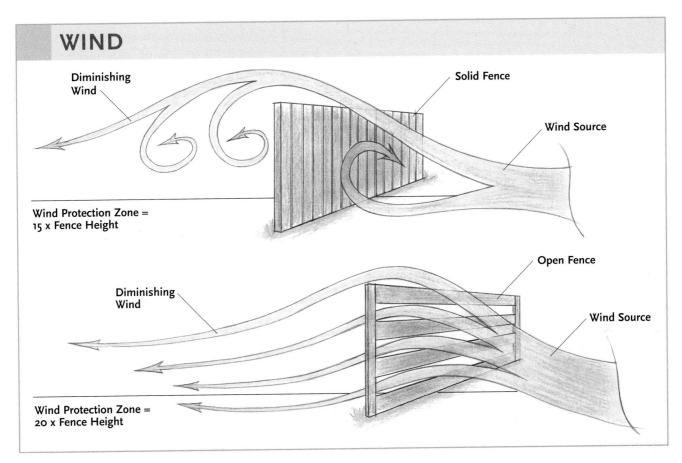

Diminishing Wind

Solid Fence

Wind Source

Wind Protection Zone =
15 x Fence Height

Open Fence

Diminishing Wind

Wind Source

Wind Protection Zone =
20 x Fence Height

SUN AND SHADE

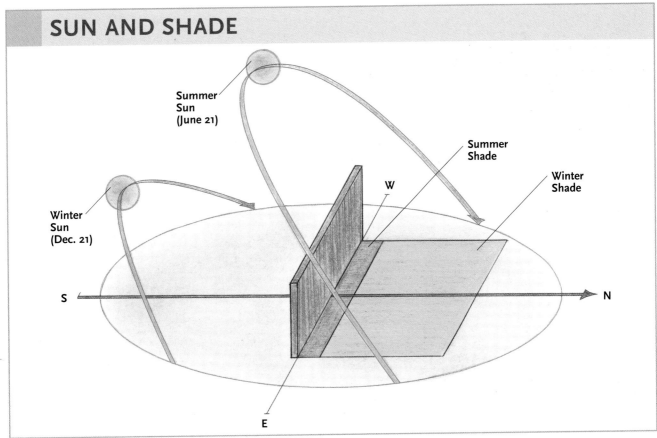

Summer Sun (June 21)

Summer Shade

Winter Shade

Winter Sun (Dec. 21)

W

S

N

E

apart in a sun-drenched yard to let in more breeze or preserve more of the view.

If privacy fences were adjustable (like the strips of glass in a jalousie window), you could adjust the slats to match the degree of privacy you wanted. And, in theory, you could build such a fence, using jalousie hardware mounted on the sides of the posts fitted with thin wooden slats instead of glass.

The Degree of Privacy

You can start with a very open design using one of the fence boards as a spacer between the components. Leaving gaps that are wider than a board generally has a marginal effect. Then try sliding the pieces closer together, leaving gaps that are about half as wide as the width of each board.

Also experiment with different patterns. Try setting boards on the diagonal or even in a V-pattern between the posts. You can use lumber ranging from 1x2s to 1x6s, generally with one size but also in combinations of sizes.

Although the installation is more time consuming, you can install boards at an angle so that from one side of the yard you would see the faces head on. From that vantage point, the boards would appear to be overlapped, creating complete privacy. But from the opposite side of the yard you would see only the narrow edges of the boards and through the spaces between them, creating only a partial screen.

If possible, also experiment with the effects of moving the fence toward or away from the area you want to protect. This can alter the overall sense of privacy as much as the space you leave between boards.

In general, the closer you are to the fence, the easier it is to see through it. The view may be interrupted by fence components, but it's easy to assemble the fragmented views into a comprehensive picture. The farther you are from the fence, the harder it is to see what's happening behind it. So if you want to preserve your long-range view, a good design would use an open board pattern in a fence built close to the private area but far from the nearest vantage point.

The best approach is to try several plans, tacking the boards with finishing nails and observing the effects of different angles and spacing from different areas of the yard. You can sketch out different plans on paper, but trial and error is the best way to find the best balance between openness and seclusion.

 ## CUTTING AND SHAPING BOARDS

Decorative fences with unusual crisscross shapes, curves, and cutouts can look spectacular. But woodworking time can mushroom when you have to create the decorative details again and again on every board. In general, it's wise to use stock-size lumber and make cuts to length using a circular saw (below left). If you do want to add accents, such as a cutout in a picket, make a template or holding jig that allows you to mass-produce the detail without measuring from scratch each time. Curves take the most time because you have to cut them with a saber saw (below right). To create a contour on many components, cut one, check to make sure it fits properly, and save the piece to use as a cutting template.

● ANGLE EFFECT

Minimum Privacy

Moderate Privacy

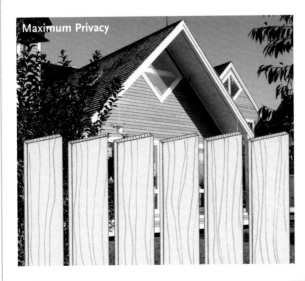
Maximum Privacy

● SPACING EFFECT

Minimum Privacy

Moderate Privacy

Maximum Privacy

DRAINAGE PROBLEMS

If possible, observe what happens in your yard during a heavy rain. Note any existing drainage problems and determine how these problems might affect the location of fences. Also consider how the fence will change drainage patterns in the yard.

Both the type of soil and the shape of the ground influence drainage patterns in your yard. Generally, good drainage means that your lot will shed water in a heavy rain and not retain puddles in low spots. Sandy soils drain well; heavy clay soils drain poorly. Contours on the lot determine where the water will drain and collect during heavy rainstorms. The water table (natural water level in the soil) also influences drainage; if the table is high, it won't take much rain to cause flooding. If you have drainage problems on your property, determine how they will affect the fence you plan to build. Then, ask yourself what kind of drainage the project requires.

Drainage for Fences

Even if your lot drains well, consider how a new structure will alter the drainage patterns. For example, fence kickboards can block water flow, flooding the area on the uphill side. One method of handling this drainage problem is to create a shallow ditch or swale to direct runoff away from the fence. In most cases, swales have gently sloping sides and often are lined with stones or concrete to prevent erosion. Very shallow swales can be planted with grass or other ground covers or ivy.

Avoiding Frost Heave

In areas subject to harsh winters, wet, fine-grained soils undergo a condition called "frost heave," in which alter-

Even low fences need to be structurally sound, which includes anchoring them with posts set in concrete. The concrete helps prevent frost heave, the freezing and thawing of the soil, that could lead to damage to the fence structure.

nate freezing and thawing causes the soil to shift, often with damaging results to any structure built on it. In severe cases, frost heave will push fence posts up, weakening the fence structure.

Where frost heave is a problem, fence posts must be set in holes with a gravel subbase that extends below the frost line. The frost line is the area below which frost doesn't penetrate in a typical winter. In areas where the frost line extends below 36 inches, consult your local building department for commonly accepted excavation practices that may save you from digging to China.

Even in areas where frost heave is not a problem, good drainage is required around fences to avoid damage to these structures. Moisture magnifies ground movement and creates erosion that will make fences sink, lean or crack; poor drainage around wood fence posts also causes rot. Gravel and sand are used to provide good drainage.

CODES AND ORDINANCES

Before you get too far along with your plans, contact your local planning council or building department to see what building codes, zoning laws, and city ordinances affect the size, design, and location of the intended fence. Most urban and suburban communities have fence-height laws — typically a maximum of 72 inches for boundary fences in back and side yards, and 36 or 48

caution

WHEN PLANNING GRADING AND DRAINAGE, AVOID DIRECTING RUNOFF INTO YOUR NEIGHBORS' YARDS. IN MOST AREAS, DRAINAGE PATTERNS IN YOUR YARD ARE, OR SHOULD BE, PART OF A LARGER DRAINAGE SCHEME FOR THE ENTIRE NEIGHBORHOOD. BE AWARE OF HOW PROPOSED LANDSCAPING CHANGES ON YOUR PROPERTY AFFECT THE OVERALL PICTURE.

inches for fences bordering the street or sidewalk. In some communities, you may be able to exceed the maximum fence height if the top portion is made of wire, lattice, or other open work. If not, you can use trees or shrubs to provide privacy.

In addition to height restrictions, codes may stipulate setbacks and easements, which require that structures be built a certain distance from the street, sidewalk or property line. This is especially true if you're erecting the fence on a corner lot, where it could create a "blind corner" at a street intersection or sharp bend in the road. Usually front-yard fences more than 36 to 48 inches high must be set back a certain distance from the sidewalk; fences more than 72 inches high usually must be set back from side and rear property lines. Check local codes.

Never assume that other fences in your neighborhood meet local codes and ordinances. If you see a design that you particularly like, you might ask the owners if there are any plans for it or where they bought the materials. You might also ask permission to reproduce the design. How-

avoiding frost heave

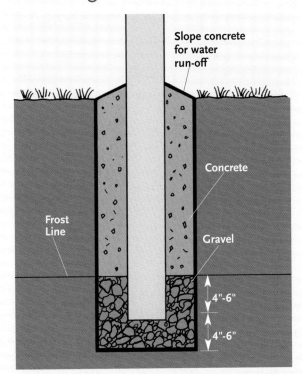

In areas subject to frost heave, dig postholes below the frost line, fill the first 4 to 6 inches with crushed stone, set the post, add more stone, and then pour a concrete collar. Slope the top for drainage.

WORKING WITH PROFESSIONALS

If your existing lot has serious drainage problems, or if you suspect that a fence will significantly affect drainage patterns in your yard, you should consider hiring a landscape architect, landscape designer, or soils engineer to calculate grading and drainage requirements. If large amounts of soil must be moved, or extensive trenches dug for subsurface drainage, you should hire a landscape contractor.

Design help. If you are unsure of the style of fence or its location, it can help to hire a landscape architect or designer to review your plans. Most do consulting work on an hourly basis, and the money will be well-spent if the professional catches errors or omissions in the plan, points out problems you may not have considered, or recommends a more cost-efficient way to build the project.

Because fencing contractors specialize in their trade and have the equipment and crew to get the job done quickly and efficiently, you might save money by hiring a fencing contractor. Most have a portfolio of their work or can show you various jobs they've done in your area. They can build the fence to your design specifications and offer advice on details that would improve the design.

Typically, when hiring any contractor, you sign a contract that specifies what work will be done and the time frame in which it will be completed.

Project management. If you plan to do a lot of the work yourself, you may opt just to hire a carpenter, mason, handyman, general laborer, or even an able-bodied college student to help you with the labor on an hourly basis. Preferably, the individual you hire should carry his own personal liability insurance; otherwise such insurance is the responsibility of the homeowner.

If you have friends or neighbors helping with the work, check with your homeowner's policy to determine the limit of your liability coverage. Also remember that children like to play on piles of dirt, stacks of boards, and in wet cement. Keep the working area off limits, and make sure you are insured against lawsuits for injury if someone is hurt while in or around your construction area.

Some building codes restrict the height of fences that can be seen from the street. Be sure to check with local building officials before starting work on your fence. Local covenants may ban certain fence materials.

Locating Utilities

Before you start digging postholes, you must know the exact locations and depth of underground utility lines. These include water and sewer lines, as well as buried gas, electrical, and phone lines. After you've located the lines that service your own house, don't assume that more don't exist. In many housing tracts, utility companies have gained the right-of-way along front or back property lines for major underground power cables, water mains, cable TV service, or fiber-optic phone transmission lines. If you accidentally break a major phone line, TV cable, or water main while digging, you could be liable for thousands of dollars worth of damage. If you hit a major power line, the consequences could be fatal.

Utility companies often will locate underground utilities free of charge. Underground utilities servicing your house (water, gas, sewer, and electric) may be indicated

ever, before you begin construction, check that the design conforms to guidelines set by your building department. In some cases, you'll need to get a building permit and arrange for one or more building inspections.

Check to see if there are any neighborhood covenants or restrictions that govern the style of fence. In some neighborhoods, homeowners' associations have gained the legal right to dictate what type of structure you can erect, what materials you can use, and even what colors you can paint it. Such restrictions are designed to maintain the architectural character of the neighborhood. Also, if your house has some historical significance in the community or is in a neighborhood designated as a historical area, you may have to get your plans approved by a local architectural review board to make sure the fence design is appropriate.

If your plans conflict with local zoning ordinances, you can apply for a variance: a permit or waiver to build a structure that does not adhere strictly to local property use laws. When you apply for the variance, there's usually a fee and often a public hearing where neighbors and others involved can express their opinions. When you present your plans to the zoning commission for review, you must prove to them that you have a valid reason for requesting the variance. Even if you go through the entire process, there's no guarantee that you will be granted a variance. It's a lot easier just to keep your design within the limits of local zoning laws.

locating utilities

WARNING:

UNDERGROUND CABLE

DO NOT DIG

Before you dig postholes, ask the local utility company to check for buried water mains, electrical cables, gas lines, etc. The inspector will flag the location of any buried utility lines with a marker similar to the one pictured here.

on the original deed map or site plan for your property. If your home was built recently, the local building department may have a record of utility hookup locations on your property. If your home is older, additional lines may have been added in previous remodels or landscaping jobs.

If you are uncertain where such lines exist within your property, hire a private wire/pipe/cable locating firm. These firms are listed in the yellow pages of your phone book under the heading "Utilities Underground Cable, Pipe, & Wire Locating Service" or similar heading. These services usually charge by the hour; a good firm can trace and mark all underground utilities on an average-size residential lot within one or two hours.

PROPERTY LINE FENCES: KNOW WHERE TO DRAW THE LINE

You need to know the exact location of the property line before you build a fence to mark it. If your fence is just 1 inch on your neighbor's side of the line, you might have to tear down the fence or face a lawsuit. In many newer subdivisions, the original survey stakes (usually a marked metal rod or wood stake driven in the ground at each corner of the property) may still be in place. If they are, show them to your neighbors and have them agree in writing that these stakes represent the actual boundaries. If you can't locate the stakes or

think they may have been moved from their original position, hire a surveyor to relocate and mark the property lines, and file a record of the survey with the county. Although a simple survey of a residential tract lot can cost a few hundred dollars, it is cheap insurance against future boundary disputes, especially if you're sinking thousands of dollars into your landscape project.

Be a good neighbor. Most property fences are centered directly on the property line. In this case, no matter who builds the structure, both you and your adjoining neighbors legally own it (the portion facing their yard) as tenants in common. This means that your neighbors can do what they want to their side of the fence—grow vines on it, paint wild murals on it or hang their laundry on it—anything short of actually damaging or tearing down the structure.

The best course of action is to inform the neighbors of your plans and enlist their cooperation, if pos-

sible. Then try to come up with a design that satisfies all parties involved. With traditional board fences, it's customary (though not legally required) to build the fence so that the board side, not the frame side, faces the neighbor's property. However, there are a variety of "good neighbor" designs that look equally good from both sides. As additional insurance, you can make a written, notarized agreement with adjoining property owners that confirms the location of the property line, the type of fence that will be built on it, and who is responsible for building and maintaining it.

If you reach an impasse with any neighbor, simply build the fence 12 inches on your side of the property line. Then you can build anything you want without the neighbor's permission or cooperation, as long as the structure meets local codes and ordinances. Bear in mind that you'll be totally responsible for maintaining the fence. But it is best to follow this course only as a last resort.

making a site plan

Now that you've got a better idea of what fences can do both functionally and architecturally, it's time to organize your thoughts by drawing a detailed site plan of your yard. This drawing forces you to think out your intentions and will save time and money when you integrate future projects into the overall scheme. When it comes time to build the fence, you can use the plan to help estimate materials. Even if you are hiring a landscape architect, the site plan will help you communicate your needs and desires.

The idea is simple: you start with a base map of the property that includes property lines, the house, and all other existing features. Then you use tracing-paper overlays—as many as you want—to sketch your ideas. Allot spaces within the yard for such features as lawns, planting beds, decks, patios, play areas, and storage areas. Then determine where fences, gates, and trellises will be needed. When you come up with a plan you like, you can make a final drawing of the site plan. Here's how to proceed:

Draw the base map. If you have an existing deed map or site plan of your property, reproduce it exactly on a large piece of tracing paper that has graph lines on it (available at stationary shops or art supply stores). For large landscape projects, draw the entire property; show its overall dimensions, its orientation (relative to North), the location of the house, and setback distances and easements from property lines, buildings, and the street. For small landscape projects, such as a backyard, just draw the portion of the property where the fence will go.

The base map should also show your house's floor plan. If you have architect's blueprints of your house, use these to show interior rooms and the location of doors and windows.

If the original site plan or blueprints aren't available, take careful measurements of the property and transfer these to a large sheet of graph-lined tracing paper. A scale of $\frac{1}{4}$ inch equals 12 inches or $\frac{1}{8}$ inch equals 12 inches should enable you to put the entire plan on one sheet. Measure from the property lines to locate a front corner of the house. Use this corner as a starting point to measure the outside dimensions of the house and transfer them to the plan.

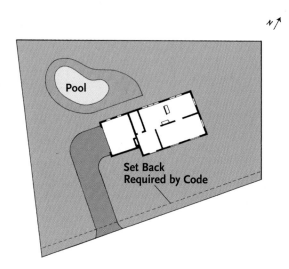

1 Use the original site plan to draw a base map showing the shape and size of the lot, the location of the house, and its floor plan. Show other major features, such as a driveway or pool, and the direction of North.

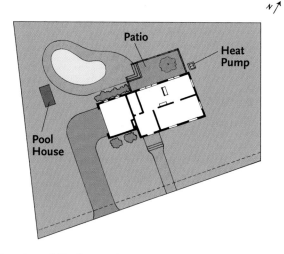

2 Add to the base map other significant details of the lot, such as large trees and shrubs, walks, patios, and outbuildings.

Locate additional features. On the base map, show the location of other buildings and permanent structures on the property, such as existing walks, walls, fences, detached garage, storage sheds, decks, patios, and the like. Show the location of underground utility lines, pipes and cables. Draw in the size and location of existing plantings, such as trees, hedges, and shrubs, as well as lawn areas, planting beds, and borders. Indicate which trees and shrubs are to be kept and which will need to be removed or relocated.

Show other factors that affect the yard. On the base map, indicate the direction of prevailing winds, and existing sun/shade patterns in the yard (direction of morning and afternoon sun). Note the existing drainage patterns, along with any outside factors that affect the yard, such as noise or privacy problems, and views that you want to retain or obscure. If you find that the base map is becoming too cluttered, you can show these features on a separate overlay attached to the map.

Locate new features on overlays. Attach an overlay of tracing paper to the base map. Draw in the exact sizes and locations of new fences, along with any other proposed landscape features. Note the heights and construction materials on the overlay. If the lot will require extensive regrading, the building department may want to see spot elevations of the lot on the final plans. This work is best left to a surveyor or landscape architect. Use as many overlay sheets as needed to come up with a suitable plan. Now is the time to experiment. When you conceive a final plan, place the overlay sheet(s) underneath the base map and neatly trace in the new features on the base map. This will be your final drawing that you will submit to the building department when you apply for a permit (if necessary).

Note: As an alternative to drawing a site plan, there are a variety of computer programs you can buy that will serve the same purpose. Some of these landscape-planning programs allow you to view your yard in three dimensions and from all angles, enabling you to "walk through" the yard on your computer screen. Others include plant lists to help you select plantings.

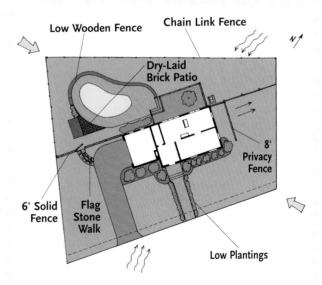

3 Complete the base map by indicating the direction of morning and afternoon sun, prevailing summer and winter winds, and views you wish to preserve or eliminate.

4 With the base map complete, attach separate sheets of tracing paper showing the proposed landscape, including the locations of fences, gates, trellises, and other structures.

2 tools & materials for fences

There are four things you need to build a fence, arbor, or other outdoor project. You'll start your project by deciding where to put the new fence. Then you will have to decide if you will be doing the work or hiring someone to do it. The third and fourth items deal with the materials and tools you will use—the subjects of this chapter. Pressure-treated southern yellow pine is generally the preferred material (with Douglas fir, cedar, and redwood used much less frequently). But you also have the option of constructing your fence of metal or vinyl. Many of the tools you'll need may already be part of your toolbox. You can rent some of the larger tools for the project.

LAYOUT AND EXCAVATION

A basic collection of rulers, squares, and levels should serve on a typical fence, arbor, or trellis project. Note that it always helps to follow the adage "Measure twice and cut once," particularly when it can save an extra trip to the lumberyard for more wood.

For measuring, you can use a classic carpenter's fold-out ruler or a measuring tape. The fold-out variety takes a little time to open and close, but some models have a handy pull-out extension that makes it easy to take accurate inside dimensions.

To square up measurements for cutting, use a combination square on smaller boards and a framing square on sheet materials. But you can also check for square by measuring the diagonals between posts. They should be equal if the posts are square.

Another trick that's good for corners is to use the proportions of a 3-4-5 triangle. If one leg is 3 feet long, another is 4 feet long, and the hypotenuse is 5 feet long, the angle between the two legs will be 90 degrees. The 3-4-5 system works at any scale.

MARKING BOARDS

Combination squares mark straight, square lines.

Sliding T-bevels mark and transfer odd angles.

LAYOUT TOOLS

Measuring Tape

Framing Square

Combination Square

Sliding T-Bevel

Try Square

Speed Square

Plumb Bob

Chalk Line

EXCAVATION TOOLS

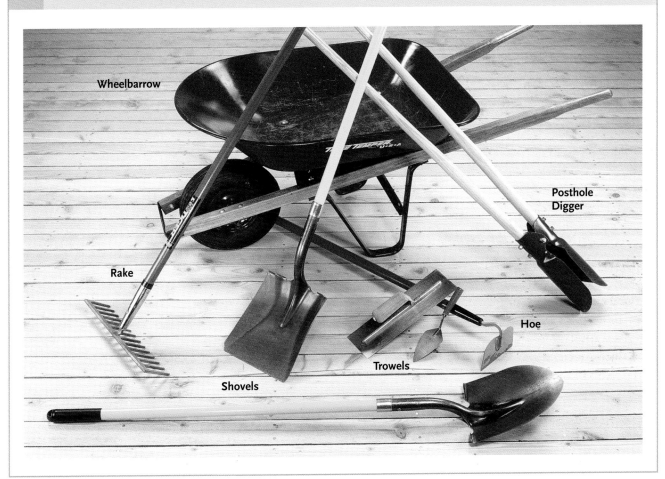

Wheelbarrow

Posthole Digger

Rake

Hoe

Trowels

Shovels

● WATER LEVEL

One of the simplest and most inexpensive tools used in landscaping work, a water level is also one of the most practical and accurate. It works just as well as an exotic laser level but uses only water and requires no special handling or calibration. The tool consists of a length of clear plastic tubing. It can be as long as you need it to be and can run up and down over rough terrain between posts. The red color in the tube (right) comes from dye that's included in some water-level kits to make it easier to read. Kits also contain clips for holding the tubing. Because water always seeks its own level, once you make sure there are no air bubbles in the line, the water at one end of the tube will be level with water at the other end.

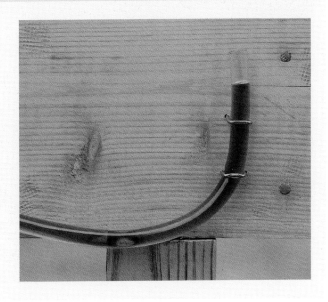

CONSTRUCTION TOOLS

Many do-it-yourselfers already own the basic hand tools required for building fences, arbors, and other outdoor projects. Unless you plan a special application, such as a fence with boards and gates with highly detailed gingerbread trim, you won't need any specialized tools.

But if you are in the process of accumulating how-to tools, consider these general buying guidelines. Naturally, the selection that's right for you depends on the work you want to do, but also on how often you'll use the tools, how expert you are at handling them, and how much you want to spend.

■ **Durability.** Buy better quality in tools you'll use often, such as a hammer and saw, that are basic requirements for building a fence. It's worth a little extra to have a set of chisels with steel-capped heads that stand up better than plastic heads. But don't pay top dollar for heavy-duty contractor tools you'll use only occasionally. Many have features you don't need. And the truth is that inexperienced do-it-yourselfers don't get professional results just by using top-notch tools. For the most part, skill is in the hand that holds them, not in the tools themselves.

■ **Precision.** Stick with basic tools designed to do one job well, and avoid multipurpose gimmick tools that are loaded with bells and whistles. That nine-in-one wrench may be handy in the car glove compartment but not so much on home-improvement projects.

■ **Strength.** Look for hammers, wrenches, pry bars, and other mainly metal tools that are drop-forged instead of cast metal. Casting can trap air bubbles in molten metal, creating weak spots that could cause the metal to fracture under stress. Drop-forging removes more bubbles and makes the metal stronger and safer to use. In general, when manufacturers take the time and money to drop-forge a tool and machine-grind its surface, they leave the fine-grained metal in plain view. Sometimes inferior cast tools are disguised with a coat of paint.

■ **Price.** If in doubt, avoid the most and least expensive models. The top end can have more capacity than you need, and the bottom end often has fundamental flaws that make work difficult—especially for a novice. There are some exceptions, of course. For example, a throwaway brush is fine for slapping some stain on a rough fence post. You don't need a high-quality and high-priced sash paintbrush for the job.

Finally, be sure to wield the tool in the store, checking the feel and comfort, to see whether it seems controllable, too heavy, or too light. If you shop in a large outlet store where there are several brands of the same tool, try one against another.

It can be difficult to compare tools you can't normally test on the spot, such as power saws. But some tools you can test. Before you buy a level, for example, check three or four on the store floor or counter, and stack them on top of each other to see whether one has a bubble that is out of line with the others.

In the end, of course, careful measurements and layouts will do more than top-notch tools to make your project both good-looking and long lasting.

smart tip

MARKING THE SITE FOR UTILITIES

BEFORE YOU START DIGGING HOLES FOR SUPPORT POSTS, CHECK INTO THE LOCATION OF UNDERGROUND UTILITY LINES, SUCH AS A NATURAL GAS MAIN OR A SEWER PIPE. ON A BIG FENCE PROJECT WHERE YOU'RE USING A CONTRACTOR TO DO THE DIGGING, YOU SHOULD MARK THE LOCATIONS OF THESE LINES AHEAD OF TIME TO AVOID AN ACCIDENT. EVEN IF YOU ARE RENTING A PORTABLE POWER AUGER AND DIGGING THE HOLES YOURSELF, YOU CAN'T AFFORD TO ACCIDENTALLY PUNCTURE A GAS LINE OR SHORT OUT UNDERGROUND ELECTRICAL CABLES. LOCAL UTILITY COMPANIES HAVE A RECORD OF THE LOCATIONS, AND IN MANY REGIONS, A UTILITY COMPANY REPRESENTATIVE WILL COME TO THE SITE AND HELP YOU LOCATE UNDERGROUND LINES, SO YOU CAN MARK THEM WITH FLAGS.

HAND TOOLS

FASTENING

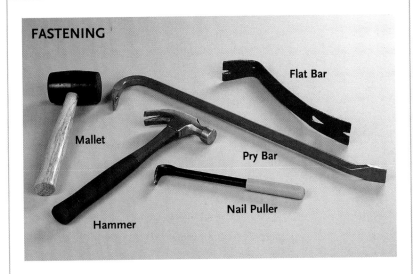

Mallet

Hammer

Flat Bar

Pry Bar

Nail Puller

SHAPING AND SMOOTHING

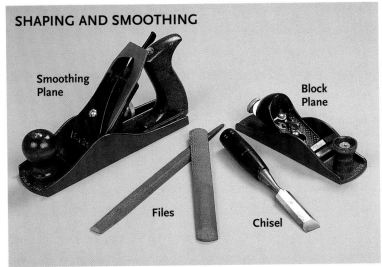

Smoothing Plane

Block Plane

Files

Chisel

LEVELING

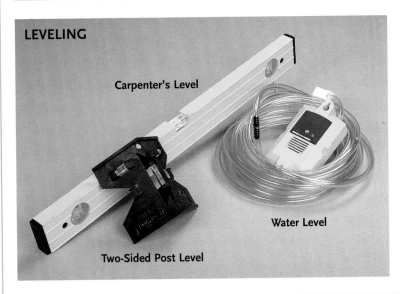

Carpenter's Level

Water Level

Two-Sided Post Level

TRIMMING BOARDS

You don't need to do much trimming and finishing on a rustic project made of rough-sawn boards. But you may need to clean up a few edges on picket styles and other types of decorative fencing. A basic smoothing plane (top) works well on most wood, but to increase your production you can use a power planer (middle). A belt sander (bottom) makes quick work of rough spots and blemishes.

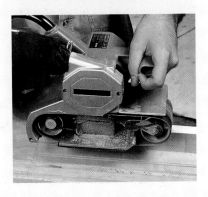

POWER TOOLS AND SAFETY EQUIPMENT

A set of basic power tools will carry you through a typical outdoor project. With a lot of wood to cut, including posts, rails, and boards, you'll probably need a circular saw. The most practical is a standard corded model with a 7½-inch blade.

In remote locations, battery-powered saws (and other tools) will save you the trouble and tangle of extension cords. But on large projects you're likely to deplete the battery fairly quickly by cutting through thick posts. Even the latest battery-powered saws can't handle continuous production cutting as well as a corded saw can. To cut large posts you'll have to get the knack of making two passes from opposing sides because most saws don't have the blade diameter to cut completely through the wood.

To make a neat, nearly seamless combination of cuts, it helps to transfer the cut lines around the post with a combination square. Another option is to bury any rough cuts you make by eye in the ground and set the cleaner, factory-cut ends up.

Whenever possible, it's wise to make repetitive cuts ahead of time. You'll find that it's most economical to shape pickets, post tops, and such in a shop (or at least on stable sawhorses). Make cuts such as angled joints on mating boards in the field.

POWER TOOLS

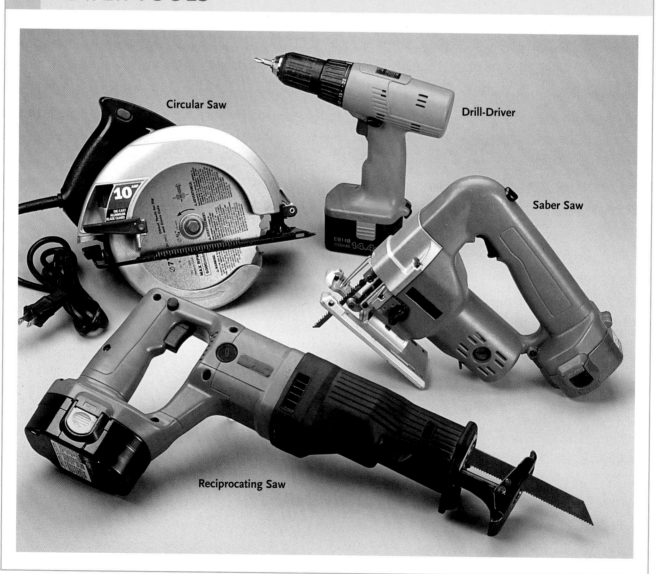

Circular Saw

Drill-Driver

Saber Saw

Reciprocating Saw

PNEUMATIC NAIL GUN

With air-powered nailers you can load many nails in one clip (near right). Then position the tool and squeeze the trigger to drive them (far right). Once you get a feel for the tool, you'll be able to drive nails quickly and accurately, which is handy on a large fence project. And the tools are safe if handled properly. Check into the safety-head feature, which forces you to set the head firmly against the work before the trigger will fire a fastener.

SAFETY EQUIPMENT

Ear Protection

Hard Hat

Rubber Gloves

Respirator

FIRST AID KIT

Safety Glasses

First-Aid Kit

Dust Mask

Ear Protection

Work Gloves

SPECIALTY TOOLS AND TECHNIQUES

Most of the tools you need for outdoor projects are the standards of do-it-yourself carpentry, such as a circular saw, drill, level, and such. But there are a few items that you may not have in the toolbox.

Among the most unusual is a come-along, which is basically a ratchet-controlled winch that allows you to apply and maintain a lot of pressure on posts or fence sections. It's handy when you need to pull a section into plumb position. Most of these tools come with two lengths of metal cable and hooks at the ends. Loop one end around a fence post, and anchor the other end to a large tree or temporary stake. Then you can ratchet increasing tension on the cables.

You also may need more than a standard carpenter's level, which is the most practical tool for plumbing and leveling posts and short lengths of rail. To establish levels over greater distances you'll need string and a line level, or a water level.

When it comes to digging postholes, you have several options. Use a shovel if you're digging only a few holes, or consider a two-handled posthole digger. This tool allows you to dig holes that are not much larger than the posts. With a shovel, you'll have to dig a larger hole and move more dirt. For big projects, rent a gasoline-powered auger.

● USING A COME-ALONG

Come-alongs have cables and hooks that you can loop around a fence section that needs straightening.

Cranking the handle turns a ratchet gear and applies tremendous pulling force through the cables.

● SPECIAL PROTECTION FROM PT CHEMICALS

Most pressure-treated (PT) lumber is made of southern yellow pine that's been treated with chemicals to keep the wood from rotting or being destroyed by insects. Until 2003, the chemical of choice was chromated copper arsenic (CCA). But it was banned that year for residential use and generally replaced with alkaline copper quat (ACQ). This treatment is available in two strengths. "Ground Contact" is created for wood members, like posts, that will be in direct contact with the ground. "Standard Grade" is less durable and is mostly used for decking boards, joists and beams.)

BRACING A POST

Attach an angled 2x4 to a ground stake, and clamp it to the post as you adjust the post into plumb position.

For accuracy, brace the post in two directions with the 2x4s at right angles. Screws make disassembly easy.

DIGGING OPTIONS

Using a shovel is the most basic way to dig piers. But you'll wind up moving more dirt than you need to.

A posthole digger has a scissor action to cut and scoop out dirt. It makes a neater, smaller hole.

You can rent a one- or two-person power auger. They churn through dirt but are a handful to operate.

FASTENERS

Besides common nails, which are the easiest to drive, you can use spiral or rink-shank nails on fence boards for more holding power. Although screws take more time to drive, they have the most holding power by far. A screw's number indicates the diameter of its shank. Common sizes are #6, #8, and #10. Of course, the length for any of these screws can vary. A #8 screw, for example, can be nearly any length up to about 3½ inches. The heavier the gauge, the more likely you are to find it in longer lengths.

You also may want to use large lag screws for making heavy-duty wood-to-wood attachments. Lag screws are heavy-duty screws that you drive with a socket wrench. Lags are sized according to the diameter of their shanks, usually $\frac{5}{16}$, $\frac{3}{8}$, or $\frac{1}{2}$ inch.

You can also use through bolts, mainly carriage bolts, which have unslotted oval heads, for attaching structural lumber face to face, such as large rails to posts. Carriage bolts have a square shoulder just beneath the head that digs into the wood as you tighten the bolt to prevent slipping. They are sized according to the diameter of their shanks as well as their length. You can also secure major joints between rails and posts with framing hardware, such as a U-shaped bracket that can support a heavy rail between posts. To prevent corrosion, hardware should be galvanized.

FASTENERS

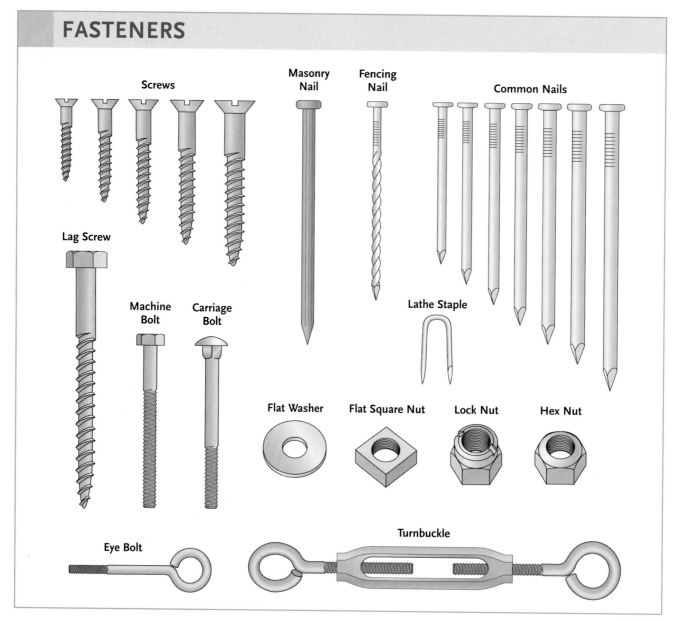

Screws · Masonry Nail · Fencing Nail · Common Nails · Lag Screw · Machine Bolt · Carriage Bolt · Lathe Staple · Flat Washer · Flat Square Nut · Lock Nut · Hex Nut · Eye Bolt · Turnbuckle

POSTS

Many lumberyards stock several types of posts, including round posts and square timbers, generally sized 4x4 or 6x6. The selection may include redwood and cedar but often is limited to rough grades of fir and pressure-treated (PT) wood. PT wood is the most durable because it is infused under pressure with an insecticide and a fungicide to ward off pests and decay. Be sure to observe the warnings of the manufacturer.

6x6 PT

4x4 Fir

PT Round Post

4x4 PT

4x4 Cedar

● TRIM POSTS

Large posts often are beyond the one-cut capacity of do-it-yourself circular saws and may be too thick for standard drill bits. But there are other options. One is to use a chain saw (observing manufacturer's cautions) or a reciprocating saw with a long wood-cutting blade. But most DIYers get by with squaring the cut line around the post and making two passes that meet in the middle (near right). You can follow the same process when drilling holes, or use longer spade-point bits (far right).

BOARD OPTIONS

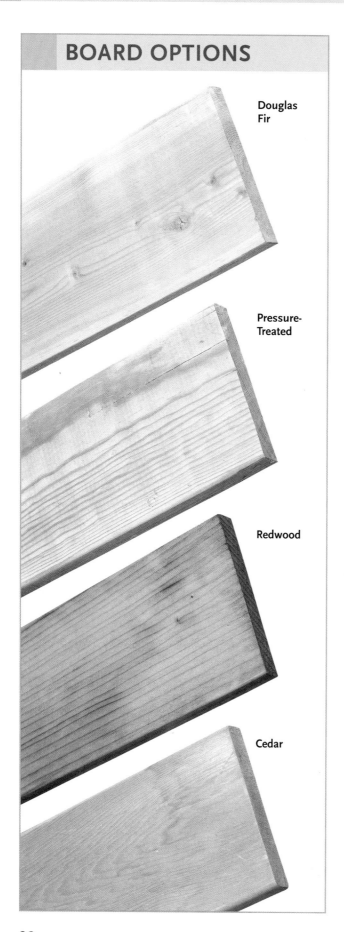

Douglas Fir

Pressure-Treated

Redwood

Cedar

LUMBER

As with any organic material that gains and loses water, wood swells when it is moist and shrinks as it dries. This can lead to warping, checking, bowing, twisting, and cupping. Softwoods like pine, Douglas fir, and cedar are particularly vulnerable. But most of these problems can be avoided by fastening boards securely and supporting them with posts, rails, and braces over their spans.

When it comes to ordering posts, rails, and boards, bear in mind that a piece of lumber has two sizes: nominal and actual. A 2x4 rail may start out at 2x4 inches (its nominal size) when it is cut from a raw log, but it soon

DECAY-RESISTANCE

Redwood and cedar are viable but pricey options to PT wood. Both combine good rot and insect resistance with an elegant appearance and are available in several grades. Less expensive grades with a rougher, saw-textured surface are generally used for fencing.

Redwood

- **Clear All Heart**
  Finest grade heartwood
- **Heart B**
  Limited knots
- **Clear (Sapwood)**
  Some defects
- **B Grade**
  Limited knots

Cedar

- **Clear Heart**
  Exposed wood
- **Grade A Clear**
  Shingles
- **Grade B Clear**
  Fencing
- **Knotty Grades**
  Closets

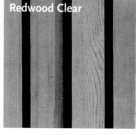
Redwood Clear

Cedar Clear

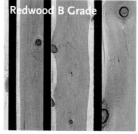
Redwood B Grade

Cedar Grade B

shrinks when it is dried. Then it becomes even smaller when it is planed. A 2x4 soon becomes 1½ x 3½ inches—the lumber's actual size. For wood lengths, the nominal and actual lengths are almost always the same. When you buy a 10-foot 2x4, it is usually 10 feet long and sometimes a bit longer.

Some lumberyards charge for lumber by the board foot, though increasingly yards are charging by the individual stick, or piece of lumber. If your lumberyard charges you by the board foot, here's how to figure it: take the nominal thickness, multiply it by the nominal width and the length, and divide by 12. A 10-foot 2x6 (usually written 2x6x10' in the industry) would be 10 board feet.

smart tip

FASTENERS FOR TREATED WOOD
THERE IS EVIDENCE THAT SOME OF THE NEWER WOOD-TREATMENT CHEMICALS ARE MORE CORROSIVE FOR FASTENERS THAN THE ORIGINAL TREATMENTS FOR PRESSURE-TREATED WOOD. CHECK PRODUCT INFORMATION SHEETS FOR SPECIFIC FASTENER REQUIREMENTS. SOME MANUFACTURERS ARE RECOMMENDING STAINLESS-STEEL NAILS OR SCREWS FOR TREATED LUMBER.

BASIC LUMBER GRADES

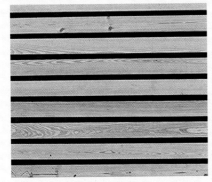 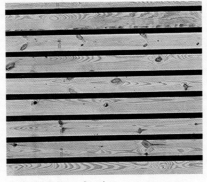 

Number 1 grade has few knots. It's not normally stocked at lumberyards.

Number 2 grade, the most common lumber, has more knots and defects.

Number 3 grade of most lumber species has knots and edge defects.

COMMON LUMBER DEFECTS

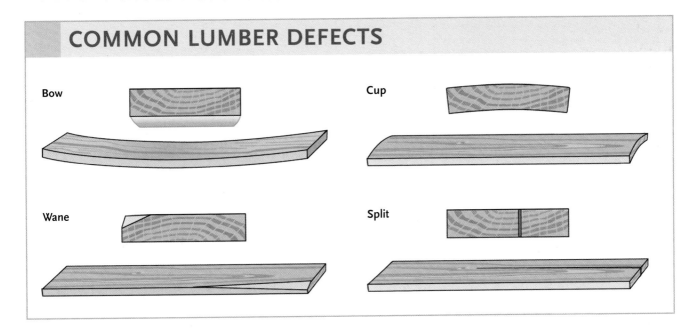

Bow

Cup

Wane

Split

3 fence designs

There are lots of different fence designs out there, from rustic split-rail types to formal privacy structures that are topped with lattice panels and supported with elaborate posts. Generally people choose designs that reflect their tastes. But other considerations also play a role. The first, of course, is the budget. Fences aren't cheap, especially when you add in the maintenance costs. Another factor is the material. Do you want a brick wall, a wood fence, or a maintenance-free vinyl (PVC) structure? And last, the contour of your property and where you want to put the fence on it has to be considered. If the site is flat, you can choose any design you like and can afford. But if the site is sloped, the installation costs go up significantly. And if you want a curved fence, the costs can be even higher.

INSTALLING A POST-AND-RAIL FENCE

The best location for a basic post-and-rail fence is on flat terrain where square (or nearly square) corners can be used. By reviewing the photo sequence here, which includes all the important steps, you can lay out and build a good-looking and long-lasting fence. Also, keep in mind the following tips to get the best results.

A. Use a flexible marking system that allows you to make an accurate layout but does not get in the way during construction.

B. Double-check your corners for square using the 3-4-5 triangulation method. When a fence corner forms a triangle with a 3-foot leg, a 4-foot leg, and a 5-foot hypotenuse, then the corner forms a 90-degree (square) angle.

C. Plan ahead to avoid odd-sized spaces between posts at the end of a run. Make sure you divide the overall length of the fence into equal sections.

D. If you use prefabricated fence panels, locate the posts so the panels will fit snugly between them or butt together on the centerline of each post.

E. Take the time to predrill pilot holes for nails and screws near the ends of boards to prevent splitting.

F. Maintain even spacing between pickets or other fence boards. But as you near a corner, adjust the gaps slightly to make a full board fit as the last board.

TOOLS & MATERIALS
▌ Sledgehammer ▌ Safety glasses
▌ Hammer ▌ Line level and 4-ft. level
▌ Circular saw ▌ Tape measure
▌ Drill and bits ▌ Mason's string
▌ 4x4 posts ▌ 1x2s for stakes ▌ 2x4 rails
▌ 2x4s for batter boards ▌ 1x4 pickets
▌ Nails ▌ 3-in. deck screws

1 Make your posts last longer by applying preservative to the in-ground section, particularly the end grain.

5 Recess the rail by cutting kerfs in the post equal to the depth of the rail. You can recess all or part of the rail. When making the cuts, hold the saw base firmly against the post to prevent accidental kickback.

2 To avoid using braces, one basic approach is to compact the backfill as you plumb the post.

3 Strike a level line across the posts for the lower rail, and drive a temporary nail to mark its place.

4 Set the lower rail on the nails; check again for level; and mark the top and bottom of the rail on all the posts.

6 Use a hammer and chisel to clear away the wood between the kerfs and flatten the base of the recess.

7 Predrill at the ends of boards to reduce the chance of splitting when you drive nails or screws.

(continued on page 38)

(continued from page 37)

8 Recess two faces on corner posts, and either lap the rails or take the time to miter the joint.

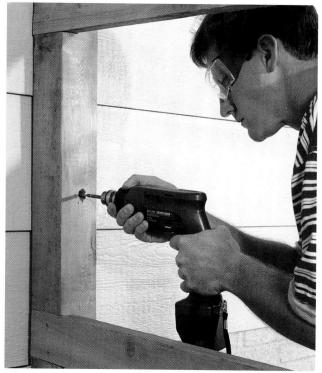

9 Tie posts to the house by counterboring and driving a lag screw long enough to reach into wall framing. If you don't hit a stud, then use toggle bolts instead of lag screws to fasten the post.

10 Speed up picket installation by leveling and installing corners; then attach pickets by using a line strung between posts as a guide. Install the pickets so they fall just below the string instead of touching it.

11 Use a spacer to keep the placement consistent. You can adjust several pickets slightly to fit final boards.

You can vary picket shape, spacing, and length on post-and-rail fences to create a custom design.

You can also vary rail sizes with a lighter rail on top and a larger rail to anchor the fence.

STEPPED FENCES

A stepped fence generally has equally spaced posts but rails that step down the slope between them. It's one of the most basic ways to handle fences on sloping ground. To start with, you need to establish a level line across the slope, using stakes (the downhill being longer), string, and a line level.

You can mark off equal increments on the string and transfer the post locations to the ground with a plumb bob or level held against a straight 2x4.

The most attractive stepped fences have the same step height at the top between sections. To figure out the step height, first you must determine the overall height (rise) of the slope and divide that by the number of sections (the areas between the posts) to determine the size of the step. For example, if the total rise is 48 inches and the fence contains four equal sections, there should be 12-inch-high steps between posts.

It pays to lay out the steps on paper so you can see the length required for each post. In theory, you could cut the posts to length ahead of time. But that generally requires a lot of adjustments when you set them. Most people find it easier to set posts long, lay out the steps, and cut the posts as needed. Bear in mind that a stepped-fence layout is often a compromise. If the steps seem too large, you may have to use more posts, which allows each step to be shorter.

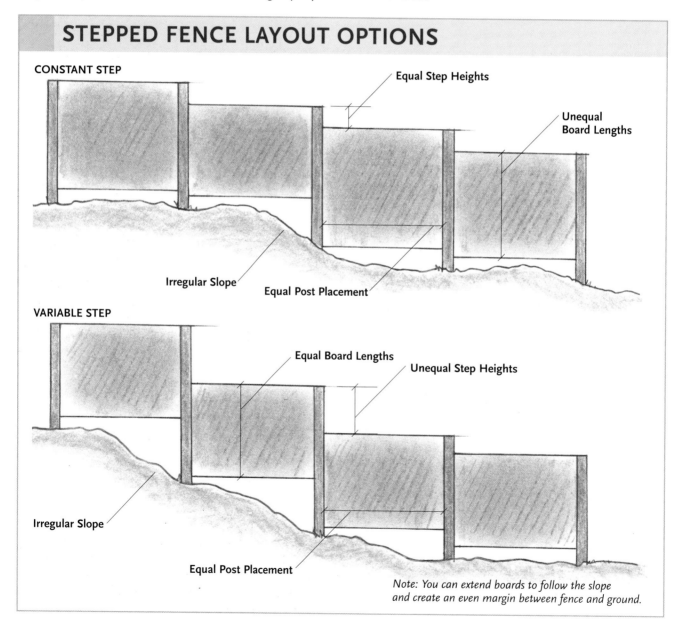

STEPPED FENCE LAYOUT OPTIONS

CONSTANT STEP

Equal Step Heights

Unequal Board Lengths

Irregular Slope

Equal Post Placement

VARIABLE STEP

Equal Board Lengths

Unequal Step Heights

Irregular Slope

Equal Post Placement

Note: You can extend boards to follow the slope and create an even margin between fence and ground.

INSTALLING A STEPPED FENCE

project

Stepped fences can be difficult to build because no piece of rolling property has a perfectly consistent slope. The trick is to make the top of the fence slope symmetrically (see opposite), while the bottom line of the fence boards follows more closely the slope of the ground. In extreme cases, where the steps down can't be equal, use the variable step approach, also shown on the facing page.

TOOLS & MATERIALS
▮ Shovel ▮ Plumb bob ▮ Circular saw
▮ Line level and 2-ft. level
▮ Tape measure ▮ Safety glasses
▮ Mason's string ▮ Long 1x2s ▮ Concrete
▮ 2x4s for batter boards ▮ Spray paint

1 Determine the overall slope of your property before you design your fence. Hold a 2x4 at the bottom of the slope, and install a mason's string near the top. Hook a line level in place, and move the string up or down until it's level.

2 Once the string is level, measure the post intervals along the string. Then transfer these marks to the ground using a lightweight plumb bob. Mark the location with a dot of spray paint.

3 Dig postholes using a hand-operated posthole digger. Or rent a gas-powered auger to drill these holes. Once a hole is complete, slide the post into it, and brace the post in a plumb position before back filling around its base. (continued on page 42)

(continued from page 41)

4 Once the post is braced and backfilled, use a level and a straight 2x4 to mark the step down at each post. Ideally the fence should drop an equal amount from one post to the next.

5 Double-check your post height marks for accuracy; then cut the posts using a circular saw. Wear eye protection, and make sure you have solid footing before turning on the saw.

CONTOUR FENCES

On a contoured fence, the rails run parallel with the slope without steps between posts. The fence follows the contour of the ground. These fences are easier to construct than stepped fences, especially on the uneven slopes of rolling terrain.

You lay out a contour fence the same way you lay out a basic straight fence. But you may need extra stakes to keep a hilly landscape from interfering with the layout lines. When installing posts for contoured fencing, set each post to the same height above the ground, and fasten each rail at the same height along each post so that they follow the contour of the slope. Install picket boards so that they are plumb, rather than perpendicular to the rails. You can extend the boards several inches below the bottom rail, and cut the ends to follow the contour of the ground.

Because sloping rails will be installed at different angles on contoured fence posts, they must be handled differently. The potential problem is most obvious if you make a plumb cut on the end of one rail along a flat section and try to join it with a plumb cut on a sloping rail. The sloped cut will be longer, sometimes significantly longer, creating a ragged, unfinished appearance.

The solution is to mark a cut through the overlapped boards. This splits the difference evenly and creates mating edges of equal size.

The posts are installed so they are plumb and cut to the same finished height to follow the contour of the land.

CONTOUR-FENCE

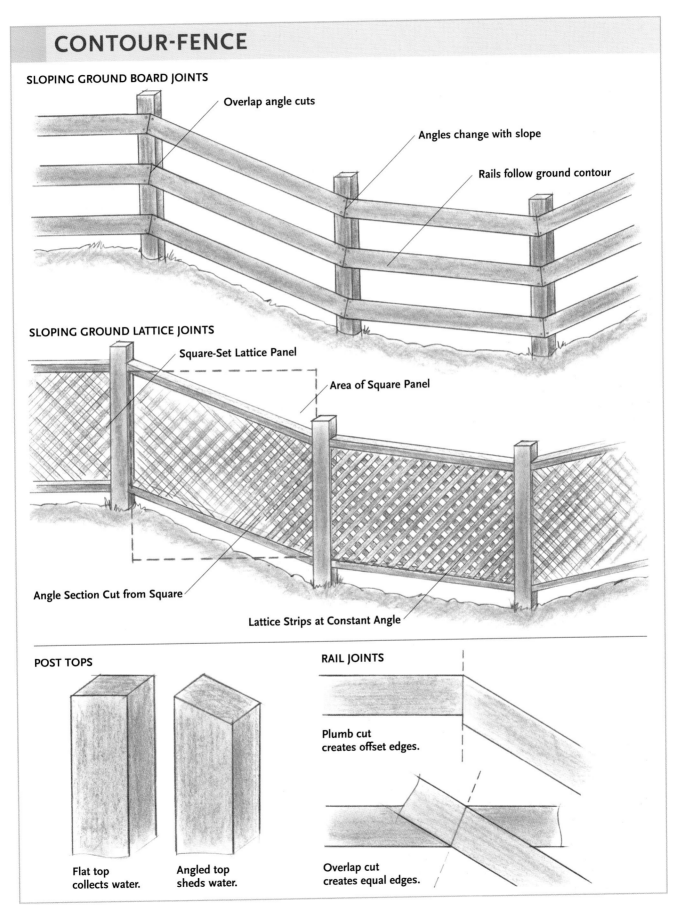

SLOPING GROUND BOARD JOINTS

Overlap angle cuts

Angles change with slope

Rails follow ground contour

SLOPING GROUND LATTICE JOINTS

Square-Set Lattice Panel

Area of Square Panel

Angle Section Cut from Square

Lattice Strips at Constant Angle

POST TOPS

Flat top
collects water.

Angled top
sheds water.

RAIL JOINTS

Plumb cut
creates offset edges.

Overlap cut
creates equal edges.

CURVED FENCES

To build a curved fence, you must set the posts 48 to 72 inches on center along an arc. You can apply either straight or curved rails, depending on the look you are trying to create.

It takes curved rails to make a truly curved fence, but making curved rails is not as difficult as you might think. There are two basic ways to do it. One is to cut saw kerfs in the back of the rail so that it can bend without splitting or breaking. The other is to make the rail out of two separate pieces of 1x4 wood strung across several posts and screwed together to form a laminated rail. The rails must span at least three posts—rails won't form a curve if they span only two. Stagger the joints so that a joint on the top rail is not on the same post as a joint on a bottom rail.

With this approach it helps to soak the rails in water before use to make them more flexible. Attach the first piece to the posts with 3-inch galvanized deck screws, using two screws at each post. Then screw the second piece over the first using 1¼-inch galvanized deck screws, spaced about 8 inches apart. Stagger the screws so that one is near the top of the rail, the other near the bottom.

For tighter arcs, you can laminate thinner strips, called bender boards, or combine the two approaches by adding saw cuts about 1 inch apart to make the boards more flexible. Placing the kerfs on the inside of the curve will help shed water and prevent rot.

Curved fences often look best with narrow, lightweight boards, pickets, or slats attached vertically to the rails. Wide boards may split when attached to curved rails.

If the extra work of kerfing and laminating is too much on your project, consider a segmented fence. Instead of curved rails, you can attach short, straight fence sections to posts plotted along a curve.

This type of construction does not result in a smooth curve. Instead, you get a series of short straight runs that roughly follow an arc. You can smooth the angled edges by mitering the rail ends and the fence boards. Because the rails are straight, you can use wide boards if you want to.

smart tip

ANGLE OPTION

Curves are difficult and time consuming to lay out accurately, and even more so to build. One efficient way around these drawbacks is to create a shallow angle at one post instead of a continuous curve over many posts. You can chamfer the post edges for better bearing or install connecting hardware. Boards can be spaced or mitered. Remember: the closer together you place the posts, the more the fence will resemble an actual contour.

Curved fences can follow natural contours, including around trees.

cutting saw-kerf curves

If you try to bend a 1-inch-thick fence rail, the unnatural stress can cause splits and other problems. To relieve some of the stress and help the board bend, cut a series of half-deep saw-kerfs about every ½ inch on one face of the board (near right). You may want to use a square to help keep your cuts even. As you gradually bend the rail between posts and fasten pickets (far right), the kerfs close up. It's best if you can cover the kerfs with pickets.

PLOTTING A SMOOTH CURVE

1. Find the corner by projecting both fence lines from last post..

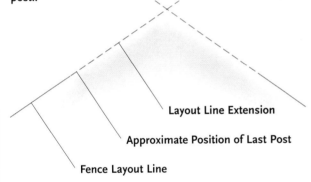

Layout Line Extension

Approximate Position of Last Post

Fence Layout Line

Note: The projected corner does not need to be 90 degrees.

2. Measure from the corner to the tangent points of curve.

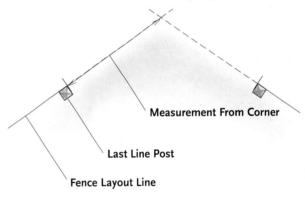

Measurement From Corner

Last Line Post

Fence Layout Line

Note: Larger distances from the corner produce larger arcs.

3. Construct lines perpendicular to the fence line.

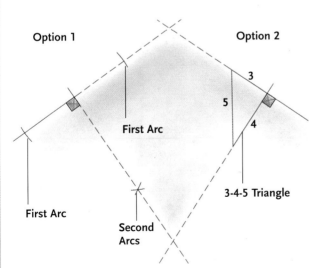

Option 1

Option 2

3

5

4

First Arc

3-4-5 Triangle

First Arc

Second Arcs

4. Drive a stake where the two lines intersect. Attach a line to it that equals the distance between the intersection point and the posts. Then swing a curve from post to post.

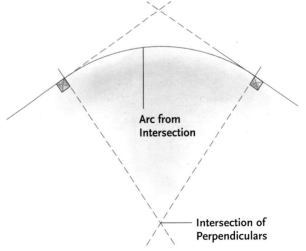

Arc from Intersection

Intersection of Perpendiculars

*Note: **Option 1:** Swing equal arcs to each side of the post, and swing a new arc from each mark. The point where those arcs intersect is perpendicular to the post. **Option 2:** You can instead use 3-4-5 triangulation.*

4 wood fences

Wood fences are popular for several good reasons. The first, and most important one, is that they represent the traditional approach to fence design. Because of this, the default white picket fence can look good next to just about any house. This takes some of the anxiety out of installing an expensive fence only to find out when it's done that it looks terrible. Second, wood can be fabricated into any number of different designs, including the picket, vertical-board, lattice, rustic, and horizontal-board examples shown in this chapter. Building these structures is well within the ability of most do-it-yourselfers, so you needn't deal with contractors to get the job done right. Finally, wood can be finished in a variety of ways, from basic white paint, to stains, to clear finishes that let the wood grain show through.

SETTING POSTS

The first step in building a fence is marking the fence location with stakes and string. Once you've done that, mark post locations along the string with tape, bright-colored chalk, or spray paint. If you're installing the fence on a property line or if the fence must meet certain setback requirements, you'll need to establish the exact location of the line to avoid disputes with neighbors or to make sure the fence meets local ordinances. Once you locate your property lines, mark the corners with surveyor's stakes or other markers.

If you're building a fence within the property, first you'll need to establish the locations of the end posts and corner posts. This is usually done by measuring out from one or more existing reference points, such as the house, the driveway, an existing fence, or other landmarks. If you haven't already done so, draw up a site plan for your project.

In most cases, you can find reliable information in your own records of the house and property. If you have ever built an addition or made major improvements requiring a building permit, chances are that you needed drawings, including a measured site plan.

You also can refer to your survey, which is generally part of any house sale. Another resource is the town clerk or the local tax office. In many areas, there is a record of your property in the town's files that includes the location, general size, and placement of buildings on the site.

After plotting the fence line, you can mark the post locations on the ground, dig the postholes, and install the posts. Once the posts are set, you'll add the rails and fence boards for the particular design you've chosen. If your design calls for you to notch, or dado, the posts, it's easier to do this before setting them. If you haven't chosen a design yet, thumb through the wood fence projects that appear later in this chapter.

As a rule of thumb, fence posts are set with about one-third of their total length in the ground and at a minimum of 24 inches deep. In areas subject to frost heave, it is recommended that you set the bottoms of the posts at least 6 inches below the frost line to avoid heaving. Average frost-depth tables are available from your local building department. It's always a good idea to check local building codes and standard practices in your particular area.

The one-third rule applies especially to gate, end, corner, and any posts that support heavy fence boards. Solid-board or panel fences exposed to high winds may also require deeper posts. However, the rule does not always make the best use of standard precut lumber lengths—a 72-inch-high fence would require a 9-foot post, for example. For this reason, most 72-inch fences can use 96-inch posts sunk 24 inches into the ground. But the end posts, corner posts, and gate posts on such a fence should be the full 9 feet long.

Lightweight pickets, like these, only need support posts every 8 to 10 feet.

POST FOUNDATIONS

Posts are typically set in tamped earth, tamped gravel, or concrete and gravel. But there are many ways to provide support, such as setting a flat stone 4 to 6 inches thick as a footing.

Whether or not you decide to use concrete depends largely on the fence design and soil conditions. Generally, you can use earth-and-gravel fill if the soil is not too loose, sandy, or subject to shifting or frost heaves, and if the fence posts don't have to support much weight. Post-and-board fences, lattice, spaced pickets, or fences less than 60 inches tall are all light enough for earth-and-gravel fill. In extremely loose or sandy soils you can attach 1x4 pressure-treated cleats to the bottoms of the posts to provide lateral stability.

Using Concrete

For added stability, use concrete, especially in areas with deep frost lines. You can even drive 16d nails partially into the post before placing the concrete to lock the post and concrete together.

If precise post spacing is required (such as when dadoing or mortising rails into posts or attaching prefabricated fence panels or sections), you'll need to set the posts successively, fitting in rails or sections as you set each post. Use fast-setting concrete mixes for this type of construction.

There are many ways to set posts in holes. You can pour concrete around the post, plumb and brace it, and attach the rails or panels when the concrete hardens. Many contractors use this approach, but for most do-it-yourselfers, it pays to plumb and brace each post securely before pouring concrete. This system keeps you from disrupting the mix (or dislodging dirt) as you add and adjust the braces. As you fill in successive sections between posts, occasionally recheck the entire fence for plumb.

If you don't use concrete to secure the posts, it's important to compact the backfill you do use, even if it's gravel. The best approach is to add fill-in layers 6 to 12 inches thick. Use a 2x4, or even a 4x4 if you can heft one, to pack down material. This step solidifies the fill around the post.

If you're not sure of local building practices, seek advice from the building department or ask several local fence contractors for recommended practices suited to the ground in your area.

BACKFILL OPTIONS

Fence posts normally are set in one of the four basic ways shown below. Posts deeply embedded in solid, compacted soil may not need a foundation stone if they carry a lightweight fence. But corner posts and posts that support heavy gates, trellises, or other additional structures need the most secure installation.

Earth

Gravel

Gravel and Cleats

Concrete and Gravel

INSTALLING POSTS

project

The hardest part of installing a wood post is digging the hole. If you have soft, sandy soil, then a posthole digger will handle the job. For many posts, a rented power auger will cut the job down to size. But rocky soil is another matter. Using a posthole digger and a 6-foot steel bar to loosen rocks will dig most rocky holes. But it's a lot easier to hire a contractor with a small auger on the back of a tractor to dig these holes.

TOOLS & MATERIALS
- Posthole digger ▪ Hoe ▪ Tape measure
- Trowel ▪ Shovel ▪ Hammer
- Level ▪ Drill-driver ▪ Wood stakes
- String ▪ Braces ▪ Concrete
- Wood posts ▪ Gravel ▪ Spray paint

1 Install layout strings that match the final location of the fence sections. If you want a square corner, make sure that the strings intersect at a 90-deg. angle. Drive a stake at the intersection point to indicate where the corner post should be.

4 Check with your local building department to learn the frost-line depth in your area. Then make sure to excavate 6 in. below this point. If you don't do this, frost heave will move the post up and either distort or break apart the finished fence.

5 Pour about 6 in. of gravel into the bottom of each posthole to create a stable base for the post and to provide some drainage for water that enters the hole.

2 Determine where the posts will fall along all sides of the fence; then mark these spots with a spray paint or chalk "X." When the marking is done, remove the string.

3 A hand-operated posthole digger works well in soft, sandy soil. But in rocky or clay-filled soil it makes more sense to rent a power auger. Or hire a contractor to dig the postholes with a tractor-mounted auger.

6 Cut the post about 12 in. longer than finished length so it can be trimmed exactly after the fence is complete. Slide the post into the hole, and use it to tamp down and compact the gravel at the bottom of the hole. Check for plumb.

7 Replace the layout string so you know exactly where to place the post. Then support the post with wood braces attached to stakes on adjacent sides of the post. Use a level to check for plumb in both directions.

(continued on page 52)

(continued from page 51)

8 For the strongest installation, fill around each post with concrete. Use premixed dry concrete sold in bags at home centers and lumberyards. Just mix it with water in a tub or a wheelbarrow using a garden hoe. For 10 or more posts, rent a concrete mixer.

9 Pour the mixed concrete into the hole around the post using a shovel. Work carefully to avoid dislodging any loose soil from the sides of the hole. When mixed in with the concrete, the soil weakens the mix.

10 Once the hole is filled with concrete, use a long stick or the shovel handle to remove any air bubbles from the mix. Use an up-and-down plunging motion to break apart these air pockets.

11 To encourage water to drain away from the post, create a beveled cap in the top of the concrete using a small trowel or wide putty knife. When the concrete dries, fill the gap between it and the post with silicone caulk.

Heavy fences, like this one, require stable posts set in concrete.

NOTCHING POSTS

Most fences are built with rails nailed to the surfaces of supporting posts. But on some fences, particularly designs with only a few widely spaced rails, you may want to dress up the installation by recessing the horizontal boards into the posts. The best tool for this job is the circular saw. By cutting repetitive saw kerfs in the surface of the posts, you can remove the wood stock and be left with a notch that matches the size of the rail. The rails will then sit flush with the post surfaces.

TOOLS & MATERIALS
- Circular saw ▪ Posts ▪ Sawhorses
- Line level ▪ Hammer ▪ Tape measure
- Chisel ▪ Safety glasses
- Combination square ▪ String

1 To notch a post so the rail will sit flush, set the depth of the circular saw blade to match the thickness of the rail. Then mark the post to match the width of the rail, and make repeated saw kerfs between these layout lines, approximately ¼ in. apart.

FANCY-CUT POSTS

IF YOU WANT TO CREATE A DECORATIVE DETAIL ON THE TOPS OF THE POSTS, YOU CAN MAKE A BEVEL CUT ALONG THE EDGES WITH A CIRCULAR SAW. MAKE A SMALL CUT ALONG THE EDGE (OR TRIM EACH EDGE WITH A PLANE), OR MAKE A DEEPER CUT THAT CREATES A WIDER BEVEL. IN THEORY, YOU CAN MAKE FOUR DEEP CUTS THAT TURN THE TOP OF THE POST INTO A PYRAMID SHAPE. BUT PARTIAL CHAMFERS GENERALLY LOOK BETTER.

4 Once the wood pieces are removed, smooth the bottom of the notch using a hammer and sharp chisel. Test fit a rail in the notch. If the notch is too shallow, remove more stock to make sure the rail sits flush with the surface of the post.

2 Start the kerfs by carefully making square cuts down the middle of both layout lines. If you have trouble making square cuts, you can use a speed square as a guide. Hold this inexpensive, usually plastic, tool against the post, and run the saw base against it.

3 Once all the kerfs are cut, break them out of the notch by striking them from the side with a hammer. If the wood sections left behind are wider than $5/16$ or $3/8$ in. they will be hard to break this way.

5 Once all the notches are cut, lower the posts into their holes and check for alignment with the notches in other posts, using a mason's string and a line level. When you're satisfied with the alignment, brace the posts in a plumb position.

To make a gate blend with the fence, make sure the pickets and rails are the same heights as those on the fence.

CUSTOMIZING POSTS

There are several easy ways to customize stock fence posts. One of the best is to decorate the surface with wood moldings. To install these trim pieces, make a series of level marks around all four sides of the post; then cut miters on the ends of each piece. Attach the moldings using exterior-grade glue and finishing nails, using the level lines as a guide. You can also build up the surface of the posts by installing one of the decorative post caps or finials shown on the facing page.

TOOLS & MATERIALS
- Hammer ▌Paint brush ▌Saw
- Router (optional) ▌Combination square
- Molding ▌Stain, sealer, or paint
- Threaded finial ▌Exterior-grade glue
- Finishing nails

1 Moldings can be placed anywhere on post surfaces. Decide what type and where by copying existing fence post designs that you like. Make sure to miter the ends of each piece, and attach each using exterior-grade glue and finishing nails.

2 Post tops can be decorated with any number of different post caps and finials. You can also make caps and finials of your own design using a router or a lathe. Use glue and screws to attach them to the posts.

3 Once the fence is assembled, coat all the parts with at least two coats of clear sealer, stain, or paint. Lightly sand away any dust and dried drips between coats, and remove all the sanding dust before recoating.

Customize posts with either multiple layers of mitered trim and/or stock ¾-in.-thick lumber. Then add one of the caps or finials (below) as a finishing touch.

● DECORATIVE POST CAPS AND FINIALS

Brass Federal

Classic

Copper Hightop

Plateau

Federal

Ball

Royal

Acorn

DEALING WITH OBSTRUCTIONS

project

If obstacles like trees, boulders, or drainage areas interfere with your fence line, you can remove the obstacle, move the fence line, or build the fence to skirt or incorporate the obstacle. The last choice is often the most practical, especially with trees. If one is in your way, set the end posts as close as possible to the tree, taking care to avoid damaging the roots when digging the postholes.Then extend the fence rails past the posts and next to the tree trunk. Add the fence boards so they fit within 2 in. of the tree.

TOOLS & MATERIALS
▌ Drill-driver ▌ Circular saw
▌ Chalk line ▌ Tape measure
▌ Sliding T-bevel ▌ Safety glasses
▌ Posts ▌ Post hardware ▌ Panel sections
▌ Braces ▌ Nails or screws

1 Set the end fence posts as close to the tree as possible. Then determine the angle that the fence boards would have to follow to avoid the tree. Do this by stretching a string from the fence to the tree and measuring the angle with a sliding T-bevel.

2 Build the fence panel that fits against the tree on sawhorses. Attach the fence boards to the bottom rail. Then cut off the bottom ends of the boards so that they follow the contour of the angle.

3 Attach the fence panel to the end post with hardware fixtures designed for this job. Also, screw a diagonal brace across the fence boards to keep the whole assembly from sagging.

Extended rails and partial pickets join a property-line tree.

Take careful measurements to fill between stone pillars.

EXTENDING A FENCE

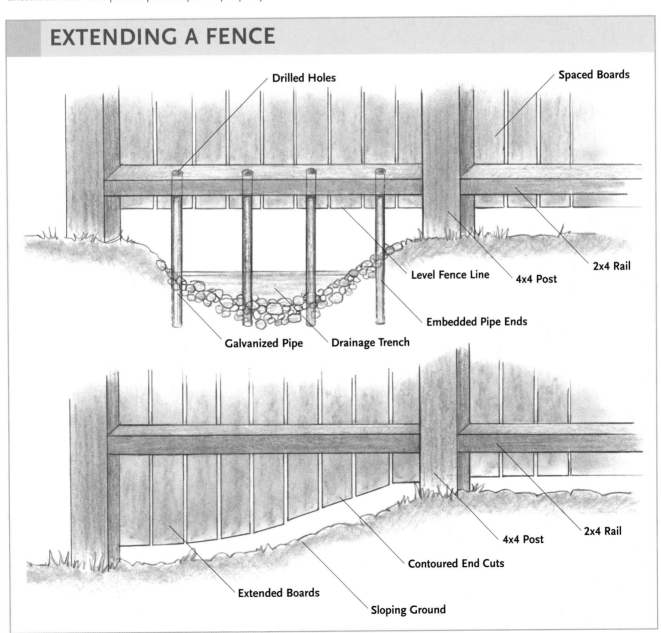

Drilled Holes

Spaced Boards

2x4 Rail

Level Fence Line

4x4 Post

Embedded Pipe Ends

Galvanized Pipe

Drainage Trench

4x4 Post

2x4 Rail

Contoured End Cuts

Extended Boards

Sloping Ground

PICKET FENCE STYLES

Picket fences are often found gracing the front yards of Colonial, Victorian, and other traditionally-styled houses, although pickets are appropriate for almost any house. As opposed to solid-board fences, the open design of a picket fence shows off plantings within the yard yet provides a definite boundary. Planting low shrubs, vines, or perennials next to the fence helps soften the design.

Some lumberyards and home centers carry precut pickets, but the designs are often limited. To make your own, clamp two or three boards together and cut the tops using a handsaw or circular saw. To make fancier shapes, cut the pattern with a saber saw.

Most picket fences are 36 to 48 inches tall, supported on a framework of 4x4 posts with 2x4 rails. Posts generally extend above the picket tops, and have some type of decorative top. But you can also run the top rail along the tops of the posts and let the pickets rise above the rail.

The pickets themselves usually consist of evenly spaced 1x3s or 1x4s attached to the outside of the rails. You can increase or decrease the spacing depending on the amount of privacy you want. It's smart to keep the bottoms of the pickets at least 2 inches above the ground to prevent decay and make it easier both to paint the fence and to remove weeds.

 ## PICKET STYLES

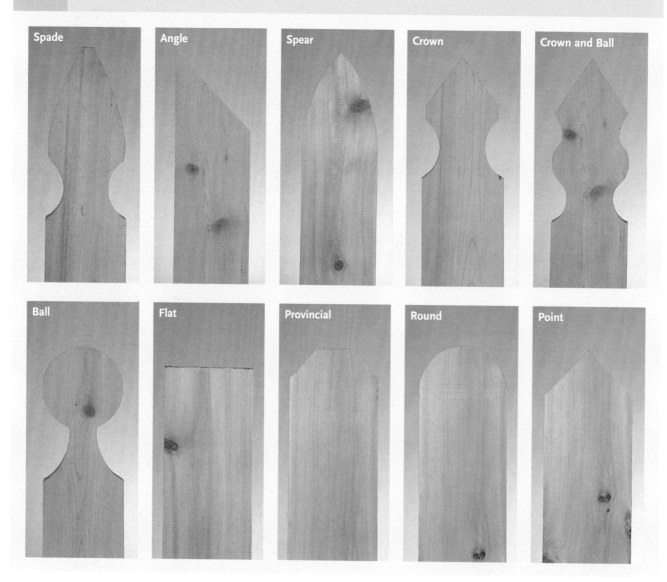

Spade   Angle   Spear   Crown   Crown and Ball

Ball   Flat   Provincial   Round   Point

RAIL CONNECTORS

Nailed Butt Joint

Nailed On Edge

Screwed Hardware

Recessed

Create a custom picket shape by making various edge cuts. Then use it as a master template to cut the others.

INSTALLING A PICKET FENCE

There are many ways to build a basic frame for a picket fence. One of the best is to notch the posts for the rails so they sit flush, and make any rail joints in the center-line of the post notches. Just make sure to drill nail pilot holes in the ends of the rails so you don't split them when they are attached. Then nail the pickets to the top and bottom rails. Space them according to your own taste, though a common rule of thumb is to use a space that's the same width as one of the pickets.

TOOLS & MATERIALS
▌ Drill-driver ▌ Plumb bob ▌ Saw
▌ Hammer ▌ Line level or 4-ft. level
▌ Tape measure ▌ 1x4s for pickets
▌ 2x4s for rails ▌ 4x4 posts
▌ Scrap for spacers ▌ Mason's string

1 Once the posts are notched and installed, begin installing the rails. The easiest way to attach these boards is to clamp them in place, drill pilot holes, and drive galvanized screws or nails through them into the posts.

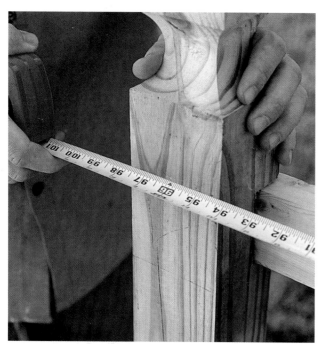

2 To determine the finished picket spacing, first measure the distance between the posts. Then divide this by the width of a picket and of a single space. If you don't come up with a whole number, then slightly increase or decrease the width of the spaces.

3 One way to keep the pickets level as you attach them to the fence rails is to install a guide string between the posts, usually at the bottom of the pickets. Draw the string tight; check for level using a line level; and install the pickets so they fall just above this line.

● POST TOP VARIATIONS

There are many ways to top posts aside from a basic square cut. Some of the best options combine decorative details with the ability to shed water, which can shorten post life by causing rot where it collects on the porous end grain. The easiest approach is to make an angled cut. Chamfering the top edges also helps. Adding a full cap rail, either chamfered or angled, also reinforces the fence.

Angle Cut

Chamfered Edges

Flat Cap with Chamfers

Angled Cap

4 Once you establish the proper spacing between pickets, cut a scrap wood spacer to match this dimension. Then use the spacer to align each successive picket. Use galvanized screws to prevent corrosion.

Some picket fences feature rod-shaped pickets.

VERTICAL-BOARD FENCES

Once you establish a basic box frame of posts and rails, you can install vertical boards in a variety of configurations. To increase privacy and wind protection, for example, you can use tongue-and-groove planks to form a solid barrier. Or you can use wide boards with equally wide spaces to create a partial screen and lattice-like support for climbing plants.

One of the most popular variations is a two-sided board design built around 4x4 posts connected by 2x4 rails. You can use smooth or rough-sawn boards of different sizes to cover the frame, but 1x6s generally have enough strength to span between rails even on a high fence. (Remember that many regions have codes that restrict fence height.) Once the posts are set, use a string and line level to mark the locations of the galvanized rail-to-post hardware. Nail the hardware to the insides of the posts and the rails to the hardware.

Plumb the first board, and use a scrap piece to lay out spaces between boards. Then create an offset version of the same layout on the other side of the rails.

The overall effect is a combination of solid protection and privacy that is lighter and airier than a solid-wood fence. And unlike many fence designs, this offset plan creates a fence that looks the same on both sides, which can be an asset if your fence plans have an impact on a neighbor.

Sturdy vertical-board fencing supports climbing vines.

Corner posts with finials, above, complement the traditional pickets. Lattice is attractive whether used alone, below, or installed over a solid fence.

INSTALLING A VERTICAL-BOARD FENCE

project

Building a vertical-board fence is much like building a picket fence except that you attach more boards to the framework. The hardest part of the planning stage is to decide if you want boards on one side or two. Covering just one side is usually less private than covering two sides. Whether you choose the single- or double-board approach, keep in mind that the more you reduce the spaces, the more you increase the privacy of the fence.

TOOLS & MATERIALS
▌Hammer ▌Saw ▌Shovel
▌Drill ▌Safety glasses
▌Tape measure ▌2x4s for rails
▌1x6 boards ▌6d galvanized nails
▌Galvanized rail hardware and nails

1 Framing hardware is an alternative to attaching the rails to the posts in notches. To install this hardware, first establish the height of the bottom rail; then nail the hardware to the side of the post using galvanized nails. Slide the rail into place, and nail it to the bracket.

2 Install the top rail bracket the same way you installed the bottom rail bracket. Then slide the rail in place, and check it with a level. When satisfied, nail the rail to the bracket.

3 Calculate the best spacing between the boards, and cut a scrap board to match the width of a single space. Use the spacer as a layout tool to mark the board locations.

4 You can install all the boards on one side first and then work on the other side, or alternate from side to side. Make sure the driven nails don't extend through the back of the rail.

LATTICE-AND-BOARD FENCES

Lattice-and-board fences are an attractive and versatile combination of two basic fence types: a solid-board fence for maximum privacy and shelter, and a see-through lattice panel on top that provides a decorative touch and an airy appearance. You can adjust the proportions, of course, using shorter boards and longer lattice panels, as desired. The combination offers good wind protection near a patio or deck, while retaining an open feeling.

Framing Lattice

You can fabricate your own lattice panels to achieve the spacing and angle you want. But there are many stock lattice configurations available, including basic squares and diamonds in plain wood, pressure-treated wood, and vinyl. Vinyl lattice is generally colored. It doesn't make a good match with naturally finished wood but does blend in if you paint or stain the fence.

For most of these fences you can build a stock assembly of posts and rails with two additions. One is a subrail that divides the board section from the lattice section. The other is an interior frame of small nailer strips that supports and captures both the edges of the lattice panel and the ends of the boards.

Once you build the basic frame, you need to add nailers inside it. The nailers support both the board and lattice but also serve to trim the panels. One option is to install only one set of nailers and nail the lower boards and upper lattice against them. For a more finished look, make a duplicate set to cover the edges of both fence sections. The best approach is to rip nailers from extra fence board material, creating 1x1 strips.

If you buy lattice panels, you'll need to cut them to fit. Use an old saw blade and wear eye protection during this operation because your saw is bound to hit a few staples that hold together the lattice panels. You can simply set the lattice in place before securing it with the trim strips set with finishing nails.

The bottom portion of the fence can be made from interlocking tongue-and-groove boards, basic slats with a space between them, or a combination of boards and covering battens.

● LATTICE STYLES

Standard Diagonal

Square PT

Diagonal PT

Privacy

Plain Vinyl

Colored Vinyl

Many patterns are available in plain and pressure-treated (PT) woods, plus white and colored vinyl that look like wood.

INSTALLING A LATTICE FENCE

project

The boards in prefabricated lattice panels are thin, usually about ¼ in. thick, which makes then easy to cut and less expensive to buy. But it also makes them relatively weak, especially when compared to a solid panel like exterior plywood. Because of this, you should provide extra support for these panels when you design your fence. One good way to do this is to hold the lattice in place with cleats nailed to the frame on both sides of the panels.

TOOLS & MATERIALS
■ Drill ■ Saw ■ Hammer
■ Tape measure ■ Level
■ 1x1 nailer strip ■ 4x4 posts
■ 2x4 rails ■ Lattice panels
■ T&G boards ■ Galvanized nails

1 Install the posts and rails for the entire fence span. Then attach nailing cleats to the rails for the fence boards and the lattice panels. Drilling pilot holes will prevent the cleats from splitting when they are nailed. Angle nails slightly (inset) to force the fence boards against the cleats.

2 Cut each lattice panel ⅛ in. shorter than the frame opening in length and height to make fitting it easier. Make sure the panel fits tight against the nailing cleats.

3 Hold the lattice in place by installing a nailing cleat on the other side. Push the panel tight against the first set of cleats, and push the second set of cleats tight against the panel. Install cleats on the top, bottom, and sides of each panel.

INSTALLING A RUSTIC FENCE

Rustic fences define space without blocking the view. And they are relatively easy to build, so you can cover a lot of ground with less effort and fewer materials than most other designs. While these fences do have some built-in adjustability—the rails can slide a couple of inches in either direction—it's still important to lay out the fence carefully. Usually the post spacing is 6 or 8 feet to match the typical length of stock rails sold in home centers. Different spacing is possible, as long as you modify the rails to fit.

TOOLS & MATERIALS
■ Drill and bits ■ Hammer ■ Saw
■ Shovel ■ Tape measure ■ 4-ft. level
■ Chisel ■ Safety glasses ■ Posts and rails
■ 2x4 braces ■ 1x2 stakes
■ Concrete mix ■ Galvanized nails

1 If you use posts that aren't pre-mortised, you'll have to cut the mortises yourself. Start by laying out the hole from both sides of the post. Then bore overlapping holes through the posts to remove most of the wood stock. Use a Forstner or a spade bit.

2 Clean up the sides of the mortise with a hammer and a sharp chisel. Work to the layout lines, and try to make the sides square to the surface of the post.

3 When the mortises are complete, dig the posthole, and lower the post in place. Make sure the mortises are at the correct height and pointing in the right direction.

4 Check the post for plumb and attach two braces (at a 90-deg. angle to each other) to keep it properly aligned when you backfill most of the hole with gravel.

● ALTERNATE RUSTIC RAILS

Rustic-style post-and-rail fences are generally available with posts already notched and rails already tapered. But you can also use rough lumber and make those cuts yourself. Another low-cost option is to use 2x4s for the rails in place of stock rails with tapered ends. Instead of making a typical side-by-side rustic joint, simply cut a half-lap so that the boards join inside the post notch. With the 2x4s on edge, the lap itself is concealed inside the post. Pressure-treated 2x4s are the best choice for economy rails. But you may want to apply two coats of preservative and penetrating stain to get a color match between the posts and rails.

5 Slide mating rails into each mortise, and pin them with a single galvanized nail driven through both rails and into the post. The nail is not required structurally. It just helps keep the rails from accidentally sliding out of their mortises.

6 Once all the rails are installed, finish backfilling the postholes. You can use soil for this job and just plant some grass seed on top. Or you can pour a concrete collar on top of the gravel. This will stiffen the posts and make the whole fence stronger.

69

HORIZONTAL-BOARD FENCES

A typical horizontal-board fence has a classic, almost formal, appearance that's well suited to contemporary home designs. It is most practical on flat ground, although you can adjust for changes in terrain by creating matching angle cuts over posts.

The basic design uses a framework of 4x4 posts set 8 feet on center and two or more rows of 1x6 rails. You can dramatically alter the appearance and function of this basic fence by using three or four horizontal rails, among other options. If necessary, you can add a 1x6 vertical board nailed midspan between posts to reinforce the horizontal rails and minimize bowing. Among other options, you can use a variety of board widths to make a repeating pattern or place a wide board near the ground and progressively narrower boards above.

You can also add a cap rail over the posts of a board fence. The best type of cap has a slight slope, which means you need to cut the post tops ahead of time. Without the angle cuts, the nails holding the cap can work loose over time, allowing the wood to cup. This tends to trap water and lead to rot.

When you install the rails (and a cap), be sure to stagger joints on a long run. You can use rough-sawn lumber or even siding boards to match your house. But stagger joints on different posts.

● ALTERNATE HORIZONTAL-BOARD STYLES

The most economical pattern, and the easiest to install, is the basic four-board fence (below). For more protection you can add a mid-board or several boards with small spaces between them. Another twist on this idea is to use different widths to create a pattern (right). But even keeping the pattern simple, alternating wide and narrow boards can sometimes create an overly busy look. Another classic board-fence pattern is the basic X-shape between posts, used in combination with top and bottom rails.

Patterned Board

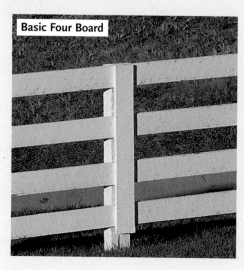
Basic Four Board

Cross Board

INSTALLING A HORIZONTAL-BOARD FENCE

project

A horizontal-board fence is one of the simplest designs around. In fact, it's just an offshoot of the standard rustic fence, albeit a slightly refined one. The posts are widely spaced for quick construction, and there are no rails at all (the fence boards do what the rails usually do) so the fence is less expensive to build. These fences are stock fixtures in horse country and are generally built to conform to the ground. The notched posts shown here do take some time. But they make the fence stronger.

TOOLS & MATERIALS
- Hammer ▍ Safety glasses
- Drill ▍ Tape measure
- Line level ▍ Saw
- Mason's string ▍ 1x6 rails
- 4x4 posts ▍ 2-in. galvanized screws

1 The fastest way to notch posts is to cut the notches beforehand on a worktable or sawhorses. Install the corner posts first, and pull a mason's string tight between them. Use this string as a guide to align the notches in other posts. Use a line level (inset) to keep the string level.

2 Join the fence boards at the centerline of a post notch. Avoid splitting the boards by drilling screw pilot holes at the ends first. If a board is slightly too big for the notch, trim the board instead of making the notch bigger.

3 Attach the boards using galvanized screws. Two per board should be enough. If the board is twisted and won't sit flat in the notch, add a screw to bring the two together.

5 metal fences

While wood may be the most versatile fence building material, it certainly isn't the only one. Metal fences—particularly chain-link, wire, and ornamental—are very popular because they are long-lived, require little maintenance, and can be installed very quickly.

Although most metal fences are put up by professionals, the average do-it-yourselfer can tackle any of these jobs. In some cases, specialized tools are required, but these can be rented at a local tool-rental shop. Just keep in mind that metal fences may look very different than wood ones (think chain-link versus white pickets), but the basic installation process is the same for both types. Start the project by laying out the fence. Then proceed to setting the posts, attaching the rails, and installing the fencing.

CHAIN-LINK FENCES

Many people think of wood pickets and boards when they think of a fence. But most buyers choose utilitarian chain-link fencing because it's strong, durable, and inexpensive compared with many wood styles. In fact, the country's largest fence manufacturer sells more chain-link fencing than any other type, and says that it is number one among the many types and styles in the $2.3 billion fence market.

A low chain-link fence is relatively easy to install. (For a tall fence, it's wise to hire a qualified fence contractor.) Even though the components are metal, you follow the basic procedures for measuring and laying out the job,

excavating the holes, and setting the posts. Bear in mind that chain-link systems (the rails in particular) are not as adjustable as wooden boards that you can quickly trim to fit. It's important to have your layout dead-on and the posts plumb.

Overall, chain-link fences consist of simple fit-together parts. You assemble them almost like plumbing pipes, fitting rails to posts with connectors and creating a frame on which you fasten the chain link.

Granted, this is not the most elegant style of fence. But on the plus side, chain-link does not require painting and doesn't warp, rot, or become food for termites. And you can weave plastic strips through the links to increase privacy and add some color. (See page 79.)

● CHAIN-LINK CONNECTORS

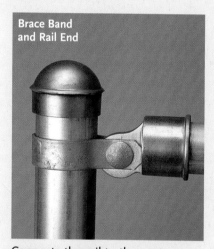

Brace Band and Rail End

Connects the rail to the post.

Loop-Top Holder, Intermediate Post

Caps intermediate post with holder.

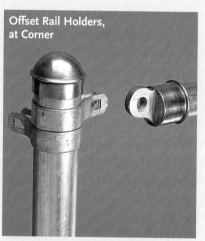

Offset Rail Holders, at Corner

Makes inside and outside corners.

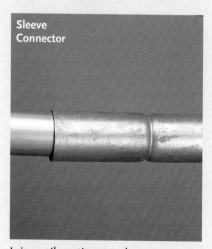

Sleeve Connector

Joins rail sections on long runs.

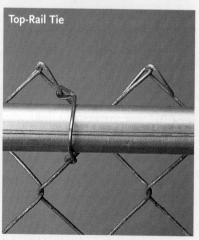

Top-Rail Tie

Secures the top row of closed links.

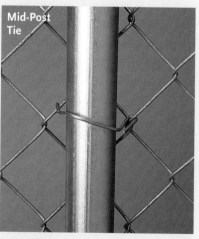

Mid-Post Tie

Pins mesh to the mid-post support.

CHAIN-LINK FENCE PARTS

GATE LATCHES

Fork Latch

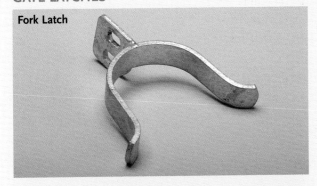

Butterfly Swing-Through Latch

GATE HINGES

Post-Mount Pin Hinge

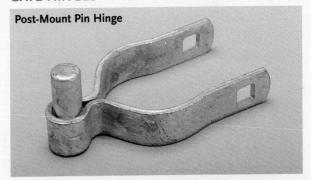

Gate-Mount Hinge

POST PARTS

Post-Mount Brace Band

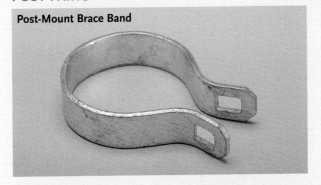

End and Top Caps

HARDWARE

Hog Rings

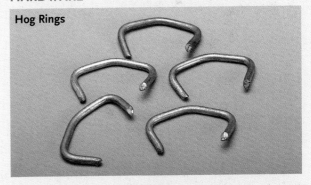

Nuts and Bolts

INSTALLING A CHAIN-LINK FENCE

project

Chain-link mesh is galvanized with zinc or coated with aluminum for a more durable finish. You can also buy vinyl-coated chain-link mesh, usually in white, black, brown, or green. Dark colors often allow the fence to blend into the surroundings, particularly if you purchase matching vinyl sleeves to cover the tubular metal posts and rails.

Galvanized mesh is usually the least expensive, but durability and price depend on the quality of the galvanized coating. Vinyl-coated chain-link mesh is the most expensive, but it offers more design choices and generally outlasts galvanized or aluminum mesh. Aluminum mesh is generally better than galvanized because it looks nicer and lasts a bit longer. You need to plan the fence project and assemble the many components. The biggest challenge may be tracking down a fence puller—the tool that stretches the chain-link mesh between the posts. A fence puller (generally used with a come-along), consists of a fence-pulling bar and hooks that grip the chain links. You may have to check several tool rental shops before you find one that carries fence pullers.

When you set the posts in concrete, bear in mind that terminal posts (end, corner, and gate posts) often have larger diameters, and are set about 3 inches higher than intermediate posts. Use a fairly stiff mix, and check to make sure that the posts are plumb.

TOOLS & MATERIALS
- Power Auger ▌Wrench and Pliers
- Hacksaw ▌Come-along ▌Fence puller
- Tape measure ▌Line level
- 4-ft. level ▌Mason's string
- 1x2s for stakes ▌Boards for braces
- Spray paint ▌Top rail ▌Chain-link mesh
- Tension bands ▌Tension bar
- Rail-end fittings ▌Eye-top fittings
- Post caps ▌Wire ties ▌Nuts and bolts

1 Use wood stakes and mason's string to lay out the location of the fence. Then determine the location of the fence posts based on the manufacturer's recommendations. Mark where each post goes with spray paint.

4 Each corner post needs hardware to hold up the rails and fencing. Begin by sliding a brace band for one rail over the top of the post (top). Then install another band for the adjacent rail and add rail ends to both bands (bottom).

2 Dig the postholes using a hand powered posthole digger or rent a gasoline-powered auger, above, to do the job. The auger works great in soft soil, but the job is quite a bit harder in rocky soil.

3 Start by installing the corner posts and bracing them from two directions so they are plumb. Then stretch a mason's string between corners to establish the proper position for intermediate posts. Plumb each in place as you fill around the post with concrete.

5 The top rails slide through loop-top holders on the intermediate posts. Install the holders first; then slide sections of rail through all the holders.

6 The rails are joined to the corner posts by sliding them into the rail ends mounted on the brace bands (top). When rail stock has to be cut, use a hacksaw for the job, and plan the splices to fall on top of a post (bottom). *(continued on page 78)*

77

(continued from page 77)

7 Rails are joined two ways. For pipe that has a reduced diameter at one end, just slide one pipe into the other (top). For pipes that have the same diameter on both ends, use a sleeve connector (bottom). Try to locate the joint over a fence post.

8 Once all the top rails are installed, attach the chain-link fence. Begin by rolling it out against the framework, starting at one corner post. Then slide a tension bar through the links at the end of the mesh. Make sure the fencing is free to move at the bottom where it meets the grass.

9 Hold the tension bar in place with brace bands. On a 4-ft. fence, three braces are typical, spaced about 1 ft. apart. Don't tighten the nuts completely until you are satisfied with way the tension bar, fencing, and post look.

10 Tighten the fence between corner posts using a pulling rod. This is a common rental item and can be used by hand. But it's easier to pull the fencing by attaching a come-along ratcheting tool to the pulling rod and the corner post.

Adding Rails and Mesh

Set the terminal posts first. The line posts are usually several inches lower and capped with eye-fittings that secure the upper rails. When the post concrete hardens (in one or two days) fit three or four tension bands (depending on fence height) on each terminal post, along with a brace band to anchor the top rail, and a terminal post cap.

Gently tap the eye tops into the ends of the line posts using a hammer and a block of wood. Bolt the rail ends onto the brace bands on the terminal posts, and then install the top rails, slipping them through the eye-top connectors on the line posts and into the rail ends. Often, one end of each rail is reduced in diameter so that you can fit the end snugly into the rail preceding it. In other cases, you may need sleeves to connect rail ends. Rail-to-rail connections do not have to occur exactly above a post, although the installation will be stronger if they do.

With a helper, unroll several feet of chain-link mesh, and weave a tension bar into the end of the mesh. Attach the bar to the tension bands on the end or corner post using the carriage bolts provided. Pull the mesh tightly by hand; then attach the mesh to the top rails and posts with galvanized ties as shown below.

11 Once the fencing is attached to the corner posts, tie the chain links to the top rail and fence posts using galvanized wire or S-shaped brackets that are available from chain-link suppliers (top). Finish up the job by installing the post caps (bottom) and any gate hardware.

STRETCHING CHAIN-LINK

You can roll out chain-link mesh and pull it reasonably taut by hand. But to remove final ripples you need some mechanical advantage. Apply it by hooking one end of a come-along to a bracket on a terminal post (below left). You can brace the post if you're pulling a lot of mesh. Attach the other end to a pulling rod woven through the links of the fencing (below right). Crank the come-along to take up any slack before fastening the loose end of mesh to the next pole.

DISGUISING A CHAIN-LINK FENCE

Chain-link fencing is certainly not the most attractive fence you can install. It may be the most durable and among the strongest, but it can't blend in with your house or yard the way a wood fence can. However, most fence suppliers carry color plastic strips that you can use to put a more palatable face on the mesh. To install them, simply weave the strips through the mesh. You can install them vertically (below left) or diagonally (below right) to help the fence blend in.

WOOD-AND-WIRE FENCES

Welded- or woven-wire mesh on a wood frame makes a lightweight, economical, easy-to-build fence that's a good choice for enclosing play areas for children or defining garden areas. Extend the posts, and this design serves well as a trellis for climbing vines.

Welded wire comes in a variety of gauges and mesh sizes, typically in 36-, 48-, and 72-inch widths, in 50- or 100-foot rolls. Choose the heaviest-gauge wire available, as thin wire can easily deform and is prone to rust. Most wood-and-wire fences have a 2 x 2- or 2 x 4-inch galvanized or vinyl-coated grid. Vinyl-coated wire is generally available in white or forest green. The darker color blends well into the landscape and can make the fence nearly invisible.

Two rails will do on fences no more than 48 inches high, but you'll need a mid-rail for extra stability on higher fences. You can enhance the fence with two options: an angled cap rail that sheds water and covers the wire tips, and a pressure-treated skirt board that keeps critters from crawling under the fence. You can backfill against this board with top soil.

INSTALLING A WOOD-AND-WIRE FENCE

project

A simple wire fence, attached to a wood post-and-rails framework, is one of the easiest fences to build. And it can be one of the most eye-catching if it's used as a trellis for growing climbing plants and flowers. As with most fences, the biggest part of the job is digging the postholes and setting the posts. A typical job calls for posts every 8 to 10 feet and fencing about 4 feet high.

TOOLS & MATERIALS
▌Hammer ▌Shovel
▌Drill-driver
▌Electrician's pliers
▌¾-in. U-staples ▌2-in. Screws
▌Wire Fencing
▌Pressure-treated 1x6 skirt board
▌Posts

3 Once the wire is rolled out, attach the leading edge to the first post using ¾-in.-long U-shaped staples (top). Use the same staples to attach the top edge of the wire to the top rail (bottom). Make sure that the top of the rail and the top of the wire align. If they don't, move the rail up or down before stapling the two together.

4 At the end of a fence, cut the wire flush to the outside edge of the post using wire cutters or electrician's pliers. If you have to splice wire rolls, do it over a post and overlap each roll by one wire grid. Use more staples rather than less to make the joint strong.

1 If you are installing the fence to keep animals out, then plan on burying wire in a trench below the bottom rail. It's easier to dig this trench before installing the posts and bottom rail. You can also do it after, especially if the soil is soft.

2 If possible, design the fence so a full width of wire will fit between the ground and the top of the top rail. This will eliminate a lot of cutting along the bottom and will allow using the top edge of the wire as an alignment tool to make sure the top rail doesn't sag down between posts.

5 Another way to reinforce the joint between rolls is to cover the post with a ¾-in.-thick pressure-treated board that matches the width of the post underneath. Use galvanized screws to attach the board. To maintain a uniform appearance, you may want to cover all the posts with the same kind of board.

6 Install a skirt board along the bottom of the fence to reinforce the lower rail and the wire that extends into the trench. This will provide increased protection against burrowing animals. Once the board is installed, backfill underneath it with top soil and spread some grass seed on the surface.

ORNAMENTAL METAL FENCES

The earliest ornamental metal fences were made of wrought iron that was heated, hammered on anvils, and twisted into curves, floral patterns, and other classic designs. These one-of-a-kind fences were largely replaced by cast iron, which allowed craftsmen to create one highly decorative mold and use it to cast many similar pieces—for example, to make many balusters for a fence or railing.

Although some craftsmen still work in wrought iron and cast iron, most ornamental metal fencing today is made of tubular steel or aluminum. You can choose from a variety of prefabricated designs and install the fence yourself, or you can have a fence custom-made and installed.

Prefabricated metal fences are generally sold through fence suppliers who can also deliver the fence to your home and install it. Designs range from ornate Victorian reproductions to sleek, modern styles. Most companies that make prefabricated fences also offer matching gates and mounting hardware.

Most prefabricated steel and aluminum fences come with a durable factory-applied finish, typically a polyester powder coating. Colors commonly available include black, white, or brown. Check the manufacturer's warranty to see how long the fence is guaranteed against rust and corrosion. If the fence you choose requires on-site painting, use a high-quality, rust-resistant paint. Often it is easier to paint the components prior to installation.

With a helper or two, prefabricated metal fences are easy to install. The prefabricated panels typically come in 72- to 96-inch lengths (and various heights) and fit neatly into prepunched holes in the metal posts. You can also buy prefabricated sections and attach them to wood posts or masonry columns with mounting brackets (supplied by the manufacturer), lag screws, and masonry anchors.

Spacing between posts depends on the size of the prefabricated panels, which must fit snugly between them. For this reason, it is best to erect the fence section by section, attaching prefabricated panels after two posts are in place.

Ornate metal fences can be landscape focal points, especially in urban settings.

INSTALLING AN ORNAMENTAL METAL FENCE

project

Although many high-end metal fences are custom made and installed, the marketplace also offers a wide range of designs that consist of prefabricated components, like those shown here. These systems are less expensive than custom fences and they are much easier to install, making them great do-it-yourself projects. Because the rails generally fit inside the posts, instead of being attached to the surface, make sure to push them into the posts before setting the posts in their postholes.

TOOLS & MATERIALS
- Drill-driver ∎ Rubber mallet
- Tape measure ∎ Mason's string
- Line level and 4-ft. level
- Concrete ∎ Sheet-metal screws

1 Many component systems recommend preassembling as many parts as possible before constructing the fence. Here a post cap is driven into place using a rubber mallet to prevent marring the parts. If you don't have a soft-faced mallet, hold a block of scrap wood on the cap and use a regular hammer.

2 To set the post, dig a hole using a posthole digger. Then lower the post into the hole, and pour concrete around it. Brace the post in a plumb position from two adjacent sides.

3 Many kit fences feature pre-assembled fencing sections. These fit into square holes punched in the side of the posts and are held in place by screws driven through predrilled clearance holes.

4 Install a post at the other end of the fence section, and brace it in place so it's plumb in both directions. Then attach the fencing to the first post using sheet-metal screws.

6 vinyl fences

Wood may be the most versatile fencing material because it can be fabricated into so many different designs. But it's not the most durable and long-lived one. These distinctions belong to vinyl, which is made of nearly indestructible PVC (polyvinyl chloride). Vinyl fencing is gaining in popularity for the same reasons that vinyl siding did: it looks good and needs just about no routine maintenance. Unfortunately, vinyl can't duplicate all the wood styles. If you have your heart set on a custom picket design, don't shop for vinyl—at least not yet. But if you want a simple horizontal-board fence or a traditional white picket fence, consider vinyl. It's more expensive than most wood products. But the difference in purchase price can be easily recouped in upkeep savings over the years.

VINYL FENCING

Vinyl fences are available in a wide variety of styles but often in only a few colors. However, they are gaining in popularity, accounting for one in five new fences, for two main reasons.

First, they are easy for most do-it-yourselfers to install because they are lightweight and sold in preformed sections that fit together without the kind of special tools and equipment you need to install some fences, such as chain-link types. Second, the vinyl is colored throughout the thickness of the material, so you don't have to paint or stain at the start of the project, nor do you have to touch up little nicks or scrapes later.

Because the color runs through the material, vinyl fences never need the attention that wood fences do. And vinyl won't decay, become a food source for wood-boring insects, or rust like metal fences.

Although vinyl fences generally are more expensive than the same styles in wood, manufacturers say the higher initial cost is offset by longer life and lower maintenance costs.

Usually, you buy the fence in what amounts to a kit that contains precut posts, rails, and siding. Lattice and other special features, including matching gates and mounting hardware, are also available. The components usually come in precut lengths, but you can cut them using a hacksaw or a fine-toothed handsaw.

Vinyl fences in traditional picket designs often look about the same as painted wood components.

VINYL FENCE PARTS

Slotted Post

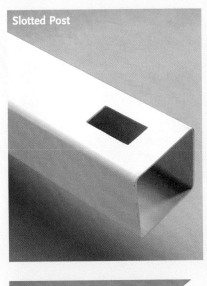

Post Cap

Upper Support Rail

Pickets

Grooved Lower Rail

Lattice

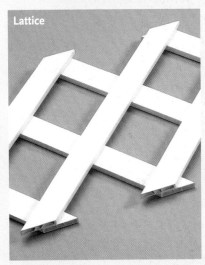

Lattice Trim Cap

Locking Rings

Splines, Screws, Caps

VINYL FENCE STYLES

Vinyl can be formed into almost any style of fence that you can build out of wood, including board, rail, and picket and combinations generally found only with wooden lattice or ornamental metal.

Vinyl fencing usually must be ordered directly from manufacturers or their distributors. The fences come in limited colors—most often white, brown, and tan—but you can dress up most installations with post caps and other decorative features modeled after Victorian, Georgian, and other styles.

You can't mix and match components from different manufacturers. But large suppliers offer options, such as a mid-rail that accepts vinyl boards or pickets below and lattice above. And some vinyl-fence designs allow you to step the installation down a slope, although you will need longer posts than you would use for a conventional project. Many assemblies can also be purposely racked to follow ground contours. Order end posts, which have holes on one side only, for all of the fence posts that will step down the hill.

Vinyl styles include offset pickets and decorative post caps.

Solid-panel vinyl fencing can step up slopes between posts to create a sheltered and private yard or garden.

VINYL FENCE DESIGN OPTIONS

Crossbuck

Alternating-Height Picket

Three Rail

Decorative Picket

Wood-Grain

Lattice Top

Open Rail

Alternating Panels

INSTALLING A VINYL FENCE

On most vinyl fence jobs, the pieces you need to assemble are stock units designed to fit into slots in posts and tracks in the rails without cutting. (Of course, you can cut as needed to modify the stock sizes. Manufacturers explain how to do this for their products.) Although basic assembly procedures do vary, generally you fit the rails into mortises in the hollow posts. And attach them with screws, clips, or special rings that vary with the specific fence design. Usually the rails are also hollow and are made with built-in channels to hold fence boards or pickets.

Keep in mind, using vinyl won't make installing the posts any easier. You still have to dig postholes, which is usually the hardest part of any fence installation. Start with a careful layout and use a posthole digger or rented power auger. Because the components are already formed, and the slots or mortises for the rails are already cut, you must install all the posts at the same height. This means you must add (or remove) fill under posts as needed to make sure the rails will fit properly. Once you firm up the posts, you can add the rails, or you can assemble subcomponents, such as rails and boards, and join them as units to the posts. In most cases, the components simply fit together with hand pressure. But when screws are used, small decorative caps are provided to hide the screw heads.

TOOLS & MATERIALS
▌ Shovel ▌ Mason's trowel
▌ Hammer ▌ Drill-driver
▌ Tape measure
▌ 2-ft. level
▌ Mason's string
▌ Concrete mix
▌ 1x2s for stakes
▌ 2x4s for braces
▌ Mixing tub ▌ Screws

1 Accurate layout is the crucial first step in any fence project. Begin by driving stakes into the ground past the corner points. Then stretch mason's string between the stakes. Make sure the strings cross at a 90-deg. angle to ensure a square corner.

3 Pour 4 to 6 in. of crushed stone or gravel in the bottom of the hole; then set the post on top of this stone. Raise or lower the posts (so the rail mortises on adjacent posts align with each other) by removing or adding crushed stone to the hole.

2 Lay out the position of all the posts along the strings. Then remove the strings and start digging the postholes. Use a shovel for shallow holes like this. But for deeper holes, where the local frost line is more than 12 in., use a posthole digger or a rental auger.

● ASSEMBLY JIG

Handling many fence parts at the same time can be difficult. Just when you have several boards or pickets coming together in a subassembly, they can fall out of position. A simple assembly jig (or a pair of them) helps. The base is a 2x4 or 2x6 a few feet long for stability. Two short pieces serve as holding blocks. Screw them to the base, allowing just enough room for the base rail between. The jig will hold the section upright as you assemble the pieces.

4 Brace the post in the plumb position from two directions that are 90 deg. apart. Attach the bottom end of the braces to stakes driven into the ground. Attach the top of the braces to the post using clamps.

5 Double-check the post for plumb using a 2- or 4-ft. level. Inspect adjacent sides, and adjust the clamps as necessary to keep the post plumb.

(continued on page 92)

(continued from page 91)

6 With the post securely braced in a plumb position, use a plastic tub and a shovel to mix dry concrete and water into a stiff consistency. Pour this concrete around the post, and taper the top surface so water will run off.

7 Once the concrete has set on the first post, slide the rails (or any rail-and-fencing subassembly) into their post mortises. Then add a post on the other ends of the rails, and plumb and brace this second post in its hole.

10 Once the panels are resting in the bottom rail groove, cover the top edges with either a top rail or—in this case—a mid rail. Spread the top of the second post slightly so the rail can fit into the mortise. After the rail is in place, the post will move back.

11 In some cases, like the one shown here, a mid rail needs to be outfitted with a channel to hold the decorative lattice at the top of the fence. It is attached using either galvanized or stainless-steel screws.

8 After installing the second post, check the rails for level using a 2- or 4-ft. level. If the ground has a gentle slope (1 to 2 in. per 10 ft. of run), and you want to follow it, then push the top and bottom rails up or down slightly to conform to this slope.

9 Some fence panel sections are joined together with splines that slide into edge groves on adjacent pieces (inset). To make the job go faster, preassemble several panels before installing them in the fence rails.

12 Cut the lattice panel to size using a circular saw with a fine-tooth blade. Slide the lattice into the mid-rail channel and push it against the post. Then hold it in place by installing the top fence rail.

13 Once all the fence sections are installed, finish up the job by installing a decorative cap on the top of each post. Generally, these caps just slide over the top of the posts. No fasteners are required.

7 specialty fences

You can build a good fence out of just about anything, from old tires to wine bottles laid up with common mortar, as long as your goal is basically decorative. But if you have special needs, such as restraining pets, livestock, or snowdrifts, you'll need what is commonly called a "specialty fence." Many different types are available. Some are sold at standard home centers, while others are usually found only at rural farm-supply stores. No matter what type you choose, remember that standard fence-building techniques don't always pertain. Make sure to get installation instructions for the product you buy, and don't forget to pick up any specialized tools that may be needed. Buy inexpensive hand tools, but rent heavier equipment unless you have a lot of fencing to install.

SPECIAL-USE FENCES

Most house styles and sites look best with a traditional fence design, such as a horizontal-board or picket fence. But there are many other types, including basic utility fencing, barbed wire, electronic fencing for pets or live-stock, fences made out of plants and other natural materials, and even fences made of recycled materials, such as one-of-a-kind fences that use old chair rungs for balusters.

■ **Utility fencing.** Utility fencing consists of wooden slats wired together. It is sold in large rolls, in heights from 36 to 72 inches. You simply unroll the fencing and nail or wire it to wood or metal posts. While not especially attractive or durable, utility fencing can provide a temporary barrier for people and animals. Utility fencing is also called snow fencing because you can place it strategically to prevent wind-blown snow from drifting across walks or driveways.

■ **Wire Pickets.** Wire picket fencing (also sold in rolls at home centers) is used as a low temporary or decorative border around planting beds and walks. These welded-wire fences are either factory painted or vinyl coated and come in heights from 12 to 18 inches. To install, you simply unroll the wire and set it into the ground. You can also find low picket sections made of wood or PVC plastic.

■ **Rope or Chain Fences.** These easy-to-install fences make attractive, economical boundary markers along paths, walks, and driveways. These fences are popular in coastal areas because they lend a nautical feeling to the landscape. To make one, drill holes through low 4x4 or 6x6 posts, and thread through a length of chain or heavy rope.

■ **Barbed Wire and Wire Mesh.** Used mainly to contain animals, both types are easy to install. With wire mesh, which is available in many gauges and sizes, you unroll and staple it to the posts. Barbed wire, which has to be handled carefully, normally comes on spools. Some pastures are bounded with mesh on posts, with a top strand of barbed wire. While barbs can be a strong deterrent to thin-skinned animals, large cows and bulls use it for scratching and can walk right through strands of barbed wire if they have the urge.

On the following pages you will also find details on hidden electric fences for pets, and the aboveground version often used around barns to contain livestock.

A wall of woven branches can define planting areas.

Utility fences can hold back leaves and drifting snow.

Barbed wire between posts can make an economical boundary.

Build a one-of-a-kind garden fence by tying together short lengths of bamboo.

You can use unusual recycled materials, such as old chair legs, in a decorative fence to define outdoor areas.

PET FENCES

To keep your pet at hand and safely in control, you need a fence in your yard and a leash when you're out for a walk. There have been a few improvements in both types of pet control, although some of the updates can have unexpected drawbacks.

In the leash department, for example, there's the long type that winds up on a reel and allows a dog to run far away without actually running away. Dog and master can be yards apart and seem like independent parties to innocent bystanders—until the dog sweeps past on the flank and trips them in the tether. Some dogs are very good at this game of bowling for bystanders.

What may seem like the latest development in pet control (actually in existence since the 1970s) is the electronic fence that's not really a fence. It does away with leashes (at home at least) and penned-in runs by creating electronic boundaries. Hidden electronic fence systems are commonly used around the perimeter of a yard. But you also can install them inside the house to keep pets out of particular areas.

System Components

Hidden-fence products have three main components: wires buried in shallow trenches around your property, a battery-powered collar with a receiver for your pet, and a controller that sends electromagnetic signals along the wires that are picked up by the collar.

The electronic system creates a fencelike boundary, but your pet can't see it to climb through, jump over, or tunnel under. Some companies have developed an electronic version of a leash that extends invisible control beyond your yard.

At first blush, the fence systems come off like a force field on an old Star Trek program—a magically strong but invisible wall off which your dog will bounce. Manufacturers' literature often reinforces the image of hidden fences as a kind of space-age doghouse in which modern technology takes the place of chain-link and electromagnetic waves put an end to swats with a rolled-up newspaper.

Electric-Fence Realities

Companies in the field have positive-sounding names such as Contain-a-Pet, DogWatch, PetSafe, and Invisible Fence, and their brochures focus on the benign beeping sound that warns your dog (or cat or almost any other pet) of the approaching boundary.

But the electronic doghouse isn't exactly benign and, in the end, delivers an electric shock to get the message across.

Industry literature says that proper training is the key to these systems, and generally claims a 98 percent or better success rate in keeping pets at home. But read further, and you're likely to find a more nitty-gritty section about how system controls and settings allow you to "give a stronger warning by increasing the rate of the electrical stimulation."

It's hard to find any literature that describes this fine point in plain language: that the system delivers an electrical shock that hurts enough to keep your pet from bolt-

● INVISIBLE PET FENCE KIT COMPONENTS

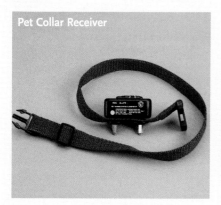
Pet Collar Receiver

Transformer and Controller

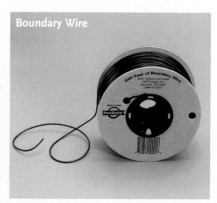
Boundary Wire

ing. But some companies are more straightforward than others about the subject and suggest that you may want to check with a veterinarian before using an electrical restraint system.

The other side of this issue is pretty simple: that an electric jolt is well worth keeping your dog from straying into the street and being hit by a car.

Basic Installation

Because the boundary wires are hidden underground, the systems can save you from adding a fence where you don't want one. You don't have to chop up a large yard with a fenced-in run or install a nearly solid boundary fence that sometimes can cause problems with your neighbors.

The systems can be tailored to fit properties ranging from ¼ acre to more than 20 acres, so you can create a safe area in part of the yard, simply follow your property lines, or create a combination plan that covers the perimeter and creates specific internal no-pet zones as well. You can also install the electronic boundaries around trees, over steep hills, and even under water across a stream or pond.

You should start with a map of the project, such as the one shown at right, to deal with the obvious catch to the system, namely, that if you have to run wires from a transformer in your house or garage out to the perimeter of the property, how will your pet cross those lines? The solution is to twist together the two wires that carry the electricity. This defeats the charge, and creates a neutral line that pets can cross without receiving a signal.

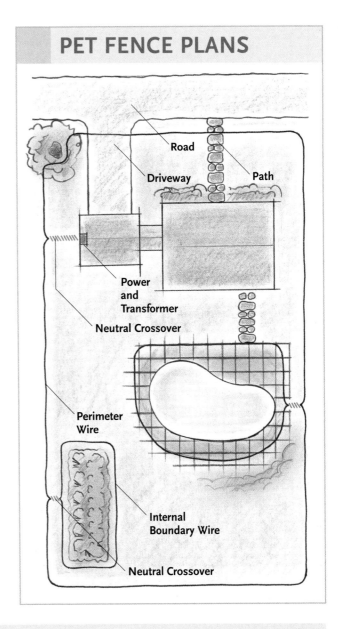

PET FENCE PLANS

Road

Driveway

Path

Power and Transformer

Neutral Crossover

Perimeter Wire

Internal Boundary Wire

Neutral Crossover

System On-Off Key

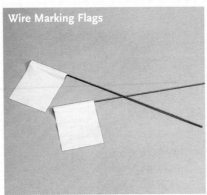

Wire Marking Flags

Instructions and Training Video

One sensible approach is to make the two wires run along the shortest stretch from the transformer to the boundary. But you can twist wires at other points in the overall plan—for example, to bring the boundary wires back into the yard to zone off a garden or swimming pool.

Most homeowners can handle these projects on their own, although many suppliers offer professional installation. You can buy basic component kits, do the trenching work for the boundary wires, and make the straightforward electrical connections.

Generally, the wires need to be only a few inches belowground, while the controller can plug into a standard outlet in your basement or garage. Many systems come with a video that covers both installation and pet training.

Costs vary widely depending on the installation, but some basic kits start at about $200. On large properties where trenches for wires extend great distances and may have to be channeled around many obstacles, the excavation work (even for relatively shallow trenches) will be most of the job.

Where your pet is concerned, installation consists of buckling on a battery-powered collar. Most weigh between 1 and 2 ounces and are suitable for all breeds from Great Danes to Chihuahuas, and cats of all sizes.

Unexpected Effects

Manufacturers understandably do not make a point of listing the drawbacks of their products. But there are a few, aside from the somewhat controversial point of delivering electric shocks to your pet. For example, some generally satisfied hidden-fence homeowners say that the shock treatment can have a negative effect on the personality of the pet. Another problem seems to be that while trainable and naturally docile or timid dogs always stop short of the electronic boundary, some more spirited animals do not.

Take the case reported by a homeowner of a dog that regularly chases rabbits out of instinct or entertainment. The owner says it's become an obsession even though he never catches them no matter how hard he tries. The urge is so strong that the dog will bolt at full speed right through the electronic barrier in pursuit. The problem is that after he calms down he won't cross the barrier to come home. One episode like this will put your pet in just the kind of trouble you were trying to avoid in the first place.

INSTALLING A PET FENCE

project

Designing a good pet-fence layout may take some time. But it's time well spent. By just accepting some common sense adjustments here and there, you can make the installation process much easier. For example, if you want the fence to cross a concrete sidewalk or asphalt driveway, you can cut a groove in both for the wires. But it's much easier to reroute them or be satisfied with a smaller fenced in space.

TOOLS & MATERIALS
▍ Circular saw ▍ Safety glasses
▍ Masonry cutting blade ▍ Dust mask
▍ Shovel ▍ Drill-driver
▍ Wire strippers ▍ Lineman's pliers
▍ Pet fence kit

4 To create a neutral line that your pet can cross without being shocked, twist the wires together using a drill driver (top). Then splice these wires to the boundary wire by stripping the insulation, twisting the wires together, and adding electrical tape (bottom).

1 Use a square-tipped shovel or garden spade to cut a trench in the sod for the fence wire. Replace the sod once the wire is in place.

2 Cut a notch in concrete walks or asphalt driveways using a circular saw with a masonry blade. Wear safety glasses and a dust mask.

3 Feed the wire into the trench around the restricted area. To splice it, strip the insulation, twist the ends together, and add electrical tape (inset).

5 Most installations start with a neutral crossover wire that extends from inside the house to the boundary line. To attach this wire to the transformer, strip off the insulation from the wires and attach them to the transformer terminals.

6 Wire the transformer into a standard house circuit. Then turn on the system and make sure that it works properly. When satisfied with the performance, bury the wires in soil, and fill in the trench with the sod that was removed originally.

INSTALLING A LIVESTOCK FENCE

project

Different animals require different types of fencing. For example, horse farms usually install expensive post-and-board fences, while cattle or dairy farms usually go with a few strands of barbed or high-tensile wire. Poultry and small animals are kept in place with woven wire or chicken wire. And goats, noted for their ability to outsmart almost any fence, often require an eight-strand electrified fence.

Aside from welded wire and barbed wire, livestock fencing often consists of economical high-tensile wire strung along a line of rustic posts. It can be electrified, but this job is best designed by a licensed electrician so that a safe, code-approved system results. If an electrified fence is necessary, you can use one that is wired directly into your house electrical service panel. Or the system can be designed for remote locations by using battery power, solar power, or a combination of both. Keep in mind that unlike other fences, electrified fences must be kept free of weeds, branches, or anything else that might cause a short circuit.

High-tensile wire is strong and resilient. It's often attached to springs at the end of long runs to allow tightening and to keep it from breaking if a branch falls on the fence. It is available in various gauges and in galvanized or aluminum-clad finishes to prevent corrosion. This wire is also rated by its breaking strength, generally between 120,000 and 200,000 pounds per square inch.

TOOLS & MATERIALS
- Drill-driver
- Electrician's pliers
- Fence strainer
- Fence posts
- Fence wire
- Screw-mounted insulators
- Mounting lags
- Tension springs

1 First install all the posts to the same depth, and establish the location of the wires so they follow the contour of the ground. Then drill a pilot hole for each mounting lag. Use a bit that's just slightly smaller than the diameter of the lag threads.

4 On long runs in wooded areas (over 20 ft.), install a tension spring between the mounting lag and the fence wire (top). This spring allows the wire to absorb the shock of a falling branch without breaking. Attach the wire to intermediate posts with an insulator (bottom).

2 Install each mounting lag in its pilot hole by turning it clockwise. Keep turning until all the threads are embedded in the wood and the hook end of the lag is pointing up. This lag comes with an electrical insulator so the fence can carry current.

3 To attach a wire to the mounting lag, loop about 18 in. of it around the lag (top), and twist it back around itself. Usually 8 or 10 twists will hold the wire securely (bottom). Use electrician's pliers to tighten the wire and to cut off any excess wire.

5 Install an inexpensive ratcheting fence strainer between the fence wire and the tension spring on the other end of long runs. Tighten the strainer to remove any wire slack; then remove the handle and leave the strainer in place for future adjustments.

smart tip

DIGGING HOLES

BY DEFINITION, LIVESTOCK FENCES ARE RURAL FIXTURES AND THEY USUALLY CONTAIN A LARGE AREA. THIS MEANS THAT A LOT OF POSTHOLES NEED DIGGING AND, UNLESS YOU ARE WORKING IN VERY SANDY SOIL, DON'T EVEN CONSIDER A CLAMSHELL POSTHOLE DIGGER. A RENTED TWO-PERSON, GAS-POWERED AUGER IS ONLY A LITTLE EASIER TO USE IF YOU HAVE MANY POSTS TO INSTALL. THE BEST APPROACH IS TO HIRE A CONTRACTOR WITH A TRACTOR-MOUNTED POSTHOLE DIGGER. THESE ARE USUALLY COMPACT MACHINES THAT CAN GET JUST ABOUT ANYWHERE BUT STILL HAVE THE POWER TO BREAK UP THE HARDEST SOIL. BE SURE TO HAVE THE POSTS ON HAND AND DROP THEM IN THE HOLE AS SOON AS THE AUGER IS BACKED OUT.

8 gates

By their very nature, fences are designed to restrict access to your property. Some, like frail pickets, do so simply by suggesting visual limits. While others, such as 10-foot-high chain-link structures, create more imposing barriers and deliver much more security in the process. No matter how substantial a fence, it needs to provide passage through at one point—a point controlled by a gate. Gates are generally built to match the overall fence design. Low-security fences can have delicate, ornamental gates. But high-security fences demand stronger structures. The challenge with every gate is to design something that is not only stable but that can also be easily opened and closed repeatedly over the years. To accomplish this, the joinery has to be strong and durable, and the hardware has to be long-lasting.

GATE DESIGN

According to an old adage, gates can tell you a lot about the people who live behind them. Gates can be simple or ornate, formal or rustic, traditional or contemporary, inviting or forbidding. The gate should complement the fence design but can break away from the uniform row of pickets or boards, which creates almost limitless possibilities.

To call attention to an opening, choose a design that contrasts with the surrounding fence. A low ornamental metal gate, for example, can soften the imposing mass of a solid masonry wall. Similarly, you can call attention to the gate by changing the size, spacing, or direction of the siding materials used on the fence. If you want privacy, gates leading to side yards or backyards, for example, can be constructed from the same materials as the fence to give the impression of an unbroken barrier.

■ **Gate Materials.** Most gates are made of wood or ornamental metal. You can choose from a variety of prefabricated designs or create your own. No matter what design you choose, the gate must be sturdy enough to swing freely without sagging or binding. The most successful wooden gates use lightweight, kiln-dried wood and heavy-duty hinges, and have sufficient bracing to prevent sagging.

■ **Gate Size and Weight.** Spacing between gate posts should be 36 to 48 inches. Generally, posts for gates leading to a house's front door should be 48 inches apart, which allows room for two people to pass through at once. Posts for gates leading to backyards or side yards should be spaced no less than 36 inches apart so that lawn mowers and other wheeled garden equipment fit through the opening.

Even for low gates, you need to set the posts a minimum of 24 inches in the ground or below the frost line in cold climates. Plumb both posts.

If you're installing a prefabricated gate, space the posts to provide clearance on the latch side and hinge side. In most cases, $1/2$ inch of clearance on the hinge side and $1/2$ to $3/4$ inch on the latch side will do. But you should use the clearances specified by the gate manufacturer. The clearances required for chain-link and orna-

GATE SWING OPTIONS

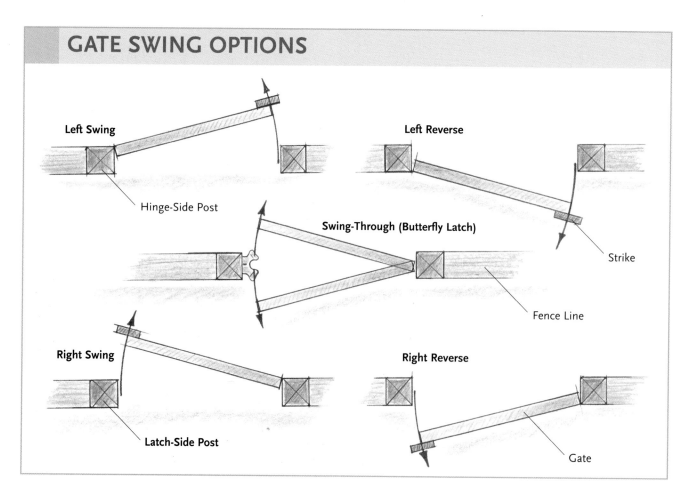

Left Swing

Hinge-Side Post

Left Reverse

Strike

Swing-Through (Butterfly Latch)

Fence Line

Right Swing

Latch-Side Post

Right Reverse

Gate

mental metal gates are usually determined by the type of hardware used to attach them.

Usually, gates are the same height as the fence or wall, but not necessarily. The gate's height depends on its function and on the fence design. If a fence or wall provides security and privacy, make the gate the same height and as difficult to climb as the adjacent wall.

Keep the weight of the gate in mind when choosing materials. The gate should be sturdy enough to stand up to continuous use but not so heavy that it's hard to open and close. Large, solid-board gates tend to be heavy and may require three or even four hinges to support them. If the gate swings over a smooth masonry walk, you can install a wheel on the bottom of a heavy gate to relieve strain on the hinges and to keep the gate from sagging.

■ **Gate Location.** Usually, gates are located where a fence or wall will cross an existing or proposed walkway or entry. In a new landscape, these elements are planned simultaneously as part of the overall scheme.

If you are installing a front boundary fence directly next to a sidewalk (especially a busy one), it is good prac-

tice to jog the fence back 36 to 48 inches from the sidewalk and install the gate there. Setting the gate back from the sidewalk provides an area where you can conveniently open and close the gate away from any traffic on the sidewalk.

■ **Gate Swing.** Entry gates traditionally open in toward the house. There is no set rule for gates, but your front door swings inward, which is generally the best design that invites entry instead of impeding it. And, somehow, pulling a gate toward you makes more sense as you're leaving.

The direction of swing also can depend on features near the gate. For example, if the gate crosses a sloping walk, it may have to swing downhill to provide clearance at the bottom of the gate. If a gate is located at the corner of a fence or at a wall, it is usually best to have the gate swing toward the structure. You can attach a hook to the structure and a screw eye to the gate to keep the gate open when necessary.

Some gates can be installed to swing through the opening, such as a chain-link gate that can be held by a two-way butterfly latch.

● GATE-CLOSING HARDWARE

Gates may swing freely on their hinges, and, of course, it's easy enough to push a gate open as you walk through the opening. But why wait to turn around and fumble with pulling it closed when you can install hardware to close the gate automatically? There are several types of spring-loaded hinges, including spring additions to standard hinges (left) and the most com-

mon type, simply a spring with screw-mounted ends (right). As you open the gate, there is slight resistance as the energy is stored in the spring. After you walk through, the energy is released and the gate closes. Some people install spring-loaded hinges and adjust the tension so that the gate stays closed against a strike without a latch.

GATE HARDWARE

Hinges and latches range from utilitarian to ornamental. Choose a style that is appropriate for the fence design, and consider whether you will mount hardware on the face or edge of the gate.

■ **Hinges.** There are four basic hinge types: butt hinges, T-hinges, strap hinges, and pin-and-strap hinges. Make sure they are designed for exterior use and are heavy enough to support the weight of the gate. A good rule is to choose the heaviest hinges you can install that are still in visual scale with the gate.

■ **Gate Latches.** You have many choices when it comes to gate latches. Most will work no matter how you build the gate to swing. Some latches are designed to be fitted with a padlock, or you can install a separate lock and hasp. On seldom-used gates, a hasp alone may suffice. Formal door-style gates, such as those leading to a courtyard or front-entry enclosure, can be fitted with conventional door locksets.

■ **Sag Rods.** On wide or heavy gates, it's wise to use sag rods or cables with adjustable turnbuckles to keep gates from sagging or binding. Install them diagonally with the high end of the rod or cable at the top post hinge and the bottom of the rod fastened to the bottom corner of the gate.

■ **Gate Springs.** Make your gate close automatically with the help of a gate spring. One bracket mounts to the gate, the other to the fence.

A wrought-iron thumb latch is traditional with picket designs.

● SAG CABLES FOR GATES

Sag cables run from lower outside corner to top hinge.

Turnbuckles allow you to increase tension over time.

GATE-HINGE OPTIONS

Butt Hinge

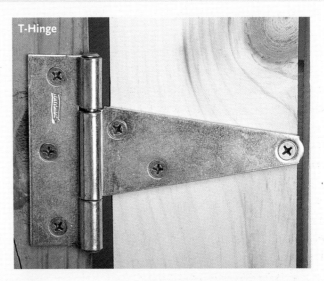

T-Hinge

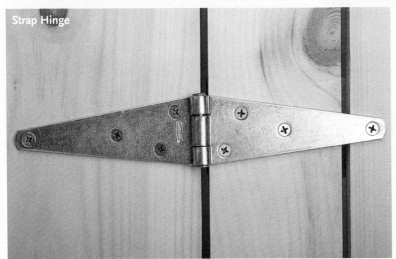

Strap Hinge

Mortised Butt Hinge

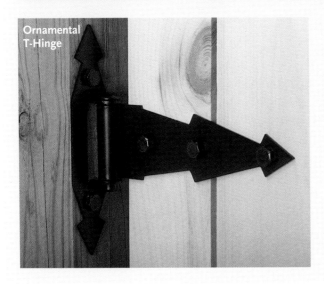

Ornamental T-Hinge

Ornamental Pin-Mount Hinge

GATE LATCHES

There are many types of hardware that will secure a gate. They range from a basic hook-and-eye, which can be somewhat inconvenient on a gate that's used frequently, to hasps that you can secure with a padlock. There are also several types of sliding bolts and traditional wrought-iron latches. You can install some types in combination with a spring-loaded hinge to close and latch automatically.

There are other alternatives, of course. One is to limit the gate swing with a strike, install a spring-loaded hinge, and use any type of decorative knob (on both sides) to easily grasp the gate from both sides.

Another approach is to build your own custom latch, such as the one shown below. You can make one out of 1x4 pine. Round over or simply sand the edges, and apply several coats of sealer or stain to protect it from the weather.

The idea is to build three keepers through which a horizontal latch bar can slide. Two of the keepers are fastened to the gate, and one to the adjacent post. With a dowel or some other type of handle between the two gate-mounted keepers, you can slide the latch back and forth across the opening to the post keeper. Because the handle protrudes, the latch won't slide free.

● MAKING A CUSTOM SLIDING LATCH

1. Find the center of the sliding latch board, and scribe an arc that rounds the end to prevent it from catching.

2. Cut the arc on the end of the latch board. This helps it slide freely through the post-mounted keeper.

3. Make keeper assemblies by predrilling and screwing a cover piece on blocks the same thickness as the latch.

4. Level the three keepers (two on the gate and one on the post); slide in the latch board; and add a dowel handle.

GATE LATCH OPTIONS

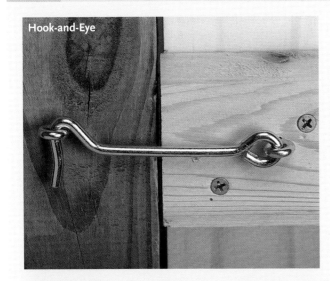

Hook-and-Eye

Thumb Latch

Barrel Bolt

Locking Hasp

Decorative Thumb Latch

BUILDING A GATE FRAME

Constructing a gate frame is a straightforward job if the opening between the posts is parallel and plumb. You start with a square frame and add diagonal bracing inside. But if the posts are not parallel and plumb, you should fix them. Either install sag cables to keep them aligned, or remove the posts and reset them properly. Don't try to make the gate fit a bad opening.

TOOLS & MATERIALS
- Drill-driver ▮ Safety glasses
- Screwdriver bit ▮ Tape measure
- Chisel ▮ Circular saw
- Framing square ▮ Pickets
- Metal L-brackets
- Pickets ▮ 2x4s
- Galvanized screws

1 Choose one of the frame corner joints shown on the facing page. Then cut the sides of the frame to size using a circular saw. Align the corners, and drill two screw pilot holes in the overlapping board. Drive galvanized screws into these holes.

4 Once you are satisfied with the fit of both diagonal braces, lay out a half-lap joint in the middle of both boards. Cut these joints using a handsaw and chisel. Then push the braces together inside the gate frame.

5 When satisfied with the fit of the half-lap joint, disassemble the parts; spread exterior-grade construction adhesive on both sides of the joint; and reassemble the parts. Reinforce the joint by driving a screw into the middle of the boards.

2 Reinforce each corner joint with a galvanized steel L-bracket. First, screw one leg of the bracket to a frame side. Then hold a framing square against the corner to align the sides. Screw the second leg in place.

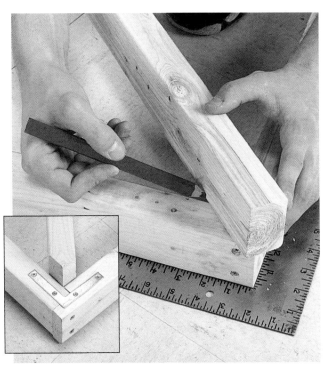

3 To install a diagonal brace, cut a 2x4 slightly long and place it on the gate frame so it extends from the middle of one corner to the middle of the opposite one. Scribe a V-shaped cut on both ends. Then make the cuts, and slide the 2x4 in place (inset).

6 Spread the pickets (or other boards) across the gate frame to establish the best spacing. Then install the pickets using galvanized screws. Predrill pilot holes for the screws to prevent splitting any of the boards.

● FRAME CORNERS

Gate frames can be constructed with three different joints. The easiest is the simple butt joint (right). The strongest is the half-lap joint (below). And the most attractive is the miter joint (below right).

Butt Joint

Half-Lap Joint

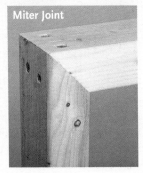

Miter Joint

BUILDING A SOLID-BOARD GATE

project

Widely spaced pickets make a gate light-weight and easier to build. But solid-board designs, whether butted together or joined with tongues and grooves, are also very popular. These treatments make the gate much heavier, which demands stronger hinges and sometimes more substantial posts. The minimum post size is usually 4x4 stock. But 6x6s installed on both sides of the gate opening are much stronger and usually look appropriate on most fences.

TOOLS & MATERIALS
▌ Combination square ▌ Screwdriver bit
▌ Framing square ▌ Drill-driver
▌ Drill and countersink bits
▌ Tongue-and-groove boards ▌ 1x6 pine
▌ 1-in. galvanized screws

1 Cut the gate frame boards to size, leaving about 1 in. of clearance from side to side for the hinges and the gate latch. Then lay the boards on a flat surface, and square up the corners using a framing square.

2 Secure the corners by attaching triangular wood gussets to the gate frame boards. Use galvanized screws and an electric drill or drill/driver to do this job.

3 Screw the gate boards to the gate frame using galvanized screws. You can mark each board and cut it to fit, or install all the boards and cut them in place.

4 To strengthen the gate and give it a more substantial look, install facing boards on the perimeter. Just cut them to length and attach them using galvanized screws.

Custom gate designs can create an unusual entry.

5 Complete the gate construction by installing trim boards around the sides. These boards strengthen the gate and provide a solid base for attaching hinges, latches, and gate-closing hardware. They also protect the end grain of the gate boards from exposure to moisture.

JOINING GATE BOARDS WITH A Z-BRACE

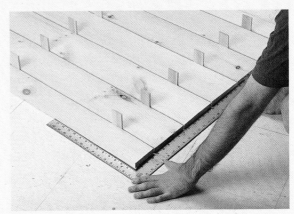

1. Lay out boards with spacers, and square up the gate. Cut equal-sized end boards to make the layout symmetrical.

2. Use a 2x3 or 2x4 top and bottom for back bracing. Predrill, countersink, and drive two screws for each board.

3. Cut the angles on a diagonal brace to complete the Z-shape. Run the brace up from the lower-hinge side.

115

● HINGING TO MASONRY

Wood-to-wood connections are easy to make. Fastening a gate post to masonry is more difficult. You need to drill through the post, set it in position, and mark the hole locations. Then you drill a hole in the masonry and insert an anchor that will capture the threads of screws or bolts that hold the post. You can dig out a hole by hand, but it's easier with a drill and masonry bit, or a rotary hammer drill. You can also use (or rent) a gun that fires hardened nails into masonry.

Hammer and Star Drill

Drill and Masonry Bit

Rotary Hammer Drill

Powder-Actuated Nailer

BUILDING A LATTICE-AND-PANEL GATE

project

Lattice is a popular building material for fences, gates, and screens because it presents a light, airy feel at the same time that it defines space and provides some privacy. Unfortunately, lattice panels aren't very substantial and can't provide the strength needed for a sturdy gate. One good solution to this problem is to install lattice at the top of the gate and solid boards at the bottom. This combination also works well for fence sections, especially if you'd like to plant vines along the top of the fence.

TOOLS & MATERIALS
▌Drill-driver ▌Safety glasses ▌2x4s
▌Hammer ▌Tape measure ▌Circular saw
▌Framing square ▌Galvanized screws
▌Tongue-and-groove boards ▌Lattice panel
▌Galvanized finishing nails

4 Place the lattice in the top opening, and hold it with a couple of nails. Then check the gate frame assembly for square using a framing square. When the assembly is square, install the panel boards in the lower section.

1 Construct the gate frame using 2x4s and galvanized screws. Install a crosspiece 12 in. from the top to separate the lattice panel from the solid-wood panel on the bottom.

2 The lattice panel and the boards below are held inside the gate frame with nailing strips on each side. Cut these strips to size, and nail them in place using galvanized nails.

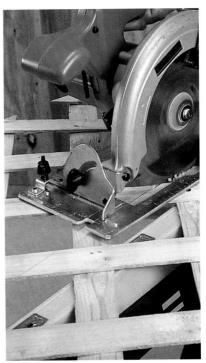

3 Cut the lattice panel to size using a circular saw. Set the blade depth so the blade extends just below the bottom of the lattice. This will make for a cleaner cut.

5 Complete the construction by attaching the second set of nailing strips to the outside of the lattice panel and the boards below using galvanized nails.

● HEAVY-DUTY GATE MOUNTS

Perhaps the strongest and most durable gate mount is a pin-mount hinge, also called a hook-and-strap hinge. The two-part system relies on a secure and solid gate post large enough to accept the L-shape pin. Some pin hardware can be bolted through the thickness of the post, while most simply screw in. The adjoining gate hinge, which can be a long, decorative leaf (top) or a short metal arm (bottom), has an eye that transfers weight onto the pin.

INSTALLING A GATE

The hardest part of installing a gate is to position it properly inside the gate opening before you attach any hardware. The easiest way to do this is to prop up the gate on some scrap boards until it roughly fits the opening. Then make final adjustments by inserting shimming shingles (a stock home-center item) between the boards and the bottom and sides of the gate. You can also clamp boards to the fence and gate to keep it from moving until the hardware is mounted.

TOOLS & MATERIALS
- Framing square ▌Drill-driver
- Combination square ▌Wrench ▌Gate
- Slip-joint pliers ▌Screwdriver bit
- Scrap wood ▌Hinges ▌Shimming shingles
- Latch ▌Lag screws ▌Galvanized screws

1 Before installing the gate, check it using a framing square. If it's out of square, determine which diagonal measurement (from corner to corner) is longer; then place a pipe clamp across this diagonal and tighten it until the gate is square. Add a brace to keep it square, and mark the hinge locations on the posts (insert).

GATE STRIKE OPTIONS

Strike Board Behind Post

Post

Gate

Fence

Strike

Fence Board on Post

Strike

Gate

Fence

Blocking Beside Post

Gate

Fence

Strike

Fence Board on Gate

Strike

Gate

Fence

2 Prop the gate inside the fence opening until it is correctly aligned. Then mark the hinge locations on the gate. Attach the hinge according to the manufacturers instructions.

3 Place the gate inside the opening, and reinstall the shims to align the gate. Check the gate appearance from both sides to make sure this alignment looks best.

4 When you are satisfied with the overall gate alignment, create some allowance for the gate eventually sagging by sliding a shingle under the lower latch-side corner.

5 Mount the other side of each gate hinge—in this case a hinge pin—on the fence post. Predrill pilot holes to make driving the screws or bolts easier.

6 Once the gate is installed and working properly, attach a strike board to the gate or the post, using one of the approaches shown opposite.

7 Finish the installation by attaching anti-sag hardware to the back side of the gate and by mounting a sturdy gate latch to the gate and the post.

9 finishing and repairs

Building a fence is only part of the job. To protect it and make it last as long as possible, you'll have to apply a finish. Transparent waterproof sealers are the first option. They are easy to apply and protect the wood against exposure to the weather. Other common choices are stains, which add some color while still letting the wood grain show through, and exterior-grade varnishes, which can provide very durable protection along with a high-gloss surface. But paint is, by far, the preferred fencing finish. Virtually any color is available, and most fences don't require a lot of paint. Standard preparation and application rules apply, as with any exterior painting. Keep in mind that it will never be easier to paint a fence than when it is first installed. So do a good job. Prime unfinished wood, and apply two topcoats of paint.

FINISHING OPTIONS

A finish does more than dress up your project. It provides a barrier against the weather, sheds water, discourages decay, and minimizes any checking and warping. There is a great variety of finishes to choose from, but all fall into one of four basic types.

■ **Water Sealer.** Most sealers contain a wax dissolved in mineral spirits. The wax lodges in the pores of the wood, sealing it against water. The finish is clear but will slightly darken the wood.

Water sealers are applied to all aboveground parts and reapplied annually to maintain a natural wood color. There are no sealers that will preserve the tone of new wood. Redwood, cedar, and other woods will weather even under coatings that contain a UV inhibiter to reduce fading from sunlight.

■ **Stain.** Semitransparent stains have pigment mixed with a preservative. Opaque stains offer more protection than semitransparent ones because they have more pigment in a mix that resembles paint. While neither type of stain is as durable as paint, stains do not crack or peel as paint does. Better yet, when it comes time to apply fresh stain in a few years, you won't have to scrape and brush off the old finish. Check the label to make sure that the stain is for exterior use and provides protection against mildew and UV rays.

■ **Varnish.** Varnish is a combination of an oil and a resin. It is durable, though prone to cracking and flaking. Polyurethane is the toughest of the varnish types but not the best for exterior use. Direct sunlight can cause

polyurethane to peel, and repairs are almost impossible. These finishes are best used indoors on floors and furniture. Outside, use a spar or marine-grade varnish that has a higher oil content.

■ **Paint.** Paint is an excellent wood preservative because it forms a surface film that seals the wood against moisture. The drawback is that you have to scrape and repaint periodically. You can use water-based acrylic latex or oil-based alkyd. Latex cleans up with soap and water. Alkyd requires paint thinner. Both types come in flat, semigloss (satin), and gloss. Better exterior paints include mildewcides that inhibit the growth of mold and decay-causing organisms.

Finishing Pressure-Treated Wood

Pressure-treating wood protects it from insects and rot but does not prevent cupping or warping. So you should protect the wood with a finish. Unfortunately, pressure-treated wood presents some finishing problems. The treatment puts moisture back into the wood, sometimes leaving a waterlogged surface that just won't hold a finish. Before you apply a finish to pressure-treated wood, sprinkle a few drops of water on it. If the wood absorbs the water, it is ready to finish. If not, you should wait until air circulation dries out some of the moisture.

Semitransparent oil-based stains generally work best over pressure-treated wood. Another option is to coat the wood annually with a water sealer. Most manufacturers advise against painting pressure-treated wood with latex paint.

wood weathering comparisons

Spruce New

Spruce Old

Cedar New

Cedar Old

A clear sealer used by itself or with a stain preserves and protects the wood against the elements.

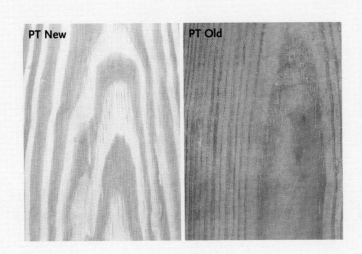

PT New   PT Old

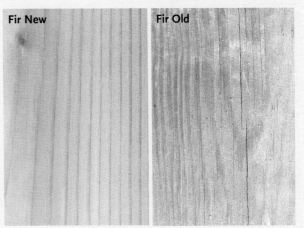

Fir New   Fir Old

APPLYING FINISHES

You can apply any type of finish or preservative with a brush, roller, or spray gun. While brushing is the most time consuming, it is often the best method for painting or staining fences with spaced boards or pickets. Rollers work well for fences made with solid boards or plywood, but you'll still need a brush to reach areas that the roller misses.

Spray guns can work well for designs that would be time consuming to paint with a brush and roller, such as those with latticework or basket weave design. But a spray gun will not save much time when painting an open design, such as a post-and-rail fence, and you'll end up wasting more paint than you would with a brush and roller. You will also need to spread drop cloths or drape plastic sheeting to prevent overspray from damaging nearby plants.

Redwood and cedar are expensive, elegant woods, so they're often stained or left to weather naturally. But some people paint these woods, especially if they're using cheaper or rougher grades. Both species bleed, which means that brownish-red tannins in the wood will seep through light-colored paints and discolor the finish. To prevent bleeding on freshly milled redwood, cedar, or even pine, apply one or two coats of stain-blocking primer to all knots and other areas that might bleed. Follow with a coat of alkyd primer to thoroughly seal the wood. If bleeding is not a concern, simply apply an alkyd or latex primer to all sides of any bare wood.

Semitransparent stain offers an evenly weathered look.

stained and painted finishes

Clear sealer protects wood and shows the grain.

Semitransparent stain adds a hue over the wood grain.

DECORATIVE HARDWARE OPTIONS

Copper Cladding

Copper caps call attention to gate posts and shed water.

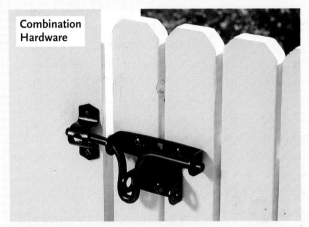

Combination Hardware

Latches with oversize handles allow easy access.

Ornamental Metalwork

Contrasting metals create ornamental details.

Ornamental Hinges

Custom wrought-iron T-hinges can support wide gates.

Full-Bodied Stain

Full-bodied stain is opaque and covers the wood grain.

Paint (two coats)

Two coats of paint are opaque but lie on the surface.

Priming before Painting

The trend with modern exterior-grade paints is a promise of long-lasting one-coat coverage over almost any type of material in any condition, whether it's raw fencing or kiln-dried boards. To be competitive, paint manufacturers outpace each other with claims about needing only the most minimal preparation work over any surface.

But no matter what type of paint you apply, two thin coats are almost always better than one thick coat. After spot-priming blemishes with a stain killer, it may be tempting to load up a brush or roller and try to do the job in one pass. While a brush or roller loaded with penetrating stain helps more material seep into the wood grain, a single thick coat of paint is likely to drip, sag, or blister under the hot sun before it dries. And no paint is immune to dull-spotting and eventual peeling where patches of rough surface grain pull excess moisture from the fresh paint as it sets and dries.

The upshot is that it's best to prime the entire fence. That provides the most uniform surface for the top coat, particularly on rougher boards. There are special priming paints, but in most cases a layer of your top-coat paint thinned by about a third will do just as well.

If you're spraying, you will have to double back on wet areas to apply a thick coat of paint. And that can increase the chance of creating drips and sags, which is one of the drawbacks of spraying in general. If you can contain the spray, this light, once-over application can produce a reasonable prime coat.

Top-Coating Tips

For best results, always keep a wet edge so that the start of one section won't dry before you get back to continue, resulting in lap marks. This isn't a problem on fences with spaced pickets or boards, but lapping can show up on solid fences. It helps to work on manageable areas at one time to reduce the amount of wet edge and the chance of creating lap marks.

Also, always work from high to low, cutting-in seams between pickets and rails, for instance, then brushing out the surfaces so that you can pick up drips on your way down. If you work on a large area and drips have hardened, scrape them off instead of trying to blend them with fresh paint. On large projects where you start early and finish late, follow the sun around the yard so that it will have warmed up and dried the fence boards of any moisture by the time you reach them.

If you're working with water-based latex paint, remember to use a brush with nylon bristles. If you're working with oil-based alkyd paint, use a brush with natural bristles. A good tool for all-around work is a 3-inch-wide long-handled brush. It offers good control, particularly when you apply a little pressure and flex the bristles to fit into a tight spot.

You may find that it saves time and effort to use a roller for basic application and a brush for working paint into seams between boards. On pickets and spaced boards, you can use a small trim-type roller (only a few inches wide) to coat the faces and edges of boards or pickets. Follow up with a brush to work the paint into joints and brush out the surfaces.

● STAIN BLOCKERS

If you use boards or pickets with knots and other imperfections and don't want them to show through, apply a stain killer. Sold under various trade names, most stain killers consist of pigmented white shellac. It looks like full-strength white paint but has the ability to hide blemishes and seal knots to reduce bleeding. Spot-prime imperfections with stain killer to start. Then apply a prime coat. The top coat should completely cover the primed patches.

A painted fence can complement the colors of a house. Plan on applying two coats over primed wood.

BRUSHING VS. SPRAYING

Painting pickets with a brush can take a lot of time because you generally need two coats, and there are all those edges to cover. Spraying spreads paint faster than a brush, but overspray can be a problem. You'll need to protect nearby vegetation with plastic sheeting. The best bet may be a combination: spray on a prime coat, and use a brush to work into the nooks and crannies and brush out the top coat.

STRAIGHTENING A FENCE POST

project

Posts that lean a bit are easy to fix. Just pull (or push) the post until it's plumb, and drive a pressure-treated wood stake next to it to keep it from moving. But more serious problems require resetting the post. To do this, dig away the soil until the post can move freely in the hole. Then attach a brace to two adjacent sides, and drive stakes in the ground next to these braces. Adjust the post until it's plumb. Then nail the braces to the stakes. Backfill around the post with concrete or compacted soil.

TOOLS & MATERIALS
- Sledgehammer ▪ Shovel
- Drill-driver ▪ Come-along
- Steel pole or stake
- Screw eye ▪ Brace

1 To straighten a leaning post, start by removing the soil from around the bottom of the post using a shovel or clamshell posthole digger. Take out enough material so the post can be pushed easily into a plumb position. If this is too difficult, use a come-along to plumb the post.

3 Attach one end of the come-along cable to the screw eye in the side of the post. Then hook the other end of the cable around the top of the angled steel pole, and tighten the ratchet handle.

4 Slowly crank the come-along to pull the post into a plumb position. The steel pole may move slightly as the post straightens. But the post will always move more. If the post is particularly stubborn, further loosen the soil at the bottom of the posthole using a 4-ft. steel bar.

2 To use a come-along, first drive a steel pole at an angle into the ground a few feet away from the post. Position it on the side of the post opposite the direction of the lean. Drive at least 16 in. of pipe into the ground. Then thread a screw eye into the side of the post (inset).

5 Once the post has been pulled into a plumb posi-tion by the come-along, attach an angled brace to the top of the post and the side of a stake that has been driven into the ground. Add a second brace if it's neces-sary to stabilize the post.

6 Backfill around the bottom of the post with con-crete. Then wait two days for it to cure; then remove the come-along and brace. If you don't want the concrete pad to show, stop it about 4 in. from the top of the hole, and cover it with topsoil and grass seed.

REPAIRING POSTS

Most fence repairs involve repairing or replacing one or more damaged posts. There are many types of wood problems that can weaken a post. Wood can be chewed away by insects or infected with a disease such as dry rot. But the most common problem is rot near the base of a post where water collects.

If your posts are set in gravel, dig around each one to a depth of about 4 inches. Check for decay by probing with a screwdriver, knife, or another sharp object. While you're at it, also check joints where rails meet posts and where boards attach to rails. Check exposed ends, such as tops of posts and picket boards.

If the tool sinks easily into the wood, you will have to repair or replace the post. If decay is less than about ½ inch deep into the surface, use a paint scraper or wide wood chisel to scrape out the decayed area down to sound wood, and treat the exposed wood with several coats of a good wood preservative, penetrating stain, or two coats of paint.

Rescuing Damaged Posts

If the post is rotted at or below ground level but the aboveground portion is still good, you can probably install a brace instead of replacing the post. Start by digging around the existing post down to the bottom. If the post has a concrete collar, break up the concrete using a pick or heavy pry bar, and remove the pieces.

Before you do any cutting, add at least one brace to hold the top of the post in position. Then you can cut off the damaged post about 1 to 2 inches aboveground and remove the rotted portion. You should be able to cut most of the way through with a circular saw, even without detaching the rails and siding. But you'll need to finish the cut with a handsaw or a hammer and chisel.

Make a permanent brace out of a pressure-treated post by cutting it just long enough to reach from the base of the hole to about 6 inches onto the old post. Clamp the stub piece in place; plumb the assembly; drill through both posts at the overlap; and secure the sections with at least three galvanized bolts. Cut the top end of the stub at an angle to aid water runoff.

If your fence design won't accommodate this type of brace, or if you simply don't like the look of it, you can also attach pressure-treated 2x4 braces on each side of the post.

smart tip
CHECKING FOR ROT

It doesn't take an expert to recognize that a dark brown patch of spongy looking wood near the bottom of a fence post is probably rot. But a lot of wood decay can be on the surface, leaving most of the wood intact and capable of supporting the fence. You can test the depth of rot by digging a knife into the wood. If the spongy material is only ½ inch or so deep on a 6-inch-diameter post, for example, scrape it away and apply several coats of preservative. If the knife sinks in deeply, it's probably time to replace the post.

diagnosing wood problems

Carpenter ants burrow.

Powder post beetles tunnel.

Termites also tunnel.

Carpenter bees bore holes.

REINFORCING A DAMAGED POST

project

The best way to repair a rotted post is to cut away the rotted section, install a pressure treated stub post next to it, and attach the two using galvanized carriage bolts. This isn't the most attractive repair and is not recommended for end or corner posts, or posts that define a gate opening. But for posts that aren't so visible or that are typically covered with shrubbery or other plants, it's the easiest and cheapest solution.

TOOLS & MATERIALS
- Cold chisel ▌Shovel
- Hammer ▌Knife or screwdriver
- Saw ▌Clamps ▌Drill-driver
- Galvanized carriage bolts
- 4x4 post ▌Concrete mix
- Galvanized nails

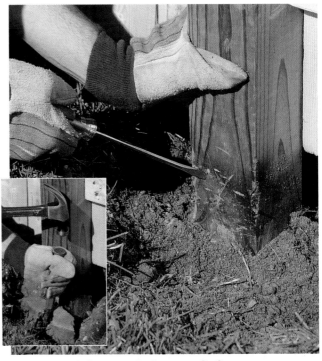

1 To check for rot at the bottom of a fence post, remove the sod using a shovel, and probe the wood with a knife. If the blade goes deeper than 1 in., the post should be repaired. With posts set in concrete, first break up the collar using a hammer and cold chisel (inset).

2 Cut off the bottom of the rotted post using a circular or reciprocating saw. Remove the old post, and install a new stub post. Clamp it securely to the side of the full post.

3 Join the two posts using galvanized carriage bolts. Predrill clearance holes; slide the bolts in place; and tighten the nuts using a socket wrench.

4 Brace the post in a plumb position, and backfill the posthole with concrete. Once the concrete cures, remove the brace and finish the post to match the rest of the fence.

131

smart tip
REINFORCE CORNERS

ONCE YOU WORK A RACKED GATE OR A SECTION OF FENCE BACK INTO SQUARE POSITION, THERE ARE SEVERAL WAYS TO SECURE THE ALIGNMENT. YOU CAN ADD GUSSET PLATES MADE OF PLYWOOD OR ADD DIFFERENT TYPES OF METAL HARDWARE. FOR BEST RESULTS, IT'S WISE TO WORK THE GATE OR FENCE SECTION SLIGHTLY PAST SQUARE BEFORE YOU ATTACH ANY BRACING. THAT WAY, THE STRESSES THAT CAUSED THE RACKING TO BEGIN WITH ARE LIKELY TO PULL THE FRAME BACK TO SQUARE BEFORE THE BRACING TAKES HOLD AND PREVENTS ANY FURTHER MOVEMENT.

Square up frames using surface-mounted brackets.

Conceal screws and brackets inside the frame.

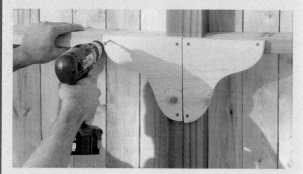

Secure corners using decorative plywood gusset plates.

UNRACKING A GATE

project

Most gate problems result from loose hinges and racked gate frames. Fixing loose hinges is generally pretty easy. If the hinge screws are loose, try tightening them using a screwdriver. If the holes are stripped, then replace the old screws with longer and thicker ones. If the bigger screws don't work, then fill the old screw holes with waterproof epoxy putty and move the hinges slightly so you can drill new holes into solid wood. To repair a racked gate frame, review the steps in this project.

TOOLS & MATERIALS
- Clamp ■ Drill-driver ■ Framing square
- Screwdriver bit ■ Power drill
- Galvanized screws ■ Tape measure
- Lumber for crosspieces and brace

3 Tighten the clamp until the gate is square. Then screw a temporary brace across one corner to keep the gate square. You'll need to loosen the clamp so you can slide the brace under the pipe. Retighten the clamp, and check the assembly for square before attaching the brace.

1 When a gate is sagging, first determine where it is racked using a framing square. Usually the latch side of the gate will sag toward the ground, and the top latch-side corner will bind against the gate post.

2 To repair the gate, first remove it from the gate opening and place it on some saw horses or a work-table. Measure the diagonals on the gate from outside corner to outside corner. Then install a pipe clamp across the corners that have the longer dimension.

4 Remove the pipe clamp, and cut a 2x4 to fit between two opposite corners. Scribe the ends so the angle cuts will fit tightly inside the corners. Tap this brace in place, and attach it at both ends using galvanized screws.

5 Instead of installing a 2x4 brace, you can attach steel cables to the opposite corners with the longer diagonal measurement. Join these cables in the middle of the gate using a turnbuckle. Tighten the turnbuckle until the gate frame is square. Then reinstall the gate.

project

RESTORING A PAINTED FENCE AND GATE

Wood will last a long time if it is protected from the weather. Unfortunately, once the paint starts cracking and peeling, the first stages of rot will not be far behind. Repainting is easiest if you catch the surface before it deteriorates too much. You can do some light sanding, touch up raw wood with primer, and add a fresh topcoat. If you have the time, it does help to wash a fence before painting. Surface deposits, such as dirt and mildew, reduce paint adhesion.

TOOLS & MATERIALS
▐ Paint scraper ▐ Power sander ▐ Hammer
▐ Scrub brush ▐ Bleach ▐ Galvanized nails
▐ Pail ▐ Pressure washer ▐ Nail set
▐ Exterior paint ▐ Sandpaper ▐ Paintbrushes

1 Begin surface preparation by scraping away any loose paint using a paint scraper (inset). Sharpen or replace the blade frequently to make the work easier. Brush off the dust; then wash the surface with detergent and warm water. Add a cup of bleach to clean off mildew.

4 Once the surface of the fence boards and gate are clean, carefully look for any protruding nailheads. Drive these heads flush using a nail set and hammer.

5 If the fence boards, posts, and gates are very rough after washing, then sand these surfaces smooth using 150-grit paper. Use a finishing sander or a belt sander.

6 Prime all the exposed wood with a good exterior primer. Once the fence is primed and dry, go back over the surface and spot prime knots using a stain-blocking primer.

2 A rented pressure washer makes short work of cleaning a fence. Some have onboard reservoirs for dispensing cleaning agents. Others, like this one, pump the agents from a container. Gas models are more powerful. But smaller electric units can easily clean a fence.

3 Pressure washers are powerful, delivering a concentrated stream of water that can easily gouge the surface of the wood. Keep the head at least 16 in. away from the surface to start. Move closer until you detect damage; then pull back 6 in. and continue working.

7 Once the priming is done, coat the surface with a topcoat of paint. Work the paint into the spaces between boards. For surfaces where most of the old paint has been removed, like this one, the best results are achieved by applying two topcoats instead of one.

smart tip

LEAD PAINT CHECK

IF YOU NEED TO SCRAPE AND REPAINT AN OLD FENCE, BEAR IN MIND THAT SOME PAINTS MADE BEFORE 1978 CONTAIN LEAD, WHICH CAN BE HAZARDOUS TO YOUR HEALTH. IF YOU SUSPECT THAT A LEAD-BASED PAINT WAS USED, TEST IT USING AN INEXPENSIVE LEAD-TESTING KIT. MOST USE A SWAB SAMPLER (BELOW LEFT) THAT YOU APPLY TO A PRETREATED TEST CARD (BELOW RIGHT). EVEN IF YOU SCRAPE AND SAND ONLY PORTIONS OF A FENCE, WEAR A RESPIRATOR APPROVED BY THE NATIONAL INSTITUTE FOR OCCUPATIONAL SAFETY AND HEALTH (NIOSH).

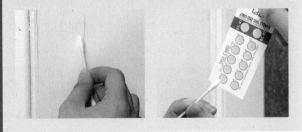

10 trellises & arbors design guide

From the simplest lattice on the side of a house to a complex pergola standing sentinel over a driveway, a trellis or arbor creates both architectural interest and vertical landscaping. With these structures, you can grow elaborate climbing plants, divide a space, lead guests down a garden path, or create a shady nook with built-in seating. As you will see from the examples shown in the following pages, well-made trellises and arbors have graceful, open designs that lend themselves to many purposes. Often, the structure is so attractive that it becomes a focal point in its own right, rather than a supporting player in the overall design of the yard.

trellises

These structures are often attached to a house or garage wall to train climbing plants, but they can also stand alone to provide vertical landscaping in the middle of your yard. In either case, be sure to select a trellis that can adequately support the plants that you choose to grow.

Many homeowners use trellises to screen an unwanted view or as a divider. In designing your trellis, choose exactly how much privacy you want. Lattice pieces that are woven tightly together effectively block views even when plants are dormant during the winter months. They also serve as a windbreak. Open lattice patterns do not provide as much privacy, but they do give the structure a light, airy appearance. When used as a fence, a trellis is a more friendly way to separate your property from that of your neighbors.

Be sure to match the size of the trellis that you are installing with its location and use. A large trellis can overpower a small area, such as an herb garden, just as a small structure plopped in the middle of a large lawn will look out of place.

Stand-alone trellises, left, provide a base for climbing plants. Choose plants that are best suited for the type of trellis you install, above. A stone wall, right, can anchor a trellis as well as a wood wall.

Wall-mounted trellises, opposite, offer the chance for creating dramatic plantings.

While trellises consist of a flat plane for supporting plants, arbors provide the added benefits of walls and a roof to create a sense of enclosure. They tend to make bolder design statements than most trellises do.

Many people use the words arbor and pergola interchangeably. Technically, an arbor is a sheltered area—even if it consists of bent twigs to support a vine; a pergola is a tunnel-like walkway supported by columns. In either case, select the structure to match its location.

Arbors make great transition points. Place one on a path and you will lead people from one point in your yard to another. Install one at the entrance to a garden, and you've created a natural separation between the two areas.

Like trellises, arbors make attractive focal points, but they also serve as inviting destinations in the yard. Set up an arbor with seating in a shady spot and you will have a secluded area to get away from it all, and you will have expanded your outdoor living area.

As with any garden structure, be sure to select one that is in scale with your yard and home.

Create a formal entry between your yard and the street or driveway, left.

Material choices for arbors range from solid wood to metal, above, to bent twigs.

Frame a doorway with an arbor and flowering vine to create a charming sheltered entry, right.

Make a landscape statement with the trellis or arbor you select. Arbors, such as the one above, can divide spaces or serve as an entry to a small garden or shaded area.

This swinging gate and high-peaked arch, right, give anyone entering this yard an open-armed welcome.

Ivy-covered arbors and landscape-tie steps soften the incline of this yard. The delicate metal framework allows the ivy to take center stage.

Highlight a view with the careful placement of an arbor, opposite, or by adding cutouts in the lattice of a trellis, right. You can also hide unwanted views of garbage bins or a neighboring street behind a trellis fence, above.

Vertical landscaping adds a new dimension to your yard. This trellis, below, supports climbing roses and separates one yard from the next.

145

used as entries

Entry arbors can give a yard or garden a sense of structure or a sense of enchantment, depending upon the materials and design involved. For instance, a rustic arbor made of entwined tree branches when used as the entrance to an abundant garden, creates a "Secret Garden" quality. The arbor you choose can also enhance a yard landscaped with a certain era in mind. A metal arbor with intricate scrollwork can be the perfect entryway to your Victorian-inspired garden. The entrance to your yard or garden should reflect the style you've created therein.

Garden entry arbors, opposite top, help define the gardens and yards to which they belong, and they beckon to passersby at the same time.

Gateway arbors, opposite bottom, can make a definite design statement. The distinctive pergola-like top of this arbor is hard to miss.

Careful placement of a trellis or arbor can create a mood or set a scene in your yard. This dramatic arbor, right, frames an attractive portion of this garden.

The simple metal design of the arbor below adds height and directs anyone strolling in this yard directly to the garden.

Even eye-catching arbors should provide practical value. Sturdy stone and metal, above, separate a formal garden from the wild. This is a good example of how imaginative you can be when designing your trellises and arbors.

The gable-type roof and unusual scrollwork contribute to the distinctive style of this secluded arbor, right. This Romanesque design echoes that of the stone pieces in the garden.

This imposing pergola, above, signals the driveway opening in this fence.

The large, curving posts and oversize dimensions of this arbor, right, echo the scale of the trees and rocks in the area.

What do you want to emphasize? If you are more interested in the plants than the structure, choose arbor and trellis materials that fade into the background when plants are in bloom. The alternative is a design where the structure always plays a prominent role, above and right.

Tower trellises come in a variety of shapes and sizes, from branches loosely bound together to the formal design shown at right. A tower trellis can add architectural interest—for instance, a trellis that resembles the Eiffel Tower— or textural interest among your plants. The abundant clematis climbing the trellis, above, creates a unique shape in the garden, as well as another level of color and character to catch the eye.

11 tools & materials for trellises & arbors

Trellises and arbors are stock items in the standard outdoor building portfolio. But in many ways, the methods used to construct them share as much with furniture and cabinetmaking as they do with traditional building techniques. For example, stock lumber sizes are the coin of the realm in the construction business. But they aren't used nearly as much in trellis and arbor construction. The light, airy feel—and the distinctive designs—of these structures almost always call for custom-cut lumber. Because of differences like these, a bench-top table saw is almost a requirement of this work. Other specialized tools come into play, too, such as routers, diverse clamps, and a full complement of power sanders.

POWER SAWS

Sliding compound miter saws offer a wide range of cutting capacities. The head rotates and tilts; it slides on a rail.

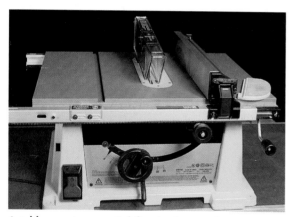

A table saw is essential for ripping stock to nonstandard widths. A good bench-top model is also suitable for many projects.

The saber saw is excellent for rip cuts and crosscuts, and is efficient at internal cuts. Its forte is the curved cut, made freehand.

POWER SAWS

Power Miter Saws. The most basic model is the traditional miter saw, which looks like a circular saw mounted on a spring-loaded hinge above a small table. The saw body rotates from a straight crosscut to a 45-degree miter cut in either direction. The majority of the saws on the market use a 10-inch blade. Most will crosscut a 2x6 and miter a 2x4 at 45 degrees. It is a simple, functional saw. To make compound miter, cuts that are simultaneously miter and bevels, you need the more sophisticated compound miter saw. It has not only a rotating table, but also a pivot to enable the head to be tilted 45 degrees (or more) to one or both sides. Cut capacities are similar to those of regular miter saws. The most sophisticated type is the sliding compound miter saw. The head assembly rotates and tilts (some models from both left and right) for compound cutting. But it also slides forward and back on a rail system, thus increasing the crosscutting capacity to about 12 inches.

Table Saws. In the typical woodworking shop, the table saw is boss. And because of this, most people who make their living working with wood don't skimp on this tool. But homeowners don't need a 3-horsepower workhorse. A bench-top model is the better choice. It's much more portable and, when adjusted properly, makes good cuts. When shopping for one of these saws, look for a tool with a 10-inch tilting blade, sturdy handwheel and knobs, and locking devices that operate easily. The blade height and bevel should adjust without any play; a lock should hold the bevel setting. Degree scales should be easy to read, and there should be adjustable stops at 45 and 90 degrees.

Saber Saws. A saber saw is a portable tool that has a narrow blade that can make straight and curved cuts. The number of teeth per inch on the blade indicates the aggressiveness of the blade's cut. More teeth yield smoother cuts. Fewer teeth make for rougher cuts. When first introduced, the saber saw cut with an "up-and-down" motion. This is known as "straight-line" action and is considered the best for smooth, tear-out-free cutting. But it can make for slow going on rip cuts and in dense materials. To accelerate the tool's cutting speed, orbital action has been added. In this mode, the blade churns forward and backward, as it strokes up and down, cutting more aggressively. You can switch this orbital action ON and OFF.

ROUTERS AND BITS

You will want to have two types of routers: a plunge router, left, and a fixed-base router, right.

Sample router bits are: straight bits (left), pattern and flush trimming bits (middle), and rounding over bits (right).

ROUTERS AND BITS

Routers are versatile tools that consist of a motor with a shaft-mounted collect that holds various cutting bits. These tools can make joints, profile edges, and duplicate parts following a template. There are two basic types of tools: fixed base and plunge.

Fixed-Base Routers. These tools are compact and very stable, which makes them the best choice for general routing jobs. Despite their name, the base can be adjusted up and down to regulate the depth of cut.

Plunge Routers. These tools are made by putting a traditional router motor in a base that can be adjusted up and down while the motor is running. This means that you can start a cut in the middle of the board simply by placing the base in the right spot, turning on the motor, and lowering the spinning bit into the work. These plunge cuts make all sorts of jobs much easier.

Bits. The more bits you have, the more jobs you can do with these tools. In every performance test, bits with carbide cutting edges are superior to high-speed steel bits. Straight bits are used to make most joiners cuts. For trimming parts to match templates, you'll need pattern and flush-trimming bits. And rounding over bits are used for smoothing sharp edges.

FEED DIRECTION

Improper feed causes a rough cut.

Correct feed produces a smooth cut.

Feed the router clockwise inside a frame.

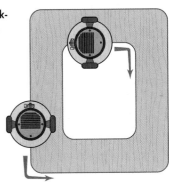

Feed the router counterclockwise outside frame.

CLAMPS

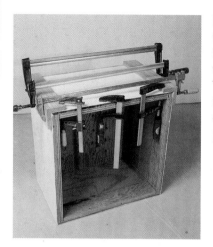

Bar clamps are the workhorses in most woodworking shops. They are available in a wide range of sizes and proportions.

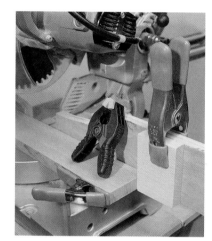

Spring clamps are plenty strong for holding small parts together during assembly, and they are great for holding stop blocks.

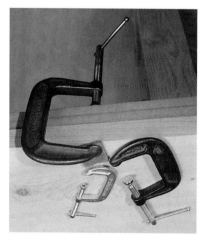

All-metal C-clamps are the strongest style. Insert wood scraps between the jaws and the work to prevent dents.

Hand screws are particularly good for laminating stock face to face because the wooden jaws are long and flat.

CLAMPS

Clamps perform the indispensable job of holding parts together while they are being assembled. There are many different styles. Here are four of the most useful.

Bar Clamps. These are the workhorse clamps. They're used for assembly work, for securing work pieces to sawhorses or worktables, for mounting temporary braces when installing fence posts, and many other jobs. These tools are designated by two capacities: the maximum length of the opening between jaws and the throat depth. Typically, the clamp's overall bulk is proportional to the throat depth. As the throat gets deeper, both the jaw and the bar get beefier. A clamp with a thicker and/or wider bar can exert more pressure with less flex.

Spring Clamps. The jaws of spring clamps are opened simply by squeezing the two handles together, typically a one-handed operation. The jaws close firmly, even on work that doesn't have parallel faces. Spring clamps are strong enough for holding things together during layout and assembly—and for glue-ups on small objects, too.

C-Clamp. These are the oldest style of all-metal clamp and gets its name from its shape. They can be slightly aggravating to use because it takes more time to install than a like-sized bar clamp. But they exert an enormous amount of pressure.

Hand Screws. While not considered to be all-purpose clamps, hand screws are particularly good for gluing-up lamination. Made of hardwood, the jaws are long and flat so you can apply pressure on board areas as opposed to isolated points like C-clamps. Because of the two screw handles, the pressure is applied evenly from end to end.

DRILLS AND BITS

Cordless drills can handle almost any job that their corded ancestors did, without the hassle of a cord.

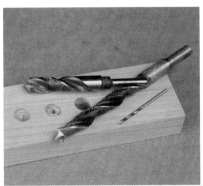

If your drill has a ³⁄₈-in. chuck, use larger-diameter bits with stepped-down shanks so that they'll fit your drill's chuck.

Forstner bits cut flat-bottomed, smooth-walled holes. They are great for cutting counterbores in soft wood.

The fastest way to drill screw holes is with a drill-countersink combo. It has a countersink bit fitted over a twist drill bit.

Use a plug cutter to make wooden plugs. Best results come with the cutter mounted in a stand or a drill press.

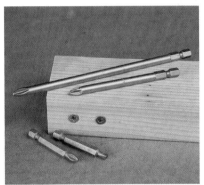

Screwdriver bits chucked into a cordless drill drive most of the screws today. It's helpful to keep some spares on hand.

DRILLS AND BITS

Corded drills are less expensive, but it makes sense to consider cordless models. Many manufacturers now have 24-volt tools with electronic brakes, adjustable clutches, and keyless chucks. Here are some of the most useful bits to use with these drills.

Twist Drills. These are the all-purpose hole makers. They're available individually and in sets, in standard and metric sizes. A good standard set has 29 bits that range from ¹⁄₁₆ through ¹⁄₂ inch, in 64ths of an inch increments.

Forstner Bits. These bits cut the smoothest counterbores. The center point keeps the bit from moving while the cutting rim removes the stock.

Countersink Bits. The fastest way to drill screw pilot holes is with a countersink drill bit that consists of a countersink bit attached to a twist drill bit with a setscrew. When the hole is drilled, the twist bit makes room for the screw shaft while the countersink creates a depression for the screw head.

Plug Cutter. To conceal a screw head below the surface of a board, you need to cover it with a wood plug. This bit cuts plugs.

Screwdriver Bits. Few people drive screws by hand these days. Usually the cordless drill/driver, using special screwdriver bits, does it instead. The most popular bits have Phillips heads and come in various lengths. Slotted and square-drive bits are also available.

● LUMBER

Lumber quality is a key component of any outdoor project. You can sometimes work around minor defects like these (left).

Allow wood to acclimate in your shop to local temperature and humidity for at least a week (right) before using it. Use 2x4s to keep lumber off of the floor; add strips between layers.

Cypress

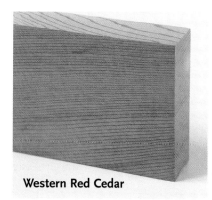

Western Red Cedar

Meranti Mahogany

LUMBER

Just about any wood species can work for outdoor projects, as long as its finish is properly applied and maintained. But this is easier said the done. Because of this most people choose wood species that stand up to weather exposure better, so if the finish is degraded the wood will not rot, at least not right away. In addition to the lumber species discussed on page 32, others were used in the construction of the trellises and arbors that follow.

Cypress. Cypress heartwood varies in color, but is usually a warm tan with some darker streaks. If left unfinished, it will weather to a charcoal color. This wood is strong, moderately hard, and straight-grained. Although cypress is resinous, it glues well, sands easily, and accepts finishes without a problem.

Western Red Cedar. Highly resistant to decay and rot, this wood has a dull red color when it's first cut but turns a handsome brown when exposed to the air. The sapwood is whitish and some boards can contain both

sapwood and heartwood. This wood is lightweight and very soft. Prolonged or heavy exposure to the dust can be irritating to some people. Rich in tannins, this wood will turn black in areas that are exposed to hardware that contains iron.

Meranti Mahogany. This is not a true mahogany but is related to lauan and Philippine mahogany. However, the color of the best boards resembles South American mahoganies. The texture is fairly coarse, and the color is highly variable. Stability does not match that of true mahoganies.

White Oak. Over 50 oak species grow in North America, and they are divided into two primary groups: red oak and white oak. White oak is stronger, harder, more durable, and better suited to outdoor projects than red oak. There is one caveat to keep in mind when working with this wood. As with cedar and redwood, white oak has a high tannin content, and iron that comes in contact with the wood will turn it black. Keep that in mind when you are matching wood with hardware.

● SANDERS

Belt sanders are best for smoothing rough boards and removing grading stamps and mill marks.

Palm sanders are finishing tools intended to remove uniform scratches left by disc or belt sanders.

Random-orbit sanders have pads that rotate in an oscillating pattern. They can smooth a surface quickly.

SANDERS

Many types of sanders are available, but the three portable models shown here should take care of most sanding chores. For the best results with the least effort, replace the sanding paper frequently.

Belt Sanders. This common power tool has an abrasive belt mounted on two rollers that are driven by the tool's motor. Belt sanders (and belts) are made in different sizes. The most common are 3 x 21 inch, 3 x 24 inch, and 4 x 24 inch. These tools are designed for aggressive stock removal, so you must pay attention when using them. A modest wobble can result in a deep gouge that can take a long time to sand out. But when used properly, no sanding tool can remove material as quickly.

Palm Sanders. These tools are also called finishing sanders or quarter-sheet sanders because they use one quarter of a standard piece of sandpaper. They provide a smooth-to-the-touch surface finish and are easy to control with one hand. They are generally used just prior to applying a finish.

Random-Orbit Sanders. Like a palm sander these tools are small and can be easily controlled with one hand. They are generally available with 5- or 6-inch-diameter pads that are designed to hold self-sticking sandpaper discs. They are, however, much more aggressive than a palm sander, and because the pad follows a random orbit, the abrasive particles never follow the same path twice. This eliminates the sanding swirls that are common with any finishing sander.

● ADHESIVES & FINISHES

Adhesives. Outdoor building calls for water-resistant glues. One is type II yellow glue that is just the water-resistant version of standard yellow wood glue. Another is polyurethane, which has a longer open time than type II yellow glue, about 1 hour versus 15 minutes.

Finishes. Exterior coatings are designed to protect structures from the damage caused by moisture, sun, and insects. Paint does the best overall job because it usually contains more pigments than other finishes. Solid-color stains have fewer pigments than paint but more than other stains. Semitransparent stains have fewer pigments than the solid-color versions but do let more wood grain show through. Varnishes, such as spar varnish and polyurethane varnish, work well when properly applied.

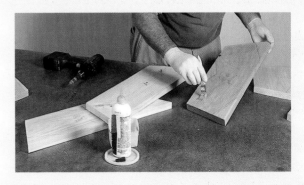

12 trellis projects

A trellis is one of the most eye-catching outdoor structures. Because it's usually built to support climbing plants (think roses), even a simple trellis can make a strong statement anywhere on your property. There are many different trellis styles, as you'll see in this chapter. But they all have three things in common. First, they must be strong enough to support the plants that will grow on them. Second, they must be firmly anchored, either with posts buried in the ground or with hardware that attaches them to a stable structure, such as a building or a fence. And third, they should feature some type of support grid that provides plenty of opportunities for vines to grip and plenty of open places for the plants to grow through. Trellises can be finished with varnish, stain, paint, or just sealed with clear wood preservative.

FAN TRELLIS

A fan trellis is a classic design that adorns countless fences and house walls. Once it's covered with healthy plants it can look like a fountain of color exploding out of the soil. As part of a larger garden design, it gives plenty of height to plants that would otherwise hug the ground. It can also lend attractive texture to surfaces that would otherwise be dull looking. Because of this, trellises are frequently found on house walls between windows where there's nothing but an unexciting expanse of clapboard siding.

A fan trellis can be made as big as you want, as long as you provide for proper support. While the stake that this unit features can support our 6-foot design, larger structures will have to be attached (usually at the top of each fan strip) to the wall or fence.

Because most trellises will eventually be covered with vegetation, the finish you use won't be very visible. And once the plants have covered the trellis, it's pretty hard to renew any finish without also coating the plants. To avoid this problem, many people choose a naturally weather-resistant wood species, like the cedar we used here, and leave it unfinished or coat it with a clear wood preservative. But if you are growing plants that you plan to prune back every few years, you can renew any surface finish, including paint and varnish, at these times.

● CUTTING LIST (See "Tools & Materials," page 164.)

Part	Quantity	Thickness	Width	Length	Stock
Fan strips	4	$3/8$"	1"	72"	$5/4$ x 6 western red cedar
Center strip	1	$1/2$"	1"	72"	$5/4$ x 6 western red cedar
Reinforcing strips	2	$3/8$"	1"	16"	$5/4$ x 6 western red cedar
Top rib	1	$1/2$"	1"	$64^{1}/_{4}$"*	$5/4$ x 6 western red cedar
Middle rib	1	$1/2$"	1"	$35^{5}/_{8}$"*	$5/4$ x 6 western red cedar
Bottom rib	1	$1/2$"	1"	15"*	$5/4$ x 6 western red cedar
Stake	1	$1^{1}/_{2}$"	$1^{1}/_{2}$"	36"	2 x 2 SYP

*These are approximate finished lengths. When cutting the pieces, cut each about 6 to 12 inches longer and trim as needed after securing the fan strips.

EXPLODED VIEW

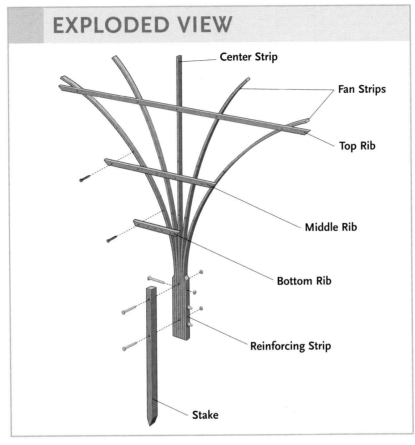

Center Strip

Fan Strips

Top Rib

Middle Rib

Bottom Rib

Reinforcing Strip

Stake

FRONT ELEVATION

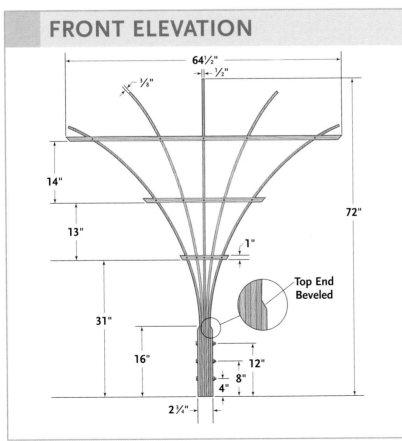

64½"

½"

³⁄₈"

14"

13"

1"

31"

16"

12"

8"

4"

2¾"

72"

Top End
Beveled

builder's notes

You can build this fan trellis fast using a table saw and a few shop tricks.

Materials

Any of a number of woods—cedar, redwood, cypress, and even treated types—can be used. You need only one board, but it must be straight-grained and free of knots. Otherwise, when you bend the fan strips, they could snap at a weak point.

The clear cedar shown requires the use of stainless-steel fasteners because they won't react to the wood the way galvanized steel will. Regardless of the wood type, the extra couple of dollars spent on the stainless-steel fasteners are a worthy investment both for durability and looks. (They won't rust.)

Tools and Techniques

A table saw, even a bench-top model, is essential for ripping the board into the slats needed for the strips and ribs of the trellis. When ripping the stock, use a pusher to protect your hand from the saw blade. The heel of a pusher hooks behind the end of the stock, and the front holds the stock flat on the saw table. When the pusher gets too chewed up, replace it. You can buy a pusher, but you can use a saber saw to cut pushers from scrap plywood.

Having two drill-drivers, one ready with a pilot bit and the other with a screwdriver bit, is handy for this project. As you're assembling the trellis, you'll need to bend a fan strip to a rib and pinch the two parts together while you drill a pilot hole and then drive a screw. A clamp would be in the way. Have the two separate drivers ready so that you can switch from one to the other without letting go of the strips.

BUILDING A FAN TRELLIS

Begin by cutting the trellis parts to size using a table saw and a pusher block to keep your fingers away from the saw blade. (The drawing on the facing page shows how to build a simple version.) Then cut the parts to length using a saber or circular saw, and bevel the top edge of the reinforcing strips that hold the bottom of the fan strips together. Make the bevel cut with a saber saw, and smooth the cut with sandpaper.

Next, lay out the bolt holes in the bottom of the center strip, the fan strips, and the reinforcing strips. These parts must be aligned carefully and their holes drilled properly for the assembly to work. Use a drilling guide (like the one we show on the facing page) to make the holes. Once the holes are drilled, stack the strips together and hold them with masking tape. Insert the bolts and tighten them with adjustable or open-end wrenches. Make sure that the beveled ends on the reinforcing strips are installed as shown in the drawing on page 163.

Once all the parts are joined together, clamp the center strip to the edge of a worktable. The center strip is the reference point for aligning the fan strips, so it must remain straight and immobile during the construction process. *(continued on page 167)*

TOOLS & MATERIALS
- Table saw ▮ Saber saw ▮ Circular saw
- Power drill and bits ▮ Hammer ▮ Bar clamps
- Adjustable wrenches ▮ Masking tape
- Tape measure ▮ Combination square
- 1 pc. ⁵⁄₄x6 8-ft. clear western red cedar
- 1 pc. 2x2 3-ft. southern yellow pine (SYP)
- 3 stainless-steel hex-head bolts,
  ¼ in. x 3½ in., with washers and nuts
- 2 stainless-steel hex-head bolts, ¼ in. x 3 in.,
  with washers and nuts
- 15 stainless-steel flathead screws, #8 x 1 in.

1 Use a table saw to rip the trellis parts to width. Adjust the saw blade so it's about ³⁄₈ in. above the top of the board, and use a pusher block to keep your fingers away from the spinning saw blade.

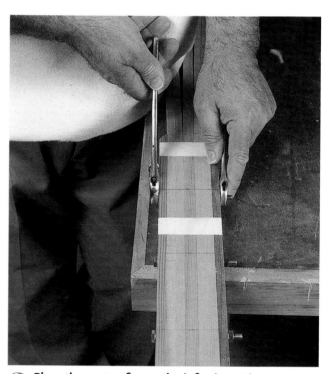

3 Place the center, fan, and reinforcing strips on a worktable; align the bolt holes; and hold the strips together with masking tape for ease of work. Insert the bolts in the holes, and tighten them using adjustable wrenches.

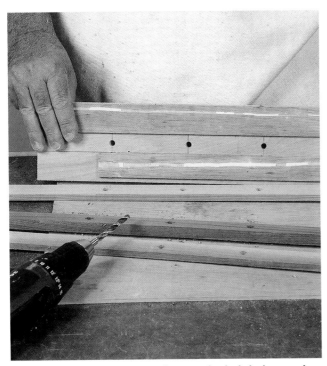

2 Once the parts are cut, lay out the bolt holes on the bottom of each and drill these holes using a drilling guide to maintain proper alignment. Remove all the wood burrs with sandpaper, and make sure the bolts slide freely through each hole.

4 Place the strip bundle on the edge of the workbench, and clamp the center strip to the table with a couple of bar clamps. Because this strip is the reference point for the fan strips on both sides, it must remain straight during construction. *(continued on page 166)*

TABLE SAW PUSHER

There are lots of pusher blocks made to protect your fingers when ripping boards. You can also make simple ones yourself using scrap plywood, as shown in the drawing below.

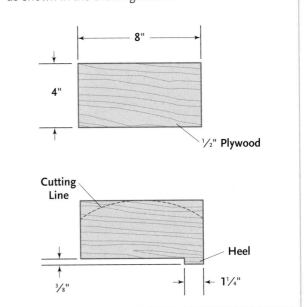

DRILLING GUIDE

Whenever you have multiple holes to drill through many parts, it makes sense to build a simple drilling guide, like the one shown here. For this project, the guide is especially useful because all the fan strips are joined together with bolts that are fed through holes in each piece. If the holes don't line up, the bolts won't fit.

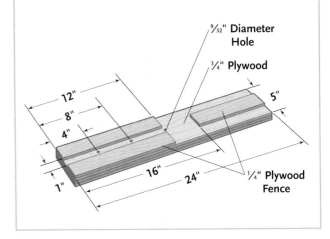

(continued from page 165)

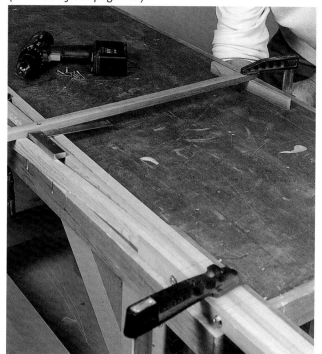

5 Attach the bottom rib to the center strip with a stainless-steel screw. Slide a scrap block that's the same thickness as the strip bundle under the end on the rib and clamp it to the worktable. Make sure the rib is square to the center strip.

6 Attach the middle and the top ribs to the center strip using stainless steel-screws. Cut two scrap blocks to act as spacers between the ribs. Just push a spacer between the bottom and middle rib, and screw the middle rib in place. Do the same with the top rib.

8 Once the outer strips are attached, lay out the location of the inside strips on the top rib. Then bend each strip to this mark, and drill a pilot hole through both parts. Attach them using a stainless-steel screw.

9 When the top rib is in place, attach the fan strips to the middle and bottom ribs. Use the same installation techniques, and make sure that each strip has the same gentle curve before screwing it in place.

TOP RIB LAYOUT

The top rib establishes the position of the other two ribs. This drawing shows the proper layout of the top rib.

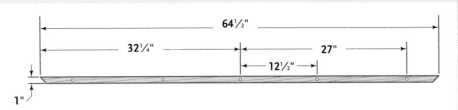

64½"

32¼"

27"

12½"

1"

7 Mark the location of the outside fan strip on the top rib using the drawing as a guide. Then slowly bend the strip until it reaches the mark. Hold the two parts together and drill a pilot hole in both boards.

10 Mark the ends on each rib to match the contour of the outside fan strips, and trim the ribs using a saber saw. Smooth each cut with sandpaper and remove the sanding dust. Then coat the trellis with paint, stain, or varnish, or leave the wood unfinished.

(continued from page 164)

Start attaching the ribs by marking the center point of each rib and the strip positions on the top rib, as shown on the drawing above. Then locate the bottom rib on the center strip 31 inches above the bottom of the strip bundle. (See the drawing on page 163.) Hold the rib in place and drill a pilot hole through this rib and into the center strip. Join the two with a stainless-steel screw. Next, pivot the rib until it is square to the center strip, and clamp the rib to the worktable. Install the other ribs in a similar way.

Once the top rib is in place, begin attaching the fan strips, starting with the outer strip. Hold it to its layout mark on the top rib. Then hold the two together; drill a pilot hole; and join the parts using a stainless-steel screw. Be careful when you bend the strip. Quick moves can break fragile strips.

Join the inner strip in a similar way, but before drilling the screw pilot hole, inspect the bend in the strip. It should follow a curve that falls between the outer strip and the straight line of the center strip. The layout marks on the top rib should establish this point. But some strips may not flex the same way due to their grain structure. So a visual check is recommended. When you are done attaching the strips and ribs on one side, join together the strips and ribs on the other side using the same construction techniques. Finish up the assembly by marking the ends of the ribs with a contour that follows the curves established by the outside fan strips. Cut the ribs with a saber saw and sand the cuts smooth.

You have several options for installing the trellis. By adding the stake shown in the drawing on page 163, you can simply drive the stake into the ground so the trellis leans against a fence or the side of a building. For lightweight plants this should be enough. The stake alone will not be able to support the trellis. But for heavy (or more mature) plants the top of the trellis should be anchored to a fence or wall. Two screws driven through the center strip and into the house siding should do the trick.

CONTEMPORARY TRELLIS

While the fan trellis, starting on page 162, is certainly attractive, it does have a traditional feel that works better with older house designs than it does with newer designs. The three trellises shown on the next eight pages are planned to complement a variety of more contemporary designs. While our plans are based on modest-sized structures, you can enlarge each by adjusting the dimensions we give you.

The first design, seen on this page, is a simple grid formed by horizontal and vertical strips that are trimmed with header boards on the top and bottom. The diamond trellis (page 173) is constructed in a similar way but is decorated with a single diamond shape nailed to the surface. The double-diamond style (page 175) is similar to the others but features two applied diamonds.

We used cypress for the first trellis and Douglas fir for the other two. You can also use cedar or redwood because they are typically straight-grained and relatively knot free. Pressure-treated southern yellow pine is another possibility. But it's difficult to fabricate because it's rarely straight and is usually filled with knots.

● CUTTING LIST (See "Tools & Materials," page 170.)

Part	Quantity	Thickness	Width	Length	Stock
CONTEMPORARY TRELLIS					
Horizontal strips	11	$1/2$"	1"	$21^1/_2$"	$5/_4$ x 6 cypress
Vertical strips	3	$3/_4$"	2"	$49^3/_4$"	1 x cypress
Headers	2	$1^1/_2$"	$3^1/_2$"	$24^1/_2$"	2 x western red cedar
DIAMOND TRELLIS					
Horizontal strips	6	$1/_2$"	$1^1/_4$"	$24^1/_4$"	2 x Douglas fir
Vertical strips	5	$1/_2$"	$1^1/_4$"	48"	2 x Douglas fir
Diamond strips	4	$1/_2$"	$1^1/_4$"	$14^5/_{16}$"	2 x Douglas fir
DOUBLE-DIAMOND TRELLIS					
Horizontal strips	6	$1/_2$"	$1^1/_4$"	$24^1/_4$"	2 x Douglas fir
Vertical strips	5	$1/_2$"	$1^1/_4$"	$54^3/_4$"	2 x Douglas fir
Diamond strips	8	$1/_2$"	$1^1/_4$"	$8^3/_8$"	2 x Douglas fir

CONTEMPORARY TRELLIS EXPLODED VIEW

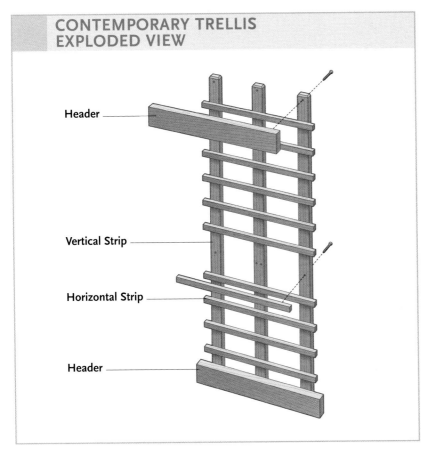

Header

Vertical Strip

Horizontal Strip

Header

CONTEMPORARY TRELLIS FRONT, SIDE, AND BACK VIEWS

builder's notes

The three trellises in this section feature basic joinery and straightforward construction techniques. With good stock and the right tools, each project should require a few hours of work.

Materials

Home centers don't carry the wood strips that these trellises require, so you'll need to rip stock on a table saw. Use stock that is straight-grained and free of defects.

Many types of wood are suitable for trellises. If you plan to paint a trellis and maintain its finish over the years, even pine can last. But an unfinished trellis will weather well only if it is made of weather-resistant wood.

Tools and Techniques

You'll use a table saw to make any of these trellises (a bench-top model is perfect). For the Contemporary Trellis, you'll also need to use a plunge router to cut dadoes into the headers of the trellis. Constructing and using a dadoing jig (page 172) will make this step easier and more accurate. Using the table saw, you'll rip the stock into thin strips and then crosscut them to length. (Reminder: Rip cuts run with the grain. Crosscuts run across the grain.)

You'll save time if you have two drill-drivers—one fitted with a countersinking bit, the other fitted with a screwdriver bit. To create a large flat work surface, you can use a sheet of plywood supported by sawhorses.

Finish

We did not finish the Contemporary Trellis. We did use white paint for the other two.

169

BUILDING A CONTEMPORARY TRELLIS

project

Begin by ripping all the parts to width using a table saw. Then cut the horizontal and vertical strips to length using a circular saw or a saber saw. To speed up this job, you can gang the strips together, clamp them under a scrap block, and make multiple cuts as shown in step 1.

Join the horizontal strips to the vertical strips with construction adhesive and stainless-steel screws. Clamp two adjacent horizontal strips to a spacer block (that is clamped to a worktable) to maintain proper alignment.

The vertical strips are held captive at the top and bottom by wide header boards. The strips are joined to the headers with dadoes, construction adhesive, and screws. You can cut these dadoes by hand with a chisel and hammer. But if you are not experienced in doing this, using a plunge router and a dado jig is the better approach. Steps 5 to 9 and the drawing on page 172 show you how to build and use one of these jigs.

TOOLS & MATERIALS
▌Table saw ▌Bar clamps
▌Power drill and bits ▌Plunge router and bits
▌Caulking gun and construction adhesive
▌Combination square ▌Framing square
▌Hammer or rubber-faced mallet
▌Framing square ▌Miter saw or saber saw
▌Backsaw or dovetail saw

CONTEMPORARY TRELLIS
▌1 pc. ⁵⁄₄x6 8-ft. cypress
▌1 pc. 1x6 8-ft. cypress
▌1 pc. 2x4 8-ft. western red cedar
▌50 flathead stainless-steel screws, #6x1 in.

DIAMOND TRELLIS
▌1 pc. 2x6 8-ft. Douglas fir
▌³⁄₄-in. stainless-steel brads

DOUBLE-DIAMOND TRELLIS
▌1 pc. 2x6 8-ft. Douglas fir
▌³⁄₄-in. stainless-steel brads

CONTEMPORARY TRELLIS

1 You can crosscut multiple strips at one time by clamping them together, and then clamping them to a worktable with a piece of scrap wood. If you align the scrap so it's square to the edges of the strips, you can use it to guide the saw as it makes the cuts.

4 Cut the spacer blocks so they're 6 in. long, and slide them between horizontal strips at the bottom and top of the trellis. Then push an outside upright against these blocks and attach it using adhesive and screws.

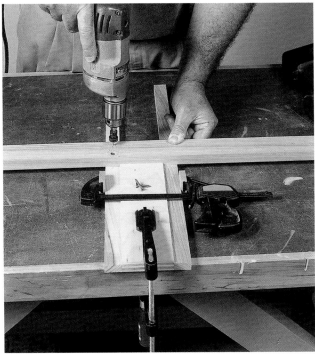

2 Clamp two horizontal strips to a square spacer block. Then clamp the block to the worktable, and place a vertical strip over the horizontal strips. Push it against the edge of the block, and hold it tight while you drive pilot holes for the screws.

3 To add more horizontal strips, just move the spacer block to the other side of the first strip and align the parts as before. Then place a dab of construction adhesive between the vertical and horizontal strips; drill pilot holes; and install stainless-steel screws.

5 To build a simple router jig for cutting the dado joints on the header boards, first look at the drawing on page 172. Then cut the parts to size and join them using screws. Make sure the first fence piece is installed square to the crossbar.

6 To position the second fence, slide a piece of scrap stock that is the same size as the vertical trellis strips into position. Place a piece of ¼-in. stock next to the scrap block, and push the second fence piece against these spacers. Attach the fence using screws. (continued on page 172)

171

(continued from page 171)

7 Mark the dadoes for the vertical strips on the edge of both header boards. Use a square and sharp pencil to make accurate marks. Make sure to center the header boards from side to side on the three vertical strips.

8 Install a template guide on the base of your plunge router. Then clamp the jig over a header board; turn on the router; and make a plunge cut. Remove all the stock within the void left by the jig. Then release the plunge mechanism and lift the router off the jig.

9 Test fit the strips in the header dadoes. If everything fits, take the joint apart; spread a small amount of adhesive on the parts; then reassemble everything. Install stainless-steel screws to secure the joints.

(continued on page 174)

DADOING JIG

The best material to use for jig making is scrap plywood left over from a recent project. It should be strong and flat, which are the two most important requirements for any accessory.

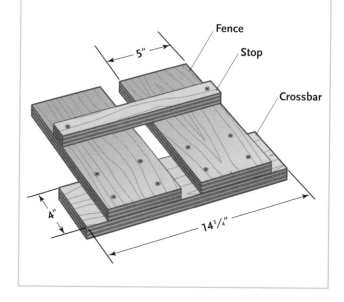

Fence

Stop

Crossbar

5"

4"

14³/₄"

Diamond Trellis

Although different from the Contemporary Trellis, this Diamond Trellis is built using most of the same construction methods. As before, start by cutting all the parts to size. (See the Cutting List, page 168.) Then cut spacers to match the various dimensions between the strips, as shown in the drawing at right. Assemble the trellis using small dabs of construction adhesive and stainless-steel brads. If any adhesive squeezes out of the joints, remove it before it dries.

Once the trellis grid has been assembled, cut the parts for the decorative diamond that is nailed to the outside surface of the trellis assembly. Cut the parts with a miter box, and test fit to make sure all the joints are tight. Then glue the parts together using adhesive, and hold them with masking tape until the adhesive is dry. Carefully glue and nail the diamond to the trellis structure.

Double-Diamond Trellis. This structure is built like the Diamond Trellis. But it is decorated with two diamonds instead of one. As before, build the diamonds separately and clamp the joints using masking tape. When the adhesive is dry, place the diamonds on the trellis and mark where they fall on the center vertical strip. Cut away the sections of this strip that fall behind the diamonds.

DIAMOND TRELLIS FRONT VIEW

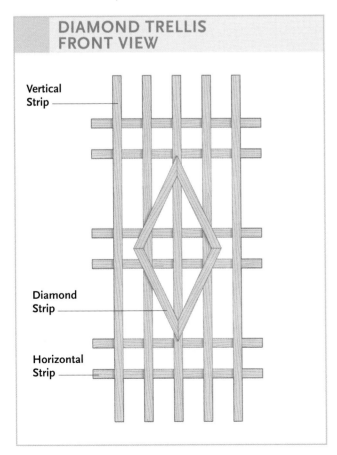

Vertical Strip

Diamond Strip

Horizontal Strip

BUILDING THE DIAMOND TRELLIS

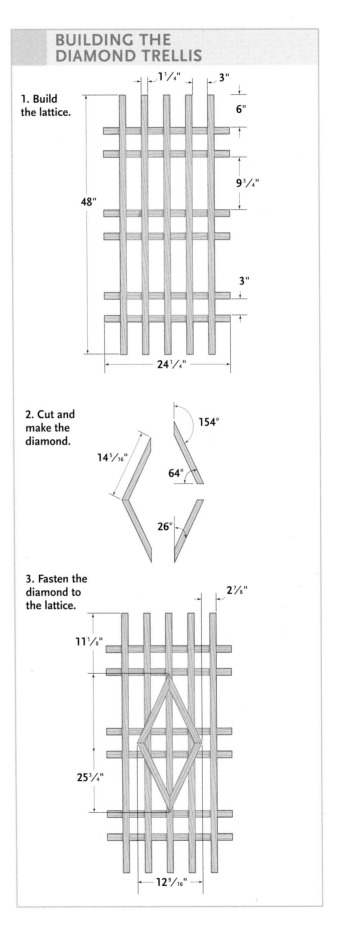

1. Build the lattice.

2. Cut and make the diamond.

3. Fasten the diamond to the lattice.

(continued from page 172)

DIAMOND TRELLIS

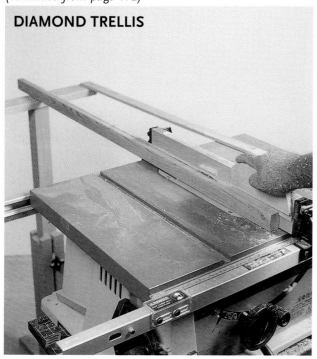

10 When ripping stock for the long trellis parts on a table saw, build an outfeed stand to support the cut piece as it exits the table. By supporting the far end of the board, you reduce the chance of the stock binding on the blade and being kicked back.

11 To assemble the lattice, place the vertical strips on a worktable and space them according to the dimensions given on the drawing. Then attach the horizontal strips using adhesive and stainless-steel brads. Make sure all the joints are square.

12 Cut the parts of the diamonds on a power miter box or chop saw. Hold like parts together with masking tape, and clamp these assemblies to a square block that's been clamped to the saw table. Make the cut slowly to get the smoothest cut.

13 Join the diamond parts with construction adhesive, and clamp them with masking tape. Let the adhesive dry; then center the diamond on the trellis and attach it using adhesive and stainless-steel brads. Remove the masking tape, and clean off any tape residue.

DOUBLE-DIAMOND TRELLIS FRONT VIEW

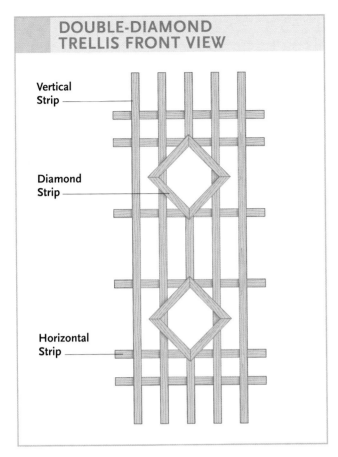

Vertical Strip

Diamond Strip

Horizontal Strip

DOUBLE-DIAMOND TRELLIS

14 Make the double diamonds like you made the single diamond. Then place them on the trellis assembly and mark where they cross the center vertical strip. Remove the diamonds; cut away sections of the vertical strip behind them; and attach the diamonds.

BUILDING THE DOUBLE-DIAMOND TRELLIS

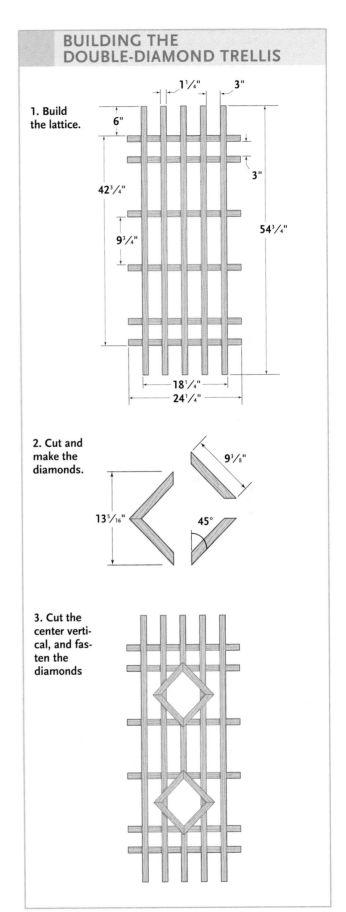

1. Build the lattice.

1¼" 3"

6"

42³/₄"

9³/₄"

3"

54³/₄"

18¹/₄"

24¹/₄"

2. Cut and make the diamonds.

9³/₈"

13⁵/₁₆"

45°

3. Cut the center vertical, and fasten the diamonds

DESIGNER TRELLIS

Although the traditional and contemporary designs that we've shown in the previous pages make for attractive trellises, they are by no means the only styles available. Just about any architectural treatment can be rendered in a trellis design. In this way, trellises are much like furniture. They can be built as one-of-a-kind expressions of your own taste. As long as you allow room for the plant to grow through the lattice and make the structure strong enough to support the plants, you can create any number of different trellises that will perform well. A good example is the attractive design we show here. The curved top piece and tapered lattice make it stand out from more common units. But with a little care in the layout stage and some patience during construction, a trellis like this is not at all difficult to build.

If you decide to design your own trellis, keep a couple of things in mind. First, if you want a large trellis, consider incorporating the existing trim treatments on your house into your trellis design. The larger the structure gets, the more it will look like a built-in feature and therefore logically would be trimmed like other parts of the house. Small units can have any design. But they can benefit from duplicating existing trim, too. You should also factor in your own carpentry capabilities. If you aren't very experienced and don't have the tools required, it's probably better to copy another design.

CUTTING LIST (See "Tools & Materials," page 178.)

Part	Quantity	Thickness	Width	Length	Stock
Frame side pieces	2	1"	$1\frac{1}{2}$"	$48\frac{1}{2}$"	$\frac{5}{4} \times 6$
Frame top piece	1	$1\frac{1}{2}$"	$2\frac{1}{2}$"	$21\frac{1}{4}$"	2×4
Frame bottom piece	1	$1\frac{1}{2}$"	$1\frac{1}{2}$"	15"	2×4
Horizontal lattice strips	11	$\frac{1}{4}$"	1"	$13\frac{1}{4}$"*	$\frac{5}{4} \times 6$
Vertical lattice strips	3	$\frac{1}{4}$"	1"	50"*	$\frac{5}{4} \times 6$
Back cleat	1	$\frac{1}{2}$"	$\frac{1}{2}$"	$10\frac{3}{16}$"*	$\frac{5}{4} \times 6$
Front cleat	1	$\frac{1}{2}$"	$\frac{1}{2}$"	$9\frac{3}{16}$"*	$\frac{5}{4} \times 6$

*Will be trimmed to fit later on.

EXPLODED VIEW

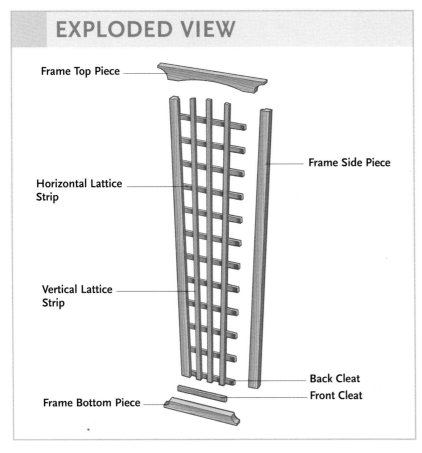

Frame Top Piece

Frame Side Piece

Horizontal Lattice Strip

Vertical Lattice Strip

Back Cleat

Front Cleat

Frame Bottom Piece

FRONT & BACK VIEWS

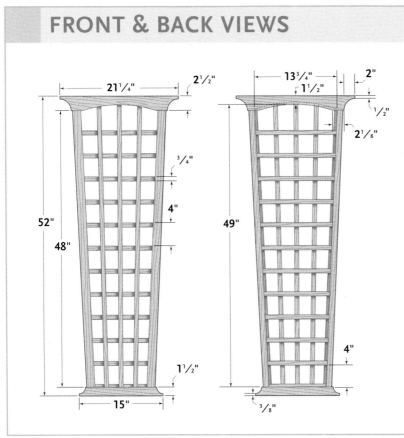

21¼" 2½"

13¾" 1½" 2"

½"

2⅛"

¾"

4"

52"

48"

49"

4"

1½"

15"

⅜"

builder's notes

Materials

We used widely available western red cedar. Other suitable woods include redwood, cypress, white oak, mahogany, and teak. For best results, select clear stock. If you choose redwood, cedar, or white oak, use stainless-steel fasteners. Tannins in these woods react with iron and produce black stains.

Because the side pieces are narrow, space closely the assembly screws that enter the end grain of the sides. To accomplish this, use finishing screws, which have small heads. These allowed me to get by with ¼-inch-diameter counterbores. Self-drilling screws are ideal for this; the point bores a pilot and the threads pull the screw into the wood.

For the top and bottom templates, I used medium-density fiberboard (MDF) because it yields crisp, smooth edges on which router-bit pilot bearings can ride. You probably won't need to buy a full 4x8 sheet of MDF; most home centers stock 2 x 4-foot pieces.

Tools and Techniques

You'll need a table saw, a router, a saber saw, and a drill-driver. One simple but effective construction technique that is used in this project deserves note here:

You will assemble the trellis's frame with screws that pass through the top and bottom pieces and penetrate the ends of the sides. Screws, however, don't hold well in end grain, so to ensure that they get a secure hold, you'll need to put dowels into the sides perpendicular to the grain of the sides. (See "Top-to-Side Fastening," page 181.)

BUILDING A DESIGNER TRELLIS

project

Begin by cutting the top and bottom frame pieces to size on a table saw. Then fabricate templates for shaping these frame pieces following the directions given at right. Once the end arcs are cut on these templates, finish the bottom piece by ripping it to a width of 1½ inches on a table saw. To shape the center arc on the top frame template, you need to fabricate a simple trammel guide. Make the trammel out of ¼-inch-thick plywood and attach your router base to one end and screw the other end to scrap block clamped to your worktable, as shown in step 2. Rout the curve by making repeated cuts, each about ¼-inch-deeper than the previous cut until the curve is complete.

Next, trace the templates onto the frame pieces and cut to within ⅛ inch of the line using a saber saw or a band saw. Then screw the templates to the frame pieces and finish the shaping using a router and a pattern bit. Adjust the base so the bearing on the cutting bit makes contact only with the template. Then rout the edge to remove the waste stock that was left behind when you rough-cut the shape earlier. Because the top and bottom frames are ½ inch thick, most people won't have a bit that will cut this whole edge in one pass. *(continued on page 181)*

TOOLS & MATERIALS
▪ Table saw ▪ Miter saw ▪ Circular saw
▪ Saber saw ▪ Router and bits ▪ Compass
▪ Power drill and bits ▪ Tape measure
▪ Bar clamps ▪ Plug cutter
▪ 1 pc. ⁵⁄₄x6 8-ft. clear western red cedar
▪ 1 pc. 2x4 8-ft. clear western red cedar
▪ ⅞-in. stainless-steel brads
▪ 2-in. stainless-steel finish screws
▪ 1 pc. ½ x 36-in. hardwood dowel
▪ Double-faced carpet tape ▪ Sandpaper
▪ Construction adhesive

Router Bit

Nail

Radius of Arc

 Cut the end arcs on the frame piece templates with a router and a straight-cutting bit. Insert a nail in the router base that fits in a hole in the template. Then lower the base onto the template so the nail slides into the hole. Turn on the router and make the cut.

● MAKING TEMPLATES

The best way to cut the shapes on the top and bottom frame pieces is to create a solid template for each using MDF (medium density fiberboard). Start by cutting the MDF to the sizes given at right using a table saw. Make sure all the cuts are smooth and square. If they aren't, sand them smooth with sandpaper. Next, lay out the end arcs on both templates using a compass. Also mark the gentle arc that connects the two end arcs on the top frame. Finish the layout by marking the finished width on the bottom frame, which will be ripped to a narrower width after the end arcs are cut. Drill a ⅛-in.-diameter hole at the center of each end arc. Then drill a corresponding hole in the router base and push a finishing nail into this hole. Cut off the nailhead; insert the pin into each radius hole; and cut the radius with the router and a straight bit.

2 Cut the center arc on the top frame template using a trammel made out of ¼-in.-thick plywood. Attach the router base to one end, and attach the other end to a scrap block clamped to the worktable. Turn on the router and swing the trammel from side to side.

3 Cut the frame stock to rough size; then screw the template to it. Using a pattern bit, cut the edge of the frame with a router. To provide extra support for the tool, you can use double-faced carpet tape to hold scrap blocks to the base. *(continued on page 180)*

TOP TEMPLATE

23¼"
3½"
1"
1"
R2"
21⅝"
Pivot Point
21¼"
2½"

BOTTOM TEMPLATE

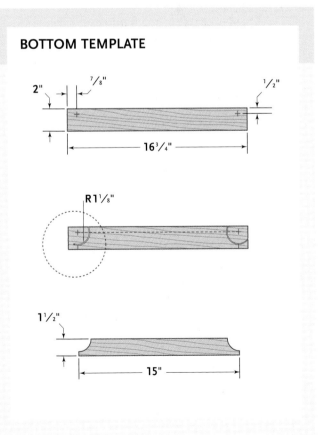

2"
⅞"
½"
16¾"
R1⅛"
1½"
15"

(continued from page 179)

4 Using a router with a ¼-in. slotting bit, cut a slot along the bottom edge of the top frame piece. Stop the slot on both ends before it reaches the flat where each side piece is joined.

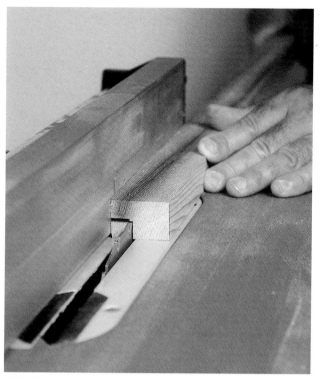

5 The side frame pieces need a rabbet along each inside edge to conceal the horizontal lattice pieces. Cut it on a table saw or use a router with a straight bit and bearing guide.

7 Attach the horizontal lattice strips to the rabbets in the side frame pieces using construction adhesive and stainless-steel brads. Hold these small brads with needle-nose pliers, instead of your fingers, while driving them into the wood.

8 Install the center vertical strip first by sliding it into the top frame slot, then lowering it onto the horizontal strips. Do the same with the side strips, making sure that they taper consistently from top to bottom.

6 Glue two dowels near the bottom and top of each side piece, as shown below. Then join the top and bottom frame pieces to the sides using screws driven into these dowels.

TOP-TO-SIDE FASTENING

Joining the top and bottom frame pieces to the side pieces requires some extra effort to achieve a strong reliable joint. Driving screws into the end grain of the sides is inherently weak. But reinforcing the side pieces using hardwood dowels provides dense stock that will hold the screws tightly. Just position the dowels so the end of your screws can easily reach them.

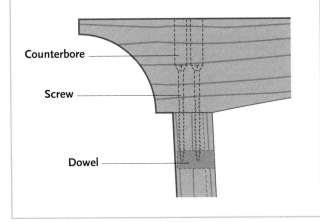

Counterbore

Screw

Dowel

To complete the cut, just make one pass with the template attached. Then remove the template and finish the cut with the bit's bearing riding along the section that's already been routed.

Next, cut a ¼-inch-wide slot in the bottom edge of the top frame piece using a slot-cutting bit in the router. This slot will receive the top ends of the vertical lattice strip. The bottom ends of the strips will be held captive by two cleats located just above the bottom frame. So no slot is required in this piece.

Cut the frame side pieces to size using a table saw. Then cut 88-degree angles on both ends using a miter box. These angle cuts are what create the tapered shape to the whole trellis. Use a table saw or router to cut rabbets on the back inside edge of both pieces. These rabbets will confine the horizontal lattice strips. Install the screw-holding dowels in both side pieces as shown in the box, "Top-To-Side Fastening," left. Then join the four frame pieces together with countersunk screws and fill the holes above the screw heads with wood plugs. Make these plugs with a plug cutter, and install them with glue. Sand the end of the plugs flush to the surrounding frame surface.

Rip the vertical and horizontal lattice strips to width on a table saw and to length on a miter box. Cut each about 2 inches long so you'll have extra stock to scribe the strips to fit. Start with the horizontal strips. Scribe and cut each piece to fit the frame. Then place a dab of construction adhesive on each joint; hold the strip in place; and attach it with stainless-steel brads. Install the vertical strips, sliding them into the slot in the top frame piece first. Finish up by installing the two bottom cleats.

Clean up any adhesive that may have squeezed out of the joints. Let the whole assembly dry; then lightly sand all parts smooth using 120-grit sandpaper and apply a finish.

smart tip

WHEN YOU USE A WOOD AS ATTRACTIVE AS WESTERN RED CEDAR, IT SEEMS A SHAME TO COVER IT WITH PAINT. BECAUSE THIS WOOD IS NATURALLY ROT- AND INSECT-RESISTANT, IT DOESN'T NEED A COATING TO LAST. BUT TO MAINTAIN ITS COLOR IT DOES. THE BEST CHOICES ARE A CLEAR WOOD PRESERVATIVE OR A COUPLE OF COATS OF EXTERIOR GRADE POLYURETHANE.

TRELLIS WALL

Many trellises are small fixtures that are designed to support only a plant or two, whether they stand alone or are mounted on a house wall. But other trellis structures are much larger (and stronger), like the one shown here. It forms a wall between the end posts that support an elevated deck. Trellises like this can hold many plants and also function as privacy screens, especially when the plants mature and fill in the lattice work.

This trellis is made to fit an 8-foot-wide opening, but the same basic design can work for wider openings. All that would be required is using heavier stock so the horizontal strips won't sag. Or you can use the same stock we used here if you make the vertical strips long enough so they can be attached to the deck joists above. In this approach the verticals would act as suspension cables to support the horizontal strips below.

Although this trellis is basically a simple grid, we did want to add a couple of distinctive elements. So we added two "windows." To make these octagonal openings, just cut a section out of one vertical and one horizontal strip and trim the openings. The size of each is just right for a hanging plant.

● CUTTING LIST (See "Tools & Materials," page 184.)

Part	Quantity	Thickness	Width	Length*	SYP** Stock
Horizontal strips	9	1"	1½"	96"	⁵⁄₄ x 6
Middle vertical strip	1	1"	1"	86¼"	⁵⁄₄ x 6
Vertical strips	2	1"	1½"	84¹⁵⁄₁₆"	⁵⁄₄ x 6
Vertical strips	2	1"	1"	83⁷⁄₁₆"	⁵⁄₄ x 6
Vertical strips	2	1"	1½"	81¹⁵⁄₁₆"	⁵⁄₄ x 6
Vertical strips	2	1"	1"	80⁷⁄₁₆"	⁵⁄₄ x 6
Vertical strips	2	1"	1½"	78¹⁵⁄₁₆"	⁵⁄₄ x 6
Blocking strips	8	1"	1½"	7"	⁵⁄₄ x 6
Triangles	8	1"	4"	4"	⁵⁄₄ x 6

* These are the lengths for this particular project. Yours will depend on the spacing of the deck posts and the height of the deck.
** Southern yellow pine

EXPLODED VIEW

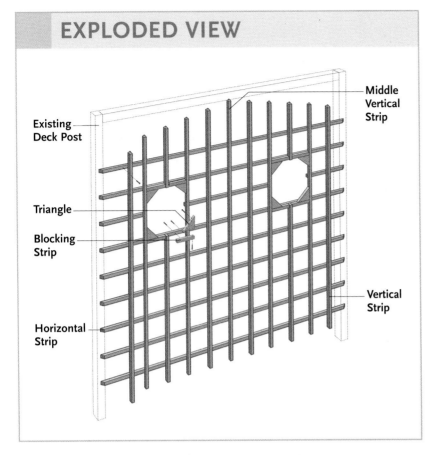

Existing Deck Post

Middle Vertical Strip

Triangle

Blocking Strip

Horizontal Strip

Vertical Strip

FRONT ELEVATION, PLAN VIEW

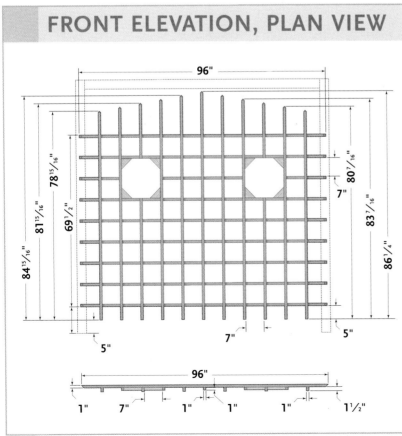

96"

$84^{15}/_{16}$"

$81^{15}/_{16}$"

$78^{15}/_{16}$"

$69^{1}/_{2}$"

$80^{7}/_{16}$"

7"

$83^{7}/_{16}$"

$86^{1}/_{4}$"

5"

7"

5"

96"

1"   7"   1"   1"   1" $1^{1}/_{2}$"

builder's notes

Adjust the dimensions and the number of slats to fit the opening you want to span.

Materials

The horizontal and vertical strips (or slats) shown here are from $^{5}/_{4}$ pine decking, which is 1 inch thick and $5^{1}/_{2}$ inches wide and has eased (rounded) edges. (Actual measurements may vary slightly from one board to another.) Because the slats for the trellis will be no wider than $1^{1}/_{2}$ inches, be sure to select boards that are free of big knots.

Treated southern yellow pine is prone to bowing, crooking, and twisting, especially when ripped into thin strips. To minimize the chance of this happening, rip and install the strips the same day. Galvanized mounting screws will keep them from warping; for additional holding power you can apply construction adhesive.

Tools and Techniques

You'll need a table saw or a bench-top model to rip the stock, and a power miter saw (preferred), circular saw, or saber saw for the crosscuts. You may be tempted to think that you can crosscut the slats on a table saw, but it's neither practical nor safe to attempt. Instead, hold the strip in position and cut it with a moving saw.

For assembly, you'll need a level, a drill-driver or two, several clamps, spacer gauges, and a vertical gauge. (See "Spacer Gauges," page 185.)

Finish

The trellis shown has no finish. You can, however, apply a water repellent, solid-color stain, or paint.

BUILDING A TRELLIS WALL

Because this project calls for using pressure-treated southern yellow pine, try to cut and install the trellis strips in a single day if possible. Once this stock is ripped into smaller pieces, the pieces tend to warp and twist quickly. If you can't do it in a single day, shoot for two days while keeping the cut pieces protected from the weather until they are attached to each other.

Begin by ripping the vertical and horizontal strips to size using a table saw. Then cut the tops of the vertical strips so they come to a point, like a small hip roof. Use a miter saw to make these end cuts. Also, leave the bottom ends of the vertical strips a little long so that you can trim them to exact size later.

Installing the Horizontal Strips

Start the installation with the bottom strip. On this job, we installed the first strip so it was at least 5 inches above the ground to provide clearance for the bottom of the vertical strips. Check your site to determine the best starting point by laying out the whole grid on the posts before you install anything. Level the first strip in place; then attach the remaining horizontal strips using the spacer block shown on right. Drill pilot holes and drive two galvanized screws in both ends of each strip. (Continued on page 187)

TOOLS & MATERIALS
▌ Table saw ▌ Miter saw or chop saw
▌ Tape measure ▌ Combination square
▌ Drill/driver with bits ▌ Power drill with bits
▌ Level ▌ Bar clamps ▌ Saber saw
▌ 7 pcs. $\frac{5}{4}$x6 8-ft. treated southern yellow pine
▌ 3-in. deck galvanized screws
▌ 2-in. deck galvanized screws
▌ $1\frac{5}{8}$-in. deck galvanized screws

1 Start this project by cutting the vertical and horizontal strips to size using a table saw. The bench-top model, shown here, works especially well because it's portable. You can work outside during good weather and in the garage when it's raining.

4 Start installing the lattice by attaching the bottom horizontal strip. Attach one end; then hold the opposite end against a post. Hold a level on top, and move the strip up or down until it is level. Attach the strip using two galvanized screws.

2 Use a power miter box or a chop saw to cut the chamfered points on the top of the vertical strips. Use a sawhorse or a small table to support the far ends of the strips while they are being cut.

3 Each vertical strip gets four miter cuts each to form its point. To get the best alignment of all these cuts, make a square shoulder line on each side that defines the bottom edge of each cut. Then carefully align the blade before starting each cut.

Horizontal Spacer Gauge

5 Install the second horizontal strip using a spacer block. Hold the block in place with a bar clamp, and rest the second strip on top of the block. Drill two pilot holes in the end of the strip, and drive two screws into these holes. *(continued on page 186)*

SPACER GAUGES

Spacer blocks make aligning trellis strips easier. The smaller one works for both strips. The larger one aligns the top of the vertical strips.

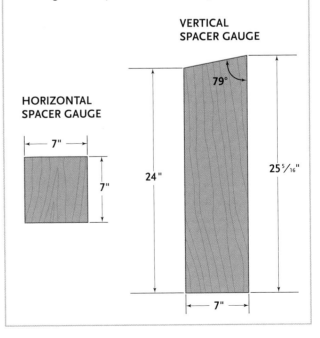

HORIZONTAL SPACER GAUGE

7"

7"

VERTICAL SPACER GAUGE

79°

24"

25$\frac{5}{16}$"

7"

(continued from page 185)

6 Start installing the vertical strips by centering the middle strip from side to side and checking it for plumb. When satisfied with the alignment, hold the strip in place with a couple of bar clamps, one at the top and the other near the bottom of the strip.

7 For a neater appearance, it's a good idea to install the screws that hold the strips together from the inside of the trellis wall. Drill a pilot hole and use 1⅝-in. galvanized screws. Always check the space between horizontal strips with the spacer block.

Vertical Spacer Gauge

9 To establish the location of the second vertical strip, clamp the spacer block against the middle strip and push the second strip against this block. Clamp the strip in place with bar clamps. Then screw the strips together.

10 If you want to install the octagonal openings we show, start by laying out the location of the openings using the drawing on page 183 as a guide. Then cut out the lattice strips that fall inside the opening using a saber saw. *(continued on page 188)*

8 Because the vertical strips taper away from the center strips on both sides, it makes sense to build a customized spacer block to make aligning these strips easier. Using a chop saw, cut a piece of scrap plywood to match the dimensions given in the drawing on page 185.

(continued from page 184)

Installing the Vertical Strips

The vertical strips are attached to the front of the horizontal strips using galvanized screws. To add some interest to the design, we used two different-size vertical strips: 1-inch square and 1 x 1½ inches. We started with a 1-inch-square strip for the centerpiece and then alternated the remaining strips on both sides. Be sure to determine the exact length you need for the center strip before attaching. You will use it as a guide for cutting the other strips. Before attaching this first strip, make sure it's plumb using a 4-foot level. Shorter levels aren't as accurate over longer distances.

Next, lay out the top horizontal strip for the remaining vertical strips. The drawing on page 183 shows the proper layout for these strips. As indicated, the center one is the longest, then the height drops on both sides with each successive strip. To determine the length of each, measure the distance from the bottom of the bottom horizontal strip to the top of the top horizontal strip. Then add the amount that each extends above the top strip, plus the amount that the center strip extends below the bottom strip.

Once you are satisfied with the layout, install these strips using the spacer block shown on page 185 to make sure the grid remains uniform throughout. For the best appearance, hold the strips in the correct position with a bar clamp. Then screw them together from the back of the trellis so the fasteners won't be as visible. The spacer block should keep the grid straight. But it only takes a minute to check each strip for level. This is a good way to keep accidental alignment problems from spreading throughout the project.

Trellis Windows

If you want only the basic trellis grid, then you're done building. You can proceed to applying the finish. But if you want to add the two "windows" we show here, now is the time to do it. Begin by laying out the position of each using the drawing on page 188 as a guide. We indicate a position that's at typical eye level. But you can place these anywhere you want. You can also make them rectangular shaped instead of the octagons that we show here. For instructions of how to build these openings, see the following page.

(continued from page 186)

11 Temporarily attach a support block to one side of each triangle with masking tape to keep the parts from moving. Then hold each subassembly in a vise and drill two screw pilot holes through the block and into the triangle.

12 Once a block is screwed to a triangle, take this assembly and clamp it inside the window opening. From the backside of the trellis, attach the block to a horizontal strip using two screws. Then drive an angled screw through the corner of the triangle into a vertical strip.

CORNER BRACKET DETAIL

Once the holes are cut in the latticework to create the "windows," cut the decorative triangles to trim out these openings on a miter box or chop saw. Make all the triangles the same size, and drill an angled screw pilot hole through one corner. Cut the 7-inch-long support blocks to length, and drill two pilot holes in them for the screws that join the blocks and triangles. Then install each of these subassemblies with screws driven into the lattice strips. Hold these parts in place using a bar clamp while you work.

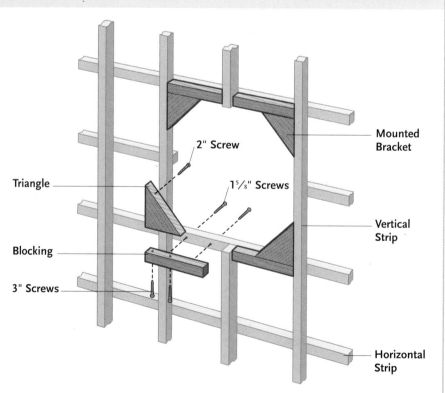

Triangle

2" Screw

1⅝" Screws

Blocking

3" Screws

Mounted Bracket

Vertical Strip

Horizontal Strip

TRELLIS WALL ON FREESTANDING POSTS

Besides serving as screening under a deck, this trellis wall can be supported by freestanding posts and be a focal point or a backdrop for a flowerbed. Here are some guidelines for making a freestanding trellis wall. To construct the lattice, refer to the general guidelines on the previous pages. For more complete instructions on installing posts, see the Grape Arbor project on pages 244-251.

▌ Use 4x4 treated posts that are long enough for the needed wall height plus the depth into the ground.

▌ Follow local building codes when digging the postholes.

▌ The measurement between the outside edges of the posts should equal the length of the horizontal strips. If the posts are slightly farther apart, adjust by centering the strips back from the post edges. If they're slightly closer together, trim off the excess that extends past the posts.

▌ Stand each post in its hole, and extend a temporary brace from about mid-height to a stake driven into the ground about 5 feet from the post. Use one screw to fasten the bottom of the brace to its stake, but don't yet attach the brace to the post. Install a second brace at a right angle to the first, attaching it to the post about one foot above or below the first. After plumbing the post with a level, fasten the braces to the post.

▌ Set the posts in concrete. Use a small trowel to slope the top of the concrete away from the post. This will ensure proper rain runoff.

▌ After the concrete has stiffened and the posts are stable, trim the tops of the posts. To do this, mark one post and carry the line across to the other post using a line or a water level. Chamfer the tops to a point using a circular saw. Be very careful when using this saw while standing on a ladder. Have a helper hold the ladder steady while you work. Also be sure to wear eye protection to keep sawdust out of your eyes.

▌ Let the concrete around the posts set overnight before installing any of the lattice strips.

TEMPORARY BRACING OF A POST

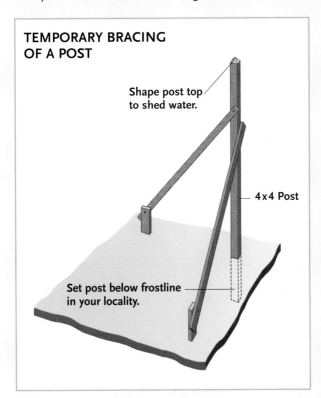

Shape post top to shed water.

4x4 Post

Set post below frostline in your locality.

TRELLIS WALL FASTENED TO FREESTANDING POSTS

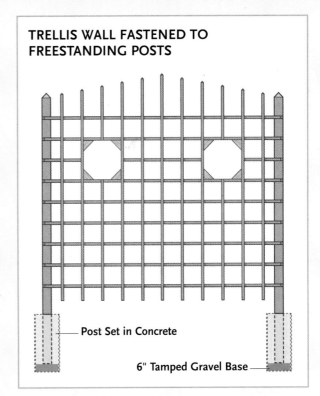

Post Set in Concrete

6" Tamped Gravel Base

TOWER TRELLIS

Gardeners have a long tradition of ornamenting their favorite spaces. Mushroom-shaped path lighting, frog-shaped fountains, and concrete urns with cascading flowered vines are just a few of the countless ways they choose to make their gardens distinctive. These days, most of these fixtures are manufactured. But in bygone days, rustic trellis towers were routinely made of long twigs lashed together with dry vines. These were built to support plants like tomatoes, cucumbers, and morning glories. They may have looked rustic, but they were strong, long lasting, and cost nothing to build.

The tower trellis we show here may be based on traditional twig structures, but it's made of stock lumber with standard woodworking machinery and tools. By weaving the vertical strips through the horizontal strips, a rough, hand-wrought feel is created. But sophistication isn't left behind in the bargain. The tower cap is made of eye-catching copper that will turn a beautiful light-green verdigris over time.

● CUTTING LIST (See "Tools & Materials," page 192.)

Part	Quantity	Thickness	Width	Length	Stock
Corner posts	4	$1^1/_{16}$"	$1^1/_{16}$"	73"	$^5/_4$ x 6 mahogany
Top crosspieces	4	$1^1/_{16}$"	$1^1/_{16}$"	$7^3/_4$"	$^5/_4$ x 6 mahogany
Bottom crosspieces	4	$1^1/_{16}$"	$1^1/_{16}$"	18"	$^5/_4$ x 6 mahogany
Horizontal strips	4	$^1/_2$"	$^1/_2$"	$12^3/_8$"*	$^5/_4$ x 6 mahogany
Horizontal strips	4	$^1/_2$"	$^1/_2$"	$14^1/_8$"*	$^5/_4$ x 6 mahogany
Horizontal strips	4	$^1/_2$"	$^1/_2$"	$15^7/_8$"*	$^5/_4$ x 6 mahogany
Horizontal strips	4	$^1/_2$"	$^1/_2$"	$17^5/_8$"*	$^5/_4$ x 6 mahogany
Horizontal strips	4	$^1/_2$"	$^1/_2$"	$19^3/_8$"*	$^5/_4$ x 6 mahogany
Vertical strips	2	$^1/_2$"	$^5/_8$"	$69^3/_4$"*	$^5/_4$ x 6 mahogany
Vertical strips	2	$^1/_2$"	$^5/_8$"	$70^5/_8$"*	$^5/_4$ x 6 mahogany
Weavers	8	$^3/_8$"	$^1/_2$"	96"**	1 x 6 cypress
Stand rails	4	$1^1/_2$"	$3^1/_2$"	$19^1/_2$"	2 x 4 SYP

* Most likely finished measurement; will be trimmed to fit.
** Working length; will be trimmed once in place.

EXPLODED VIEW

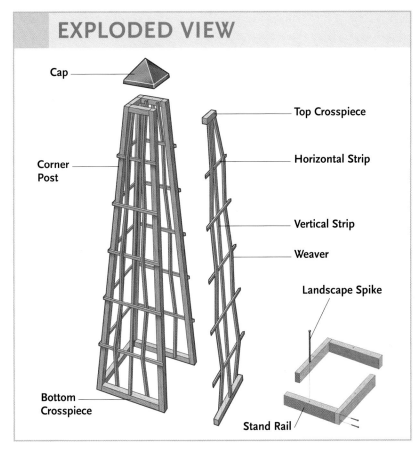

Cap

Top Crosspiece

Corner Post

Horizontal Strip

Vertical Strip

Weaver

Landscape Spike

Bottom Crosspiece

Stand Rail

FRONT AND SIDE VIEWS

12"

12"

12"

12"

11⁵/₈"

8⁵/₈"

4⁵/₈"

20¹/₄"

9⁷/₈"

3¹/₂"

72³/₄"

76¹/₄"

¹/₂"

20¹/₄"

builder's notes

There are no elaborate joinery cuts in this project, but it does require miters and compound miters.

Materials

This project employs woods of contrasting hues that are relatively decay resistant. Most of the tower is of meranti mahogany; the weavers are of cypress. You could instead use redwood for the mahogany or combine western red cedar and white oak.

We chose to use 28-ounce copper sheeting for the cap. Check roofing and building supply entries in the classified section of the phone book to locate a source. You could instead use other sheet metal, such as aluminum flashing. Before tackling the pricey copper, practice cutting and bending on less expensive aluminum flashing. If you use copper, diligent shopping should also lead you to copper escutcheon pins (nails, really) to fasten the cap to the tower.

Tools and Techniques

All parts in the tapered frames are mitered, and most of the lattice pieces are compound-mitered. You can cut all the pieces using a table saw, but a compound miter saw will make the crosscutting easier.

The only special tool required for making the copper cap is a pair of straight-cutting aviation snips. We used a special sheet-metal seamer to fold the tabs, but you can fold it against a piece of hardwood, too.

Finish

The tower can be varnished, stained, or painted, but do it before you install the cap.

BUILDING A TOWER TRELLIS

Begin by cutting the stock for the framework and lattice strips to width. Leave each strip about 6 inches long at this point, so it can be trimmed to fit exactly later on. Also cut the bottom and top crosspieces to size. Because each side of the tower is tapered (86 degrees on both sides), none of the frame pieces are cut square on the ends. Adjust a compound miter saw to the proper angles; then make the end cuts on the frame pieces.

Once all the parts are cut, lay the frame pieces from one side on a worktable with the bottom and top crosspieces between the two side members. Place a dab of construction adhesive between the parts; then clamp the joints together; and clamp the assembly to the top of the table. Position all the clamps so you can easily drill pilot holes for the screws that finish the joints. Then drill the holes; drive the screws; and keep the assembly clamped until the adhesive is dry. (continued on page 195)

TOOLS & MATERIALS
▮ Table saw
▮ Compound miter saw
▮ Bar clamps
▮ Power drill with bits
▮ Steel straightedge
▮ Utility knife
▮ Tin snips
▮ Ball peen hammer
▮ 3-lb. sledgehammer
▮ 2 pcs. $^5/_4$x6 8-ft. meranti mahogany
▮ 1 pc. 1x6 8-ft. cypress
▮ 1 pc. 2x4 8-ft. treated southern yellow pine (SYP)
▮ 1 pc. 16 in. x 20 in. of 28-oz. copper sheeting
▮ 3-in. galvanized screws
▮ Stainless-steel screws, #6 x 1 in.
▮ 12 brass screws, #6 x $^3/_4$ in.
▮ 3 brass sheet-metal screws, #6 x $^1/_2$ in.
▮ 1$^1/_2$-in. aluminum nails
▮ 4 10 in. landscape spikes
▮ Construction adhesive

1 Begin by ripping the corner posts, crosspieces, strips, and weavers to size on a table saw. For same size parts, set the fence away from the blade to the desired thickness. Then make repeated rips until all the same-size parts are cut.

4 Once the sides are assembled, begin installing the horizontal strips by holding a strip in place and scribing it to exact length. These strips are joined at each corner with miter joints, so the length of each has to be marked precisely and cut accurately. (continued on page 194)

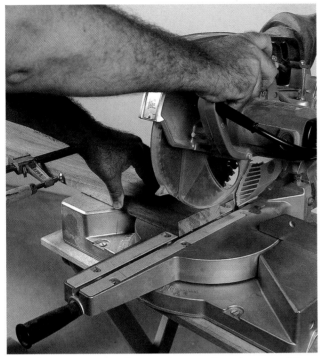

2 Cut the posts and crosspieces to length on a table saw. You can make these 86-deg. cuts individually on a miter saw or you can clamp together several parts and cut them in one pass.

3 To assemble the sides, first clamp the corner posts to the ends of the crosspieces using bar clamps. Keep the clamps a couple of inches away from the end of the posts so you can drill pilot holes for the screws that hold these joints together.

ASSEMBLY SEQUENCE

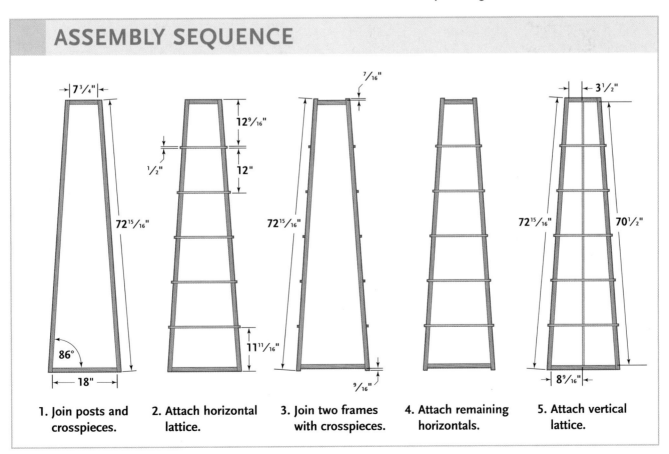

1. Join posts and crosspieces.
2. Attach horizontal lattice.
3. Join two frames with crosspieces.
4. Attach remaining horizontals.
5. Attach vertical lattice.

(continued from page 192)

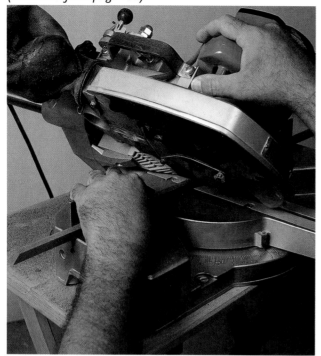

5 Use a compound miter saw to cut compound miters on both ends of each horizontal strip. To make this cut, tilt the saw blade to 45 deg. and swing the table to 4 deg. to the right and make a cut. Then swing it 4 deg. to the left and cut the other end.

6 Use a spacer made of scrap plywood to position the horizontal strips. Push the spacer tight against the previous strip; then place the next strip against the spacer; and attach the strip using galvanized screws. Drill pilot holes first to prevent splitting the strip.

8 Once both side frames are assembled, join the two with the top and bottom crosspieces on the remaining sides. Hold each joint together with masking tape until you can install a bar clamp. Use this clamp to squeeze the joint tight.

9 When the sides are all joined, install the horizontal strips on the two open sides. Hold each strip against the miters on the adjacent strips, and scribe it to length. Cut it precisely on the compound miter saw.

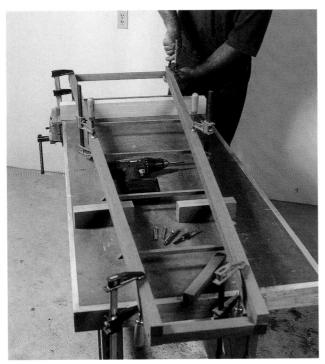

7 To build the second trellis frame, lay its parts on top of the assembled side and clamp the two together. This will ensure that both sides will be aligned identically. Screw the corner posts to the crosspieces as before.

10 Attach the vertical strips between the bottom and top crosspieces using aluminum nails. Slide each strip into place, and drill a pilot hole for the nails to prevent splitting the strip. *(continued on page 196)*

(continued from page 192)

Next, cut the horizontal strips to size. Note that the end of each strip needs a compound miter because it meets the other strips at the corners with a mitered joint that must match the taper of the tower. Position each strip, using a plywood spacer, so each is aligned the same way on each side. Attach the strips with a dab of adhesive and a galvanized screw. Follow the same procedure for assembling the opposite side frame.

To form the tower structure, join the top and bottom of the two sides with crosspieces using glue and screws. Then hold the joints together with bar clamps until the adhesive is set. Next, add the horizontal strips that connect both sides using glue and screws. These strips form miter joints at the corners. Make sure these joints are tight. (The overall assembly sequence is shown in the drawings on page 193.)

When all the horizontal strips are installed, attach the vertical strips to the crosspieces using aluminum nails and the horizontal strips with small dabs of construction adhesive. Drill pilot holes to keep the wood from splitting when it is nailed. Let the adhesive dry thoroughly and scrape off any excess. Then lightly sand the whole structure to ease the edges and reduce the chance of getting splinters.

The weaver strips on this trellis are made of cypress stock that is cut into $3/8$ x $1/2$-inch pieces. This thin size makes it possible to weave these strips through the horizontal strips that are part of the basic trellis frame. To weave them into the trellis, start at the bottom and feed one of the strips under the bottom crosspiece. Then slide it up and over the first strip, under the second strip, over the third, and so on until it slides under the top crosspiece. Do the same thing for the other weaver strips. Then align them so they have the gentle taper shown in the drawing on page 191.

Mark the finished location of each weaver. Then lift each up slightly where it crosses a horizontal strip, and place a dab of adhesive between the parts. Squeeze the pieces together so they fall next to the mark, and hold the joints with small clamps or stainless-steel brads. Fabricate the copper top as shown on page 197; then install the trellis. The easiest way to do this is to build a simple pressure-treated wood frame and install it (in a level position) on the ground with landscape spikes. Then screw the bottom crosspieces of the trellis to the top edge of the pressure-treated frames.

(continued from page 195)

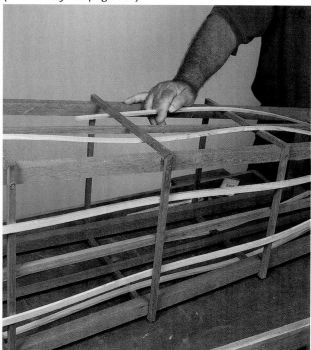

11 Rip the weaver strips to width, and cut them to approximate length. Weave them above and below the horizontal strips on each side of the trellis, and attach them using adhesive or stainless-steel brads. Cut the top and bottom flush with the crosspieces.

12 Use the pattern (at right) to mark the shape of the cap on the copper sheet. Use a felt-tip marker and straightedge to draw the cut lines and the bend lines.

13 Bend the sheet metal using a hardwood block with at least one square, straight edge. Place the block over a line, and pull the metal up against the block. Pulling up works better than pushing down because you can watch for proper alignment of the block and the line.

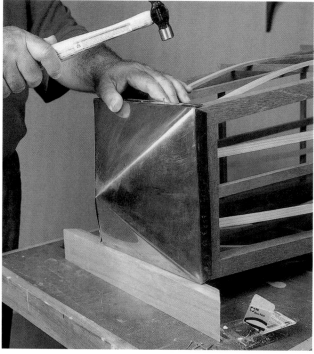

14 Join the ends of the cap with sheet-metal screws. Then slide the cap over the top of the tower, and push the tabs flat against the crosspieces. Drill clearance holes; then use copper or stainless-steel brads to attach the cap.

MAKING THE CAP

SINGLE SEGMENT

7³/₄"

6"

10"

1¹/₈"

FOUR SEGMENTS COMBINED (WITH TAB)

15⁵/₈"

1¹/₈"

16¹¹/₁₆"

Attach the Cap

The cap for this tower was made of a copper sheet from a roofing supply store. It's very attractive, but if you have trouble finding it in your area, you can also build the cap with standard aluminum flashing that's available at lumberyards and home centers.

To make the cap, first transfer the pattern (at left) onto the sheet with a felt-tip pen. Then bend the sheet along these lines using a metal straightedge or a small hardwood block with a straight edge on at least one side. Once the cap is shaped properly, tape the seams together and test fit it. If it fits, then remove the cap and tape and join the ends using sheet-metal screws. If the cap needs adjustment, take apart the assembly; modify the folds; and try again. When the cap is screwed together, slide it over the top of the tower and attach it by driving copper or stainless-steel brads through the side tabs into the top crosspieces.

With the tower assembled, you can build a simple base for it made of pressure-treated 2x4 lumber. For stability, drill pilot holes and then drive 12-inch-long landscaping spikes through the lumber and into the ground.

15 Build a base frame for the trellis using pressure-treated 2x4s. Join the sides with galvanized screws or nails; then level the frame on the ground. Attach it with landscape spikes driven into the ground through clearance holes in the sides.

smart tip

THE MAHOGANY AND CYPRESS WE USED FOR THIS JOB CAN BE EXPENSIVE. FORTUNATELY THIS JOB DOESN'T USE MUCH OF EITHER. BUT IF YOU WANT TO BUILD SEVERAL OF THESE TOWERS AND WANT TO SAVE SOME MONEY, CONSIDER USING PRESSURE-TREATED SOUTHERN YELLOW PINE DECKING. THIS LUMBER MEASURES A LITTLE OVER 1-INCH THICK AND CAN BE USED FOR THE CORNERS AND RIPPED TO SIZE FOR THE STRIPS. BECAUSE THIS WOOD TENDS TO HAVE LOTS OF KNOTS, IT TAKES A LITTLE PLANNING TO AVOID THE BIG ONES. AND AVOIDING THEM DOES CREATE SOME WASTE. BUT EVEN WITH THE WASTE, YOU'LL BE AHEAD FINANCIALLY. ALSO, MOST LUMBERYARDS AND HOME CENTERS LET YOU SELECT THE BOARDS YOU BUY. SO BE SURE TO PICK THE STRAIGHTEST ONES WITH THE FEWEST KNOTS.

TRELLIS BENCH

Trellises are usually designed to support nothing more than some lightweight plants. But they can easily be built to hold you and a friend comfortably. All it takes is beefing up the support members and building a bench between the two trellis sections. Once the lattice is covered with climbing plants, you'll have a cozy, shaded spot to relax outside. All the components are made of pressure-treated southern yellow pine joined with galvanized screws. Most people can build this project in a couple of days.

● CUTTING LIST (See "Tools & Materials," page 200.)

Part	Quantity	Thickness	Width	Length	Stock
Bench posts	4	$1\frac{1}{2}$"	$3\frac{1}{2}$"	84"	2 x 4
Wide beams	2	$1\frac{1}{2}$"	$5\frac{1}{2}$"	$69\frac{1}{2}$"	2 x 6
Narrow beams	2	$1\frac{1}{2}$"	$3\frac{1}{2}$"	$61\frac{3}{4}$"	2 x 4
Side rails	2	$1\frac{1}{2}$"	$3\frac{1}{2}$"	$33\frac{5}{8}$"	2 x 4
Back rail	1	$1\frac{1}{2}$"	$3\frac{1}{2}$"	$47\frac{1}{2}$"	2 x 4
Seat rail	1	$1\frac{1}{2}$"	$3\frac{1}{2}$"	$47\frac{1}{2}$"	2 x 4
Backrest posts	2	$1\frac{1}{2}$"	$3\frac{1}{2}$"	$23\frac{7}{16}$"	2 x 4
Back side-rail doubler	2	$1\frac{1}{2}$"	$3\frac{1}{2}$"	$4\frac{9}{16}$"	2 x 4
Front side-rail doubler	2	$1\frac{1}{2}$"	$3\frac{1}{2}$"	$26\frac{3}{16}$"	2 x 4
Seat boards	3	1"	$5\frac{1}{2}$"	$50\frac{1}{2}$"	$\frac{5}{4}$ x 6
Backrest boards	3	1"	$5\frac{1}{2}$"	$47\frac{1}{2}$"	$\frac{5}{4}$ x 6
Top backrest board	1	1"	$5\frac{1}{2}$"	$47\frac{1}{2}$"	$\frac{5}{4}$ x 6
Side lattice horizontal strips	14	$\frac{3}{4}$"	$1\frac{1}{2}$"	$32\frac{7}{8}$"	1 x 2
Side lattice mounting strips	4	$\frac{3}{4}$"	$1\frac{1}{2}$"	$33\frac{5}{8}$"	1 x 2
Side lattice vertical strips	12	$\frac{3}{4}$"	$\frac{3}{4}$"	$65\frac{7}{8}$"	1 x 4
Side lattice mounting blocks	8	1"	2"	$1\frac{1}{2}$"	$\frac{5}{4}$ x 6
Nailers	2	$\frac{3}{4}$"	$1\frac{1}{2}$"	$44\frac{1}{2}$"	1 x 2
Short roof blocks	9	$\frac{3}{4}$"	$\frac{3}{4}$"	$36\frac{5}{8}$"	1 x 4
Long roof crosspieces	6	$\frac{3}{4}$"	$1\frac{1}{2}$"	50"	1 x 2

EXPLODED VIEW

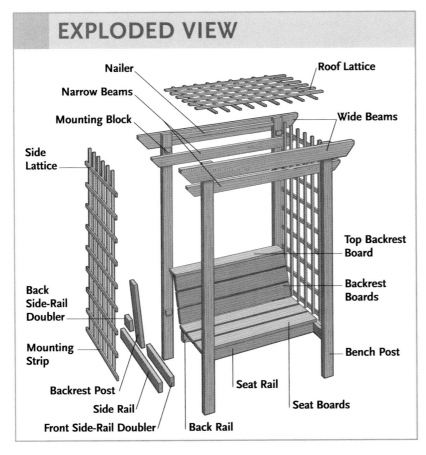

Nailer
Narrow Beams
Mounting Block
Side Lattice
Back Side-Rail Doubler
Mounting Strip
Backrest Post
Side Rail
Front Side-Rail Doubler
Back Rail
Roof Lattice
Wide Beams
Top Backrest Board
Backrest Boards
Bench Post
Seat Rail
Seat Boards

FRONT AND SIDE VIEWS

69½"
61¾"
84"
76⅛"
17"
44½"
51½"

39⅝"
77⅜"
34⅝"
12½"
17⅜"
33⅝"

builder's notes

Materials

We used treated southern yellow pine. You need 2x4s, a 2x6, some ⁵⁄₄ boards, and ³⁄₄ inch stock for the lattice strips.

Some home centers, however, do not stock one-by lumber because it warps readily. So, bear potential warping in mind when you shop and when you work. Remember also that commercial lumber designations indicate dimensions before milling. For example, nominal 1x2s are actually ³⁄₄ x 1½ inches, the same dimensions as several of the pieces for this project. Using 1x2 stock will save the time needed to rip larger boards. For the ³⁄₄-inch-square parts, rip 1x4s (actually ³⁄₄ x 3½ inches). If you can't find one-by stock, you can rip two-by stock into the ³⁄₄-inch strips.

During assembly, you will need to make several gauges from plywood or hardboard to act as spacers when placing the strips that make up the lattice. I used scraps of various thicknesses. If you need to buy material for spacers, buy a precut quarter-sheet of hardboard. It's flat and inexpensive.

Tools and Techniques

Except for the lattice strips, you can crosscut all the parts with a circular saw or a saber saw. For this, you'll appreciate an adjustable speed square. The speed square was designed primarily for layout work. But clamped to the workpiece, it is sturdy enough to serve as a saw guide, both for crosscuts and the project's miter cuts.

Finish

Pressure-treated wood doesn't need a protective finish. But you may want to give it some color, using a semitransparent or solid-color stain.

199

BUILDING A TRELLIS BENCH

project

Cut the posts and beams to length. Note that the beams need a decorative miter cut on both ends. Lay out these miters using the drawing on the facing page, and make the cuts with a circular saw or a chop saw. To assemble these parts takes a little setup. We used a couple of sawhorses placed about 6 feet apart so they could support a wide beam on the top and a seat rail on the bottom. Once you have these boards on top of the horse, place two posts on top and clamp the parts together so they are all square. Join them with galvanized screws. Build the post-and-beam frame for the other side of the project the same way.

The two sides of the trellis structure are joined with the bench. Cut the bench parts to the size and shape indicated in the drawings on page 202. Start by attaching the back and seat rails to each side frame using pilot holes and galvanized screws. Hold the parts together with bar clamps while you are working to prevent them from slipping out of alignment. Next, place one of the side

TOOLS & MATERIALS
- Circular saw ▌Tape measure
- Adjustable speed square
- Power drill with bits ▌Bar clamps
- Framing square
- Saber saw
- 5 pcs. 2x4 8-ft. treated southern yellow pine (SYP)
- 2 pcs. 2x4 10-ft. SYP
- 1 pc. 2x4 12-ft. SYP
- 1 pc. 2x6 12-ft. SYP
- 4 pcs. $\frac{5}{4}$x6 8-ft. SYP
- 15 pcs. 1x2 8-ft. SYP
- 5 pcs. 1x4 8-ft. SYP
- 1 box galvanized screws, $1\frac{1}{4}$ in.
- 1 box galvanized screws, $1\frac{5}{8}$ in.
- 1 box galvanized screws, 2 in.
- 1 box galvanized screws, 3 in.

frames on the sawhorses, and clamp temporary braces to this frame to support the other side frame. Then lift the second side on top of these braces and clamp it in place. Check for square; then screw the second frame to the bench seat frame.

Get some help to turn the trellis upright. Be sure to place it on a level section of ground, or shim it so it's level while you work on it. (Cedar shim shingles are inexpensive and easy to use.) Cut the seat boards to size, and attach them using galvanized screws. Install the front board first, the back board second, and the middle board third, centered between the other two. Finish up the seat by installing the backrest posts and boards. Notch the top board at both ends to fit around the bench posts. Make sure all the screws that are used to attach the seat boards are countersunk below the surface of these boards. Otherwise, they might catch clothing when people sit on the bench.

Next, cut the lattice strips to size using the drawings on page 204 as a guide. Use a table saw for this job, and try to cut the stock out of clear section of the lumber so it will stay as straight as possible. *(continued on page 205)*

1 **Cut the wide beams, side rails, and bench posts to size and place them on a pair of sawhorses as shown. Hold the parts together with bar clamps and compare opposite diagonal measurements to check the assembly for square.** *(continued on page 202)*

POST-AND-BEAM ASSEMBLY

Our trellis bench was built using one of the oldest building techniques around, namely post-and-beam construction. This system creates shelter by using vertical posts to support horizontal beams, which (in turn) support a roof. This method was used for building just about every old barn and for some new high-end houses that feature open floor plans. It yields a strong structure that is relatively lightweight. And it uses lumber more efficiently than other building systems.

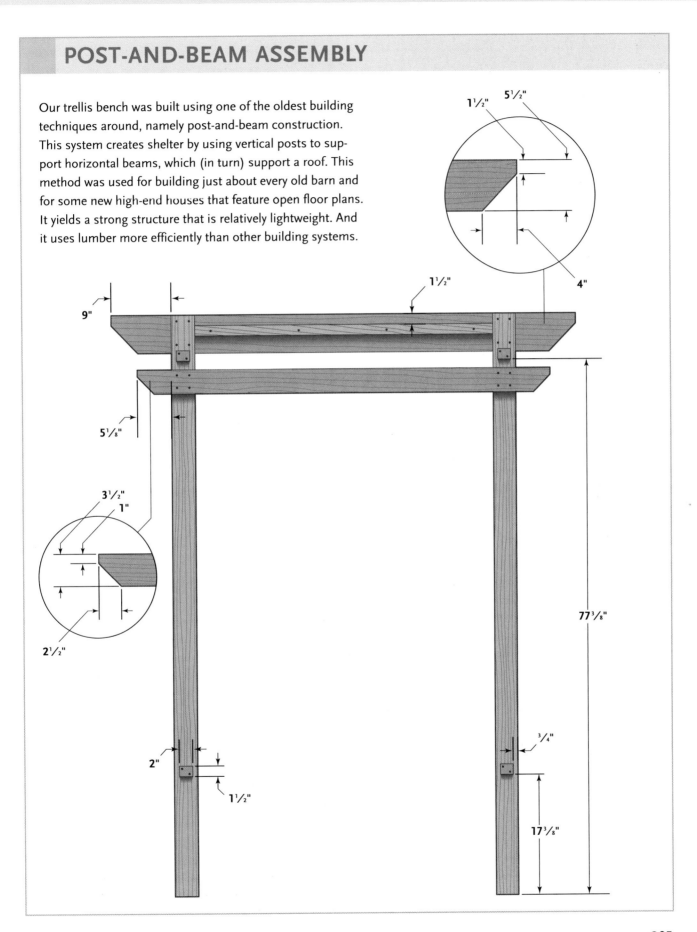

12 trellis projects

(continued from page 200)

2 Once the side frames are assembled, cut the parts for the bench seat using a circular saw (inset). Then attach the back side-rail doubler and the backseat post to the side rail using galvanized screws. Also attach the front side doubler.

3 Attach the front and back seat rails to the side frames using galvanized screws. Pre-drill pilot holes and drive the screws at an angle. Make sure these joints are tight so the bench seat will have solid support.

SEAT FRAME

BACKREST POST LAYOUT

1/4"
78°
1⁵⁄₁₆"
23⁷⁄₁₆"
78°
12°

Backrest Post

Back Side-Rail Doubler

Back Rail

78°

15³⁄₈"

Seat Rail

78°

3¹⁄₁₆"

Front Side-Rail Doubler

Side Rail

6 Have someone help you lift the second side frame onto the bench frame and the temporary braces. Clamp it in place; make sure all parts are aligned; and join the two sides using galvanized screws.

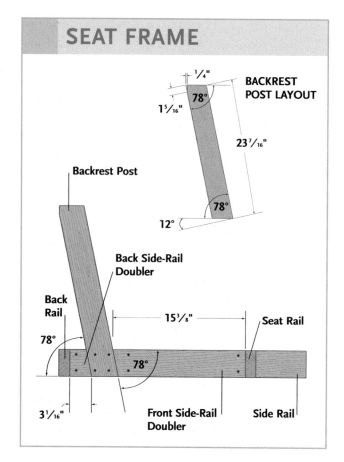

4 Place one post-and-beam assembly on the saw-horses, and position the seat frame on top of it. Make sure the parts are aligned properly; then attach the seat frame using galvanized screws.

5 To attach the remaining trellis frame side, you need to clamp temporary braces to the top of the frame side that's on the sawhorses. Cut these braces the same length as the side rails, and clamp them to the sides of the posts.

7 Place the trellis on a flat and reasonably level section of ground. Then cut the bench seat boards to size, and attach them to the seat frame. Make sure the screw heads are countersunk below the surface of the boards.

8 Attach the back seat boards to the back rest posts, making sure (again) to countersink the screw heads. Cover the top board on the seat back with a trim board that's notched on both ends to fit around the frame posts. *(continued on page 204)*

(continued from page 203)

9 Position the vertical strips for the lattice panels on a worktable, and use spacers made of scrap plywood to keep the strip aligned. Clamp them against the table. Cut the horizontal strips to length and position them on the vertical strips.

10 Join the strips on each lattice panel using galvanized screws. Make sure these assemblies are square. Then install the mounting strip on the bottom edge of both panels. Lift the panels onto the sides of the trellis and push them against the mounting blocks.

LATTICE LAYOUT

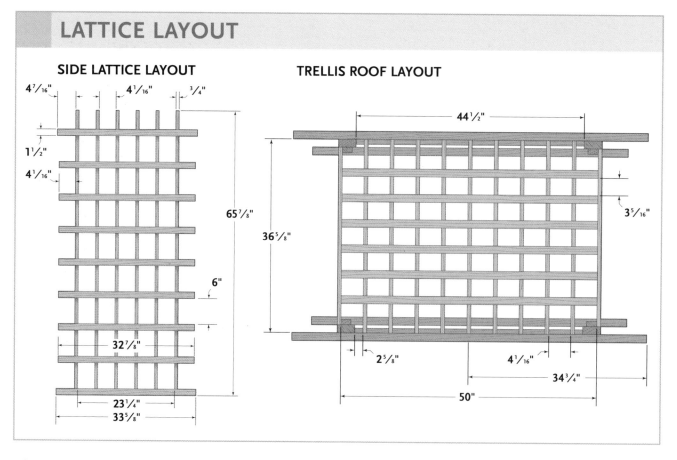

SIDE LATTICE LAYOUT

4⁷/₁₆" 4¹/₁₆" ³/₄"

1½"

4¹/₁₆"

65⁷/₈"

6"

32⁷/₈"

23¼"
33⁵/₈"

TRELLIS ROOF LAYOUT

44½"

3⁵/₁₆"

36⁵/₈"

2⁵/₈" 4¹/₁₆"

34¾"

50"

11 Check the top of each panel to make sure the vertical strips won't hit the roof lattice. If any of the strips are too high, place a guide board on top of the wide beams and scribe the strips. Take down the panels and cut off the waste using a circular or saber saw.

12 For the best alignment of the strips, build the roof lattice in place. Screw nailers to the wide beams and attach crosspieces to the nailers. Then add the longer crosspieces to the top. Attach the strips to each other using galvanized screws.

(continued from page 200)

Preassemble the side lattice panels by laying out the vertical strips on a worktable. Clamp these strips to the table, then place the horizontal strips on top of the vertical strips. Use spacer boards, cut from scrap plywood, to make sure the gap between the strips remains consistent, and join the strips using galvanized screws. Finish up each panel by attaching a mounting strip to the bottom of both sides. Install the four mounting blocks that are shown in the drawing on page 201. Then attach the side panels to these blocks using galvanized screws.

You can preassemble the roof lattice panel as you did the sides and simply mount it on the nailer strips attached to the backside of the wide beams. Or you can build it in place, as we did, to ensure the best fit. To do it this way, install the nailers first; then cut the cross strips to length; and attach the short ones to the nailers using galvanized screws. Once these are in place, lay the long cross strips on top of them. Align these strips with the vertical strips on the side panels for a neat, crisp look, and then join them to the shorter cross strips below using galvanized screws. Do a dry run before attaching the strips.

smart tip

THERE ARE MANY DIFFERENT PLACES YOU CAN PUT A TRELLIS BENCH LIKE THIS. IF YOU HAVE A NICE VIEW, AS WE DO, IT MAKES SENSE TO PLACE IT WHERE YOU CAN TAKE ADVANTAGE OF IT. BUT THIS PIECE ALSO WORKS WELL IN AN EN-CLOSED GARDEN, ESPECIALLY IF IT'S PLACED IN A QUIET CORNER WHERE YOU CAN HAVE A CUP OF COFFEE, READ A BOOK, OR MAKE YOUR FUTURE GARDEN-ING PLANS. AND IF YOU REMOVE THE BENCH AND INSTALL LONGER POSTS THAT ARE ANCHORED IN THE GROUND, YOU CAN INCORPORATE IT INTO A FENCE AND USE IT AS AN ARBOR. YOU CAN ALSO BUILD A GATE TO FIT BETWEEN THE POSTS AND MAKE AN ELABORATE PASSAGEWAY INTO YOUR GARDEN. NO MATTER WHERE YOU PLACE IT, JUST MAKE SURE IT'S IN-STALLED SO IT'S LEVEL AND PLUMB.

MODULAR CORNER TRELLIS

A corner trellis is a great way to define property lines or to establish the borders of an outside room. And they work well in big yards and small. The wide open lattice doesn't feel claustrophobic, but if you do want some privacy, planting a dense climbing plant next to the trellis will provide the barrier you want. This particular design was based more on fence installations than on traditional trellises. In fact, if you like this design, consider incorporating it into the corner of an existing fence. This structure also mimics a typical fence because it must be self-supporting. This means the posts have to be installed in postholes that extend below the frostline. If you don't know how deep this is where you live, just call your local building department and get their recommendations. Where we built this project, the required depth was 18 inches. So we dug our holes about 24 inch-deep and put 6 inches of gravel in the bottom of each. Then we compacted the gravel by tamping it down with the end of a 2x4. We lowered the assembled trellis into these holes; adjusted it until the bottom rails were level and the posts were plumb; and backfilled the postholes.

● CUTTING LIST (See "Tools & Materials," page 208.)

Part	Quantity	Thickness	Width	Length	Stock
Frame tops/bottoms	4	3/4"	2 1/4"	27 3/4"	1x6 white oak
Frame sides	4	3/4"	2 1/4"	39 1/4"	1x6 white oak
Vertical lattice strips	6	1/2"	1/2"	39 1/2"	1x6 white oak
Long filler strips	4	1/2"	1/2"	39 1/2"	1x6 white oak
Horizontal lattice strips	20	1/2"	1/2"	26 3/4"	1x6 white oak
Short filler strips	16	1/2"	1/2"	6"	1x6 white oak
Corner post	1	3 1/2"	3 1/2"	96"	4x4 8' red cedar
End posts	2	3 1/2"	3 1/2"	72"	4x4 12' red cedar
Bottom/top rails	4	1"	3 1/8"	27 3/4"	5/4x4 12' red cedar
Brackets	2	1 1/2"	5 7/8"	24 3/16"	2x8 8' red cedar
Post trim	12	1 1/16"	1 1/2"	4 7/8"	1x6 8' red cedar

EXPLODED VIEW

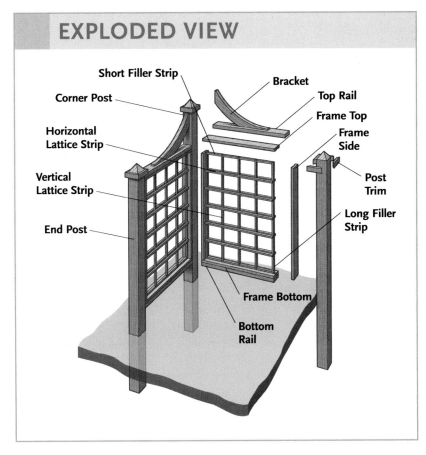

Short Filler Strip
Corner Post
Horizontal Lattice Strip
Vertical Lattice Strip
End Post
Bracket
Top Rail
Frame Top
Frame Side
Post Trim
Long Filler Strip
Frame Bottom
Bottom Rail

SIDE VIEWS

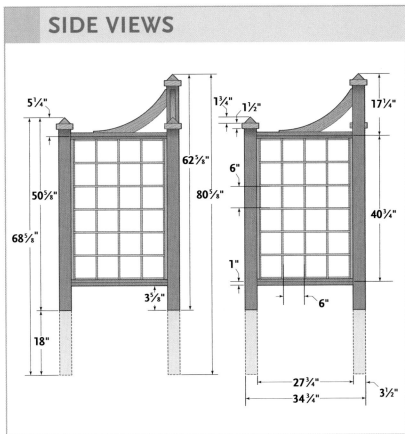

5¼"
1¾"
1½"
17¼"
62⅝"
6"
50⅝"
80⅝"
68⅝"
40¾"
1"
3⅝"
6"
18"
27¾"
34¾"
3½"

builder's notes

Contrary to appearances, this modular corner trellis is easy to make. In addition, it doesn't require a great deal of material or an extensive array of tools.

Materials

For woods, we chose western red cedar and white oak. Both are durable outdoors, and they provide a contrast in hues, with the generally dark cedar framing the blond oak. I also needed the strength of white oak for the slender lattice strips. White oak is probably a material you'll have to order, as it is not always in stock. Red oak is widely available, but it fares poorly in the outdoors and will deteriorate quickly. You could use other woods, of course. For the darker hue, redwood, mahogany, or teak, would be appropriate; for the lighter hue, cypress would work well.

Be sure to use stainless-steel (or aluminum) fasteners with the cedar and oak. Both woods contain tannins that react with iron to produce black stains.

Tools and Techniques

More than any other tool, you will need a table saw to construct this trellis. It is essential for ripping the stock for the latticework. You will also need a circular saw, router with bits, and a miter box or chop saw.

To stabilize the posts, dig holes using a clamshell posthole digger or a shovel. Make the holes deep enough so that the posts reach below the frostline in your area. Check with the local building department to find out how deep to dig.

BUILDING A MODULAR CORNER TRELLIS

Begin by cutting all the parts that make up the two frames to size on a table saw and a miter saw or chop saw. Then rout a $1/2$-in.-wide by $1/8$-in.-deep groove down the middle of the four frame pieces on each panel. Clamp the board to a worktable while you rout this groove.

Next, start cutting the lattice strips to size on a table saw. After cutting the first one, make sure it fits properly in all the frame grooves before cutting the rest of the strips. Glue and nail a long filler strip into the groove in each side frame side. Then clamp one of these frame sides to a worktable and place a $3/8$-in.-thick panel of plywood or particleboard next to it. The panel should measure about 16 x 36 inches so it can fit within the frame boards and support the horizontal lattice during assembly.

Spread the horizontal strips along the frame side and on top of the spacer panel. Keep the space between strips consistent. Then place a spacer panel, again made of $3/8$ plywood or particleboard, on top of (continued on page 210)

TOOLS & MATERIALS
- Table saw ▮ Circular saw ▮ Saber saw
- Miter box or chop saw ▮ Router with bits
- 4 pcs. 1x6 8-ft. white oak ▮ Bar clamps
- Power drill with bits ▮ Pipe clamps
- Spring clamps ▮ Waterproof glue
- Half sheet of $1/4$-in. hardboard
- 1 pc. 4x4 12-ft. western red cedar
- 1 pc. 4x4 8-ft. western red cedar
- 1 pc. $5/4$x4 12-ft. western red cedar
- 1 pc. 2x8 8-ft. western red cedar
- 1 pc. 1x6 8-ft. western red cedar
- Stainless-steel screws, #8 x1$5/8$ in.
- Stainless-steel screws, #8 x 2 in.
- 2 stainless-steel screws, #10 x 3 in.
- 17-gauge, $3/4$ in., 1 in., and 1$1/4$ in. stainless-steel brads ▮ Waterproof glue

1 Cut the frame parts to size and cut a groove down the middle of each using a router with an edge guide. Clamp the frame piece to a worktable, and move the clamps as necessary to allow the router to move along the board.

3 Once all the horizontal strips are in place, lay the vertical strips over them. Maintain the space between vertical strips with a 6-in.-wide spacer panel. Mark the intersection point of the strips on the edge of the vertical strip.

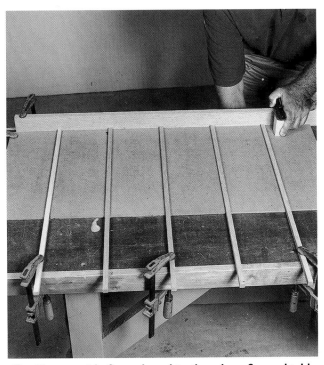

2 Clamp a side frame board to the edge of a worktable and slide a ³/₈-in.-thick panel against it. Then place the ends of the horizontal lattice strips against the frame board and clamp them in place. Make sure the space between the strips is consistently 6 in.

TOP VIEW

This top view provides essential dimensions for the assembly of the parts that fall above the lattice panels. It indicates the position and length of the decorative brackets as well as the trim pieces that ornament the posts.

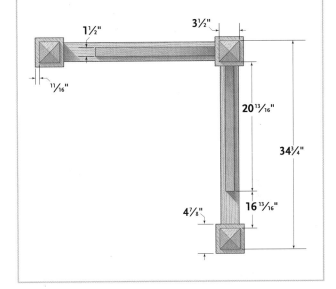

4 Remove the vertical strip, and squeeze a dab of waterproof glue at each intersection point. Don't apply too much glue because it will squeeze out when the strips are nailed together—and cleaning up the excess is an annoying job.

5 Drill a pilot hole for the brads that hold the strips together to avoid splitting these thin pieces of wood. Match the drill bit to the diameter of the brads, or simply cut the head off one of the brads; chuck it in the drill; and use it to drill the hole. (continued on page 210)

(continued from page 209)

6 Use ³/₄-in.-long stainless-steel brads to join the strips. Carefully drive them with light strokes. If you have a 13-oz. hammer, use it. It's easier to control and strikes that miss the brad won't do as much damage.

7 Install the second layer of horizontal strips so they align exactly with the first layer of horizontal strips. Glue and nail them to the vertical strips.

(continued from page 208)

the horizontal strip and against the frame side. Then push a vertical strip against this spacer and mark where it intersects the horizontal strips. Lift off the vertical strip; place a dot of waterproof glue at each intersection point; and lower the vertical strip into place again. Join it to the horizontal strips below with stainless-steel brads. Be sure to drill pilot holes to keep the brads from splitting the strips. Install the rest of the strips in the same manner.

Joining the Frames

Once the lattice panels are complete, join the frame parts and these panels as shown in steps 8 to 11. Basically, you will be building a frame to hold the lattice sections in place.

Then cut stock to size and shape for the decorative brackets that sit on top of the trellises. Join the lattice panels to the posts; install the brackets; and add the small mitered trim pieces at the top of each post. Finish up by installing the trellis posts in postholes that reach below your local frostline. Level and plumb the structure before backfilling the postholes.

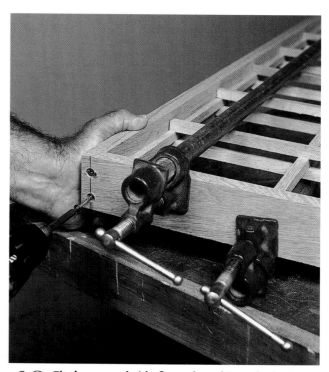

10 Fit the second side frame board into the lattice panel and against the top and bottom frame pieces. Hold this assembly tight with clamps as necessary. Then join the corners of the frame boards using stainless-steel screws.

8 Once the lattice panel is complete, join one frame side to a bottom and a top frame piece to form a U-shaped assembly. Use a pipe clamp to hold a scrap board between the bottom and top frames to make driving the corner screws easier.

9 Remove the temporary brace and carefully place the U-shaped frame on top of your worktable. Slide the lattice panel into the frame so the vertical strips slide in the router grooves in the top and bottom frame pieces.

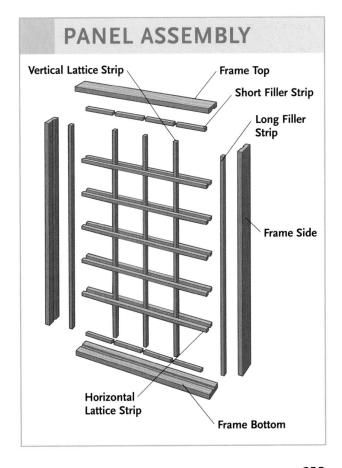

PANEL ASSEMBLY

Vertical Lattice Strip

Frame Top

Short Filler Strip

Long Filler Strip

Frame Side

Horizontal Lattice Strip

Frame Bottom

11 Fill the grooves between the vertical strips on the top and bottom frame boards with short filler strips that are the same width and thickness as the other filler strips. Glue and clamp them in place.

(continued on page 212)

(continued from page 211)

12 The top of each trellis post must be shaped to a point. To do this, cut a 45-deg. bevel at the top of each of the 4 posts sides. Clamp the post to a worktable to keep it from moving when you make these cuts.

13 Lay out the decorative brackets that appear on the top of both lattice frames using the drawing on the facing page as a guide. Draw the curves with a trammel arm and the straight sections with a framing square.

15 Lay out the sides of all three posts for the proper location of the lattice panels. Then lift each panel in place and attach it with stainless-steel screws.

16 Once the first lattice panel is attached to one side post and the corner post, lay this assembly on the worktable and lift the second panel onto the corner post. Clamp it in place, and attach it using screws driven through the side frame.

14 Cut the bracket arcs using a router attached to a plywood trammel. Bolt one end of the trammel to the router base. Screw the other end to the same spots where the trammel arm used for drawing the arcs was attached.

BRACKET LAYOUT

This pattern shows the shape of the two brackets that sit on top of the lattice panels. The red "X's" indicate the sections that abut the trellis parts.

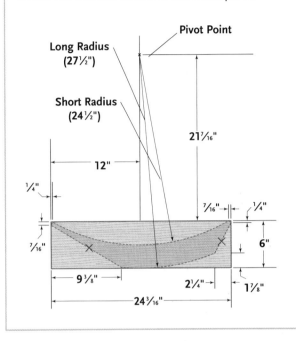

Pivot Point

Long Radius (27½")

Short Radius (24½")

21⁷⁄₁₆"

12"

¼"

⁷⁄₁₆" ¼"

⁷⁄₁₆"

6"

9³⁄₈"

2¼"

1⁷⁄₈"

24³⁄₁₆"

17 Attach the brackets to the top of the lattice frames and to the sides of the corner posts. Use a couple of screws to join each bracket to its top frame and a single 3-in. screw, driven at an angle, to join the top of the bracket to the corner post.

18 Cut miters on the ends of all the trim pieces that decorate the top of the posts. Make sure these pieces fit properly; apply waterproof glue; and nail them in place with stainless-steel brads.

pre-built trellises

In addition to building one of the great trellises or arbors presented in this book, you can also purchase ready-made designs. Check at home and garden centers for structures that you can buy and take with you right away. There are also a number of mail-order catalogs and Web sites that feature these types of structures. (See the Resource Guide, page 278.) Many fence companies will construct a custom trellis or arbor for you or build one based on its portfolio of designs.

Materials range from traditional wood to some you may not have thought of using, such as copper or aluminum. No matter which you choose, look for quality materials, such as cedar and redwood products and metals whose components are joined together securely. Finishes should be able to protect the structure from the elements.

Prices vary greatly, so it is best to shop around before making a final decision. Simple trellises can range from under $20 for a plastic model to several thousand for a large redwood arbor.

A simple design, when combined with high-quality materials and workmanship, yields a distinctive structure, opposite top.

Combining trellises and an arbor that have the same curved-top design can create a one-of-a-kind fence, opposite bottom.

Large pre-built trellises and arbors, above, are usually delivered in sections and assembled on site.

The large round trellis, right, is striking on its own. But it can easily be incorporated as an open gate on a matching fence.

No matter how nice a wall-mounted trellis looks, above, it's the plant that grows on it that becomes the focal point.

The area in front of a trellis can act as a colorful introduction to the plants that grow on the lattice itself. See the hydrangeas at left.

A series of wall-mounted trellises can be used to frame the windows and doors of any house, as these climbing roses show, opposite.

13 arbor projects

Arbors come in many different sizes and shapes and can be installed in several different locations. They often function as gateways to gardens, but they are just as likely to act as destination points, especially if they include benches or a swing. Wherever they are located, and no matter what other purpose they serve, they are usually built to support climbing plants. Because of this, they invariably feature some lattice panels on the sides and the top. This latticework is made of wood strips and is often similar to the latticework on a trellis. But where the trellis is often supported by a house wall or fence, an arbor is always a freestanding structure. It has posts that either sit on top of the ground or are installed in postholes, usually to a depth of one-third the post height.

MODULAR ARBOR

This modest-size arbor was designed to work as an entry-way to a garden or backyard. Its modular design makes it easy to build because both side panels are identical. And the top is made of beams and crosspieces, which are easy to install. The techniques used on this project are almost identical to those employed on our Corner Trellis project (See page 206.)

We used a combination of weather-resistant woods, cedar and white oak, to build this project. Both should be long lasting even if they aren't finished. But it makes good sense to apply a couple coats of wood preservative to all the parts before you apply (or don't apply) a finish. The preservative will make everything last longer. We also built this project to sit on top of the ground. All this required was creating four level spots on the ground for the legs. But if you want a more permanent installation, dig a posthole for each post. The usual recommendation is to dig below the frostline or to a depth one-third of the post height above the ground.

● CUTTING LIST (See "Tools & Materials," page 222.)

Part	Quantity	Thickness	Width	Length	Stock
Posts	4	$1\frac{1}{2}$"	$3\frac{1}{2}$"	$88\frac{3}{8}$"	2 x 4 cedar
Bottom rails	4	$1\frac{1}{2}$"	$5\frac{3}{8}$"	$29\frac{3}{4}$"	2 x 6 cedar
Top rails	2	$1\frac{1}{2}$"	3"	$29\frac{3}{4}$"	2 x 4 cedar
Stiles	4	1"	3"	$66\frac{3}{4}$"	$\frac{5}{4}$-cedar
Lattice frame tops and bottoms	4	$\frac{3}{4}$"	$2\frac{1}{4}$"	$27\frac{3}{4}$"	white oak
Lattice frame sides	4	$\frac{3}{4}$"	$2\frac{1}{4}$"	$65\frac{1}{4}$"	white oak
Vertical lattice strips	6	$\frac{1}{2}$"	$\frac{1}{2}$"	$65\frac{1}{2}$"	white oak
Horizontal lattice strips	36	$\frac{1}{2}$"	$\frac{1}{2}$"	$26\frac{1}{4}$"	white oak
Long filler strips	4	$\frac{1}{2}$"	$\frac{1}{2}$"	$65\frac{1}{2}$"	white oak
Short filler strips	16	$\frac{1}{2}$"	$\frac{1}{2}$"	6"	white oak
Beams	3	$1\frac{1}{2}$"	$7\frac{3}{8}$"	$76\frac{1}{4}$"	2 x 8 cedar
Roof crosspieces	7	$1\frac{1}{2}$"	$2\frac{1}{2}$"	$45\frac{3}{4}$"	2 x 6 cedar

EXPLODED VIEW

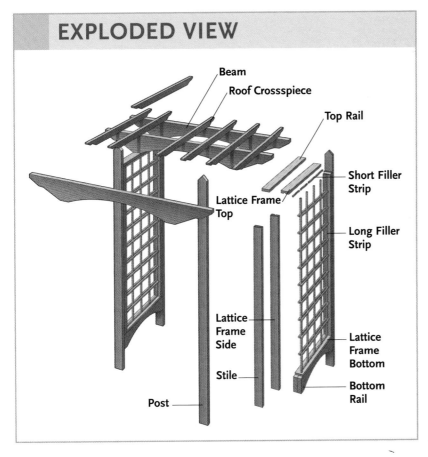

Beam

Roof Crossspiece

Top Rail

Short Filler Strip

Lattice Frame Top

Long Filler Strip

Lattice Frame Side

Lattice Frame Bottom

Stile

Bottom Rail

Post

SIDE AND TOP VIEWS

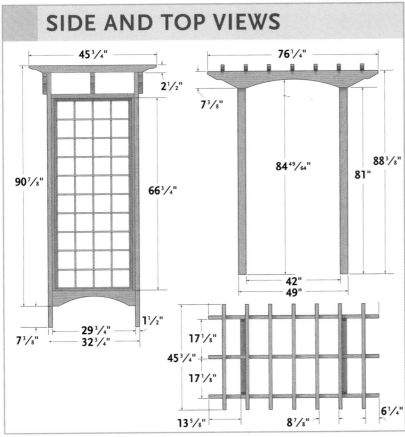

45³/₄"

2¹/₂"

76¹/₄"

7³/₈"

90⁷/₈"

66³/₄"

84⁴⁹/₆₄"

88³/₈"

81"

42"

49"

1¹/₂"

29³/₄"

32³/₄"

7³/₈"

17¹/₈"

45³/₄"

17¹/₈"

13⁵/₈"

8⁷/₈"

6¹/₄"

builder's notes

Building the modular arbor has much in common with the modular corner trellis (See pages 206–213.)

Materials

This arbor is made of western red cedar and white oak, both durable woods for outdoor projects. We used white oak for the framed lattice panels (modules) because of its strength. Other woods used for outdoor projects—such as cedar, redwood, and cypress—are too frail for the ¹/₂-inch-square lattice strips. When shopping for oak, avoid buying the less durable red oak.

For the other pieces of the arbor, you could also use redwood, cypress, and more exotic imported woods like teak.

Be sure to use stainless-steel (or aluminum) fasteners. If you mistakenly use iron fasteners, the tannins in both cedar and oak will react with the iron to produce black stains.

Because the beam template is more than 6 feet long, you need to buy a full sheet of MDF (medium-density fiberboard) for that template. Bear in mind that a sheet of MDF is an inch wider and longer than 4x8 paneling. If that size presents a transportation problem, have it cut where you buy it.

Tools and Techniques

You'll need a table saw and a pusher to rip the stock for the lattice strips and the filler strips. You'll have to rip stock for the top rails, stiles, and roof crosspieces. You'll also need a router.

Finish

Use a penetrating oil formulated for outdoor use. It is easy to apply and cleans up with water.

BUILDING A MODULAR ARBOR

Start by ripping all the parts for the two lattice panels to size on a table saw, and cut them to length using a miter saw or chop saw. Then, using a router with an edge guide attached, cut a groove down the middle of the side, top, and bottom frame pieces. This groove is ½ in. wide and just ⅛ inch deep.

Clamp a side frame to the table, and butt the horizontal strips for each lattice panel against the frame piece. Make sure they are evenly spaced; then clamp them to the table so they won't move during assembly. Next, mark the horizontal strips where the vertical strips will intersect. Then squeeze a dab of waterproof glue on the spots and lower the vertical strips in place. Join the strips with stainless-steel brads.

Once the lattice is assembled, join one side frame to its top and bottom frame pieces to form a large "U-shaped" frame. Set this frame, open side up, on the worktable, and lower the lattice into the frame. Then complete the frame by (continued on page 225)

TOOLS & MATERIALS
▌ Table saw ▌ Miter saw or chop saw
▌ Power drill with bits ▌ Bar clamps
▌ Framing square
▌ Saber saw
▌ Router with bits
▌ Lightweight hammer
▌ 5 pcs. 2x4 8-ft. clear cedar
▌ 3 pcs. 2x4 8-ft. clear cedar
▌ 4 pcs. 2x6 8-ft. clear cedar
▌ 1 pc. ⁵⁄₄x4 12-ft. clear cedar
▌ 5 pcs. 1x6 8-ft. white oak
▌ 2 pcs. ½-in. x 36-in. hardwood dowel
▌ Box stainless-steel screws, #8 x 1⅝ in.
▌ Box stainless-steels crews, #8 x 2 in.
▌ Box stainless-steel screws, #10 x 3 in.
▌ Box 17 gauge, ⅞-in. stainless-steel brads
▌ Box 17 gauge, 1¼-in. stainless-steel brads
▌ Waterproof glue

1 Cut the frame pieces to size, and rout a ⅛-in.-deep x ½-in.-wide groove down the middle of each part. Then cut the lattice strips to size. Check the first one in one of the frame grooves to make sure you have the table saw fence adjusted correctly.

BOTTOM RAIL TEMPLATE

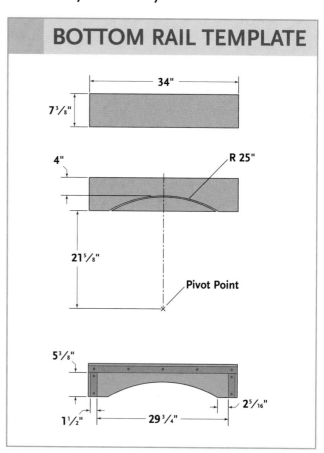

34"

7³⁄₈"

4"

R 25"

21⁵⁄₈"

Pivot Point

5³⁄₈"

1½"

29³⁄₄"

2⁵⁄₁₆"

2 Clamp a side frame to the edge of the worktable, and butt the horizontal strips against this board. Make sure the strips are spaced evenly. Clamp these strips in place; then glue and nail the vertical strips to these horizontal strips using stainless-steel brads.

3 Assemble the top, bottom, and one side frame to form a U-shaped enclosure. Then clamp this assembly to a worktable so the open side points up. Lower the lattice panel into the frame. Install the second side frame.

4 To fabricate the bottom rails, first make a router template to cut the curve on the bottom of each. Lay out the template stock according to the drawing at left; then cut the curve with a router mounted on a simple plywood trammel.

5 Scribe the perimeter of the template onto a piece of bottom rail stock, and cut out the rough shape with a saber saw. Attach the template to the stock, and use a router and a pattern bit to cut the finished shape of the bottom rails. *(continued on page 224)*

(continued from page 223)

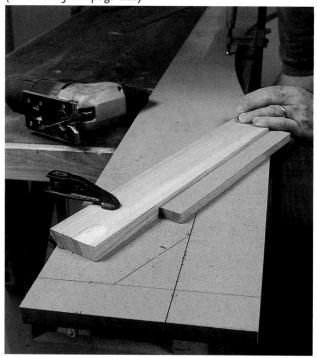

6 To cut a roof beam to shape, make a template as shown in the drawing on page 227. Cut the curve using a router and trammel and the straight cuts with a saber saw. Clamp a straight strip in place to guide the saber saw.

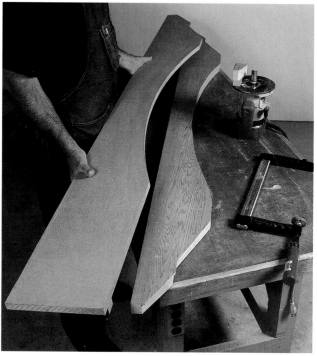

7 Because the template has an end profile on only one side, you have to rout the whole beam in two steps. First, clamp the template on one end of the beam and rout the shape. Then flip the beam end-for-end; clamp the template in place; and rout the other end.

9 Cut medium density fiberboard (MDF) stock to size for the roof crosspiece template, as shown in the drawings on page 227. Join the parts with screws.

10 Join a bottom rail assembly to one of the post-and-stile assemblies using waterproof glue and stainless-steel screws. Clamp the parts in place to keep them from moving during assembly. Then install the top rail in a similar way. *(continued on page 226)*

8 If your pattern bit doesn't cut all the way through the beam stock, turn the beam over and mount a flush-cutting bit in your router. Use it to cut off the remaining waste.

(continued from page 222)

joining the remaining side frame to the top and bottom frame boards.

Cut the posts and stiles to size, and shape the point of top of the posts using a miter saw. Also cut the parts for the top and bottom rails to size, and cut the roof crosspieces and beams to length and width. Wait to cut their decorative shapes until you build the appropriate templates.

Building Templates

The rail at the bottom of both side panels is made of 2x6s with a curve cut in the bottom. The best way to do this is to create a template and use it to cut a uniform curve in each piece. We used medium-density fiberboard (MDF) to make this template (and other ones) because it is dense and stabile. Cut the template blank to the dimensions shown in the drawing on page 222. Then cut the curve using a router and straight bit attached to a plywood trammel. Make the cut in ⅛-inch-depth increments. Once the curve is cut, screw ½-inch blocks to three sides of the template, as shown in the drawing. These blocks will hold the bottom rails to the template when they are being routed. Insert each blank into the template and curve the curve.

Next, make the roof beam template using MDF, as shown in the drawing on page 227. Cut the MDF to size; rout the curve on the bottom of the template; and cut the ends with a saber saw. Clamp the template to each roof beam, and cut the beam to shape using a router and a saber saw. Then fabricate the template for cutting the roof crosspieces, following the instructions in the drawing on page 227. Use a router and saber saw to shape the template; clamp it to the crosspiece stock; and cut these pieces with a router and saber saw too. Once all the roof parts are cut, dull their edges slightly with sandpaper to reduce the chance of splinters.

Assembly

Join the stiles to the posts with glue and stainless-steel screws. Then attach one of these post assemblies to each bottom rail. Clamp this assembly to a worktable, and slide the lattice panel against the stile and bottom rail. Clamp the panel in place, and attach it to the bottom rail with stainless-steel screws. Then install the other post-and-stile assembly against the lattice panel and screw it in place. *(continued on page 227)*

(continued on page 227)

smart tip

WHEN YOU ARE WORKING ON A PROJECT LIKE THIS, WHICH CALLS FOR CUTTING PARTS USING A ROUTER AND A TEMPLATE, CONSIDER GETTING A PLUNGE ROUTER FOR THE JOB. BECAUSE A ROUTER CUT MUST BE MADE IN SHALLOW INCREMENTS OR YOU WILL BURN THE BIT OR OVERLOAD THE ROUTER, A FIXED BASE ROUTER DOESN'T WORK VERY WELL. EACH TIME YOU LOWER THE BIT FOR A DEEPER CUT, YOU HAVE TO STOP THE TOOL, REMOVE IT FROM THE GROOVE, READJUST THE BASE, RESTART THE TOOL, AND RETURN TO THE GROOVE. A PLUNGE ROUTER LETS YOU LOWER THE CUTTER IN SET INCREMENTS WITHOUT TURNING IT OFF OR REMOVING IT FROM THE WORKPIECE. THIS MAKES WORK FASTER AND SAFER.

(continued from page 224)

11 Place the post-and-rails assembly on the worktable so the open side is pointing up. Slide one of the lattice panels into this frame, and clamp it in place. Then join it to the rails and post with stainless-steel screws.

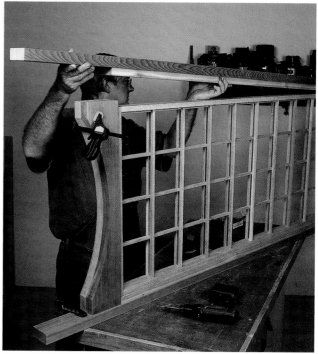

12 Finish up the side assembly by adding the second post-and-stile unit. Clamp the parts together to make tight joints between all the parts. Then join them with stainless-steel screws. Assemble the other side panel in the same way.

13 Stand the side panels on sawhorses, and clamp them in place. Also cut a scrap board to fit between the bottom of the panels and temporarily clamp it in place to provide more stability. Then install the roof beams to the posts and the top rails.

14 Lay out the roof beams for the location of the roof crosspieces. Clamp each crosspiece in place, and join it to the beam underneath with stainless-steel screws driven down through the top edge.

ROOF BEAM TEMPLATE

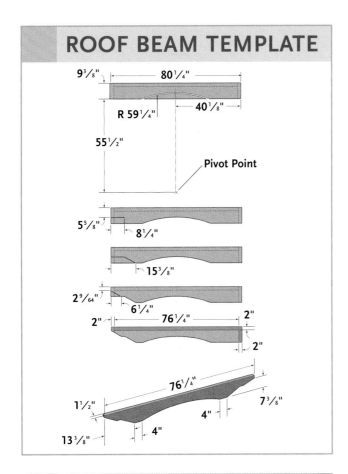

CROSSPIECE TEMPLATE

(continued from page 225)

Finish up the side assemblies by installing the top rail on both side panels.

Assembly

At this point you need to decide if you want to finish the project inside or on site. We decided to work outside because the parts were easier to carry this way. But if you have help and can fit the finished project through your doorway, then working inside is usually more convenient. If you choose working outside, then the first step is to place a pair of sawhorses far enough apart to support the side panels. Make sure the sawhorses are reasonably level so that the assembly is easier.

Begin by clamping the side panels to the top of the sawhorses. Then install the outside roof beams by attaching them to the top of the posts, and install the middle beam by screwing it to the top rails on the side panels. Once the beams are installed, lay out their top edges for the roof crosspieces. Clamp each crosspiece in place; then attach it to the beams with screws driven down through the top of the crosspiece. Finish up by placing the arbor on the ground, taking care to make sure that it is level and plumb.

smart tip

BECAUSE THIS ARBOR IS MADE OF NATURALLY WEATHER-RESISTANT CEDAR, YOU CAN PLACE THE POSTS DIRECTLY ON THE GROUND AND NOT WORRY FOR A LONG TIME ABOUT ANY ROT OR INSECT DAMAGE. BUT YOU CAN CREATE A MUCH BETTER BASE FOR THIS PROJECT BY JUST IN-STALLING A 4 X 8 X 16-INCH SOLID CONCRETE BLOCK UNDER EACH POST. THESE INEXPENSIVE BLOCKS ARE AVAILABLE AT LUMBERYARDS, HOME CENTERS, AND MANY GARDENING STORES. TO INSTALL THEM, DIG AN 8-INCH-DEEP HOLE FOR EACH. THEN, PUT 4 INCHES OF GRAVEL IN THE BOTTOM OF THE HOLE; PLACE THE BLOCKS ON TOP OF THE GRAVEL; AND LEVEL EACH IN PLACE WITH THE OTHER BLOCKS. BACKFILL AROUND THE BLOCKS WITH EXCAVATED SOIL.

GATEWAY ARBOR

This classic arbor has all the appointments of a traditional piece. It has a substantial square post at each corner with a plinth block (baseboard) on the bottom and box beam above. It has a massive open arch top for supporting climbing vines, and square, pointed balusters on the sides to carry the vines from the ground to the top. And in the middle of the arbor hangs a beautiful two-part arched gate. When the half-arch formed by the top of the gate is combined with the half-arch defined by the top of the arbor, a full circle is created that is a great welcoming touch to any yard or garden.

In keeping with the classic design of this arbor, it was primed and painted with two coats of acrylic paint in a brilliant white color. Even though this finish created a stunning appearance, it can be difficult to maintain once a mature vine covers the arbor. Because of this, some people chose a climbing plant that is less dense rather than more dense. Others prune the vine regularly to keep it under control. While others simply tie back the sections of the vines to repair the paint underneath; let it dry; and then tie back other sections and repeat the process. This last option can be a nuisance, but it doesn't really take that long because most arbors don't have much structure that actually needs repainting. As with many other jobs around the house, patience is a virtue when painting an arbor.

Building this project is bound to challenge your construction skills. But it looks more complicated than it actually is. By carefully making each component should go smoothly when it comes time for assembly everything.

● CUTTING LIST (See "Tools & Materials," page 231.)

Part	Quantity	Thickness	Width	Length	Stock
ARCHES					
Arch segments	28	1"	$7^1/_4$"	$24^1/_2$"	$^5/_4$ x 8 10' pine
Arch half segments	8	1"	$7^1/_4$"	$12^1/_4$"	$^5/_4$ x 8 10' pine
Rungs	5	2"	2"	$39^7/_8$"	laminate $^5/_4$ x 8 12' pine
Loose tenons	4	1"	2"	$2^3/_8$"	$^5/_4$ x 8 12' pine

(continued on page 230)

EXPLODED VIEW

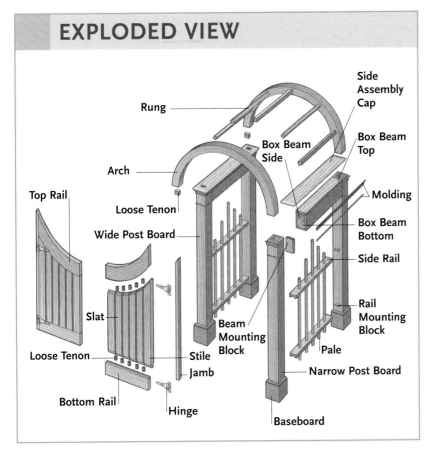

Rung

Side Assembly Cap

Box Beam Side

Box Beam Top

Arch

Molding

Top Rail

Loose Tenon

Box Beam Bottom

Wide Post Board

Side Rail

Slat

Rail Mounting Block

Loose Tenon

Beam Mounting Block

Stile

Jamb

Pale

Bottom Rail

Narrow Post Board

Hinge

Baseboard

FRONT AND SIDE VIEWS

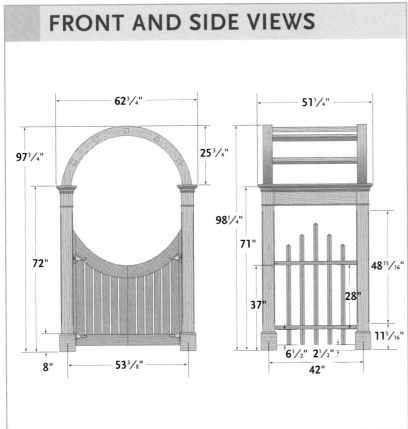

62³/₄"
97³/₄"
72"
8"
53³/₈"
25³/₄"

51¹/₄"
98¹/₄"
71"
37"
28"
48¹⁵/₁₆"
11⁵/₁₆"
6¹/₂" 2¹/₂"
42"

builder's notes

Although this project involves some unusual techniques, it isn't especially difficult if you work methodically.

Materials

Because this project requires quite a bit of wood and top-grade outdoor woods can be pricey, use white pine for almost all parts. For arches and rungs, posts, gates, and some of the trim, use ⁵/₄-by stock, which ranges from 1 to 1¹/₈ inches thick. Select nominal one-by stock (actually ³/₄ inch thick) for the box beams. For the side rails and pales, glue-laminate one-by to create 1¹/₂-inch stock.

Tools and Techniques

You need a well-equipped shop, including a table saw, a good router (or two) with an assortment of bits, a couple of drill-drivers, a power miter saw, a saber saw, and sanders. To clamp the side assemblies and the arch assembly, you'll need bar or pipe clamps.

Constructing the two arches is the most time-consuming task (several days) in this project. Each finished arch consists of four layers of arch segments. You start by forming four double-layer and glue-laminated arch blanks assembled from segments, cutting each to shape, and then layering and gluing pairs of them to form the two quadruple-layer arches. For the laminations, I used polyurethane glue, which dictates a clamping cycle of about four hours. I wound up using about 25 clamps at a time, of different varieties, including C-clamps, bar clamps, quick-action clamps, hand screws, and even short pipe clamps.

● CUTTING LIST *(continued from page 228)*

Part	Quantity	Thickness	Width	Length	Stock
SIDE ASSEMBLY					
Wide post boards	8	1"	$5\frac{1}{2}$"	$71\frac{1}{2}$"	$\frac{5}{4}$ x 8 12' pine
Narrow post boards	8	1"	$4\frac{1}{4}$"	$71\frac{1}{2}$"	$\frac{5}{4}$ x 8 12' pine
Box beam sides	4	$\frac{3}{4}$"	$8\frac{1}{4}$"	$36\frac{5}{8}$"	1 x 10 10' pine
Box beam tops	2	$\frac{3}{4}$"	$5\frac{3}{8}$"	$36\frac{5}{8}$"	1 x 10 10' pine
Box beam bottoms	2	$\frac{3}{4}$"	4"	$36\frac{5}{8}$"	1 x 10 10' pine
Beam mounting blocks	4	1"	4"	$6\frac{3}{4}$"	$\frac{5}{4}$ x 8 10' pine
Side rails	4	$1\frac{1}{2}$"	$3\frac{1}{2}$"	$36\frac{5}{8}$"	1 x 8 8' pine
Center pales	2	$1\frac{1}{2}$"	$1\frac{1}{2}$"	$54\frac{1}{2}$"	1 x 8 8' pine
Intermediate pales	4	$1\frac{1}{2}$"	$1\frac{1}{2}$"	$51\frac{1}{16}$"	1 x 8 8' pine
Outside pales	4	$1\frac{1}{2}$"	$1\frac{1}{2}$"	$47\frac{9}{16}$"	1 x 8 8' pine
Rail mounting blocks	8	$\frac{3}{4}$"	2"	1"	1 x 8 8' pine
Side assembly caps	2	1"	$9\frac{3}{8}$"	$51\frac{3}{8}$"	$\frac{5}{4}$ x 10 10' pine
Baseboards	16	$\frac{3}{4}$"	8"	7"	1 x 10 10' pine
Post extensions	4	$3\frac{1}{2}$"	$3\frac{1}{2}$"	48"	4 x 4 8' treated
MOLDING					
Cove molding, long	4	$1\frac{3}{8}$"	$1\frac{1}{2}$"	52"*	1 x 8 10' pine
Cove molding, short	4	$1\frac{3}{8}$"	$1\frac{1}{2}$"	10"*	1 x 8 10' pine
Bead with fillet, long	4	$\frac{5}{8}$"	$\frac{7}{8}$"	52"*	1 x 10 10' pine
Bead with fillet, short	4	$\frac{5}{8}$"	$\frac{7}{8}$"	10"*	1 x 10 10' pine
Bead, long	4	$\frac{1}{4}$"	$\frac{1}{2}$"	52"*	1 x 10 10' pine
Bead, short	4	$\frac{1}{4}$"	$\frac{1}{2}$"	10"*	1 x 10 10' pine
GATE	* Finished length. Cut a few inches longer, and trim to fit during assembly.				
Bottom rails	2	1"	$5\frac{1}{2}$"	$22\frac{1}{2}$"	$\frac{5}{4}$ x 10 10' pine
Top rail blanks	2	1"	$9\frac{1}{4}$"	$29\frac{1}{2}$"	$\frac{5}{4}$ x 10 10' pine
Stiles	2	1"	$3\frac{1}{2}$"	$26\frac{1}{4}$"*	$\frac{5}{4}$ x 4 10' pine
Stiles	2	1"	$3\frac{1}{2}$"	$37\frac{3}{8}$"*	$\frac{5}{4}$ x 10 12' pine
Slats	8	1"	3"	$32\frac{13}{16}$"*	$\frac{5}{4}$ x 4 10' & 12' pine
Jambs	2	1"	$1\frac{1}{2}$"	$54\frac{1}{4}$"	$\frac{5}{4}$ x 10 10' pine

BUILDING A GATEWAY ARBOR

project

Begin by cutting the arch segments to size, using the drawing on this page as a guide. Then join the segments with glue and plenty of clamps, and build the arch template shown on page 233. This template is used to cut not only the finished shape of the arches, but also as a jig for cutting the mortises in the arches to receive the arbor rungs that join the two arches together.

Once the arches are complete, cut the rungs to size on a table saw, and shape the tenons on the ends of the rungs with (continued on page 235)

TOOLS & MATERIALS

- Table saw ▮ Miter saw or chop saw
- Saber saw ▮ Steel rule
- Combination square
- Power drill with bits
- Adjustable bevel gauge
- Tape measure
- Bar, spring and pipe clamps
- Router with bits ▮ Soft-faced mallet
- Level ▮ Posthole digger ▮ Wheelbarrow
- Shovel and hoe
- 7 pcs. ⁵⁄₄x8 10-ft. #2 common eastern white pine (arch segments)
- 1 pc. ⁵⁄₄x4 10-ft. select eastern white pine (gate parts)
- 2 pcs. ⁵⁄₄x4 12-ft. select eastern white pine (gate parts)
- 8 pcs. ⁵⁄₄x8 12-ft. #2 common pine (posts)
- 2 pcs. ⁵⁄₄x10 10-ft. select pine (caps, gate parts)
- 5 pcs. 1x8 8-ft- select pine (rails and pales)
- 1 pc. 1x8 10-ft. select pine (cove moldings)
- 4 pcs. 1x10 10-ft. select white pine (box beams, moldings, baseboards)
- 2 pcs. 4x4 8-ft. treated southern yellow pine
- 2 pr. strap-type decorative gate hinges
- 2 gate handles/pulls
- 1 gate latch,1 gate stake
- 1 box 1⁵⁄₈- and 2-in. galvanized screws
- 1 box 6d galvanized finishing nails
- 1 box 1¹⁄₄-in. stainless-steel brads

ARCH SEGMENT LAYOUT

The distinctive top arches on this arbor were made by laminating multiple layers of pine boards comprised of angled segments. Each segment matches the drawing below. The arches need 32 of these segments, 28 of which are full-size, while 4 are cut in half to yield 8 half-size segments. Make the angled end cuts on a miter saw or a chop saw.

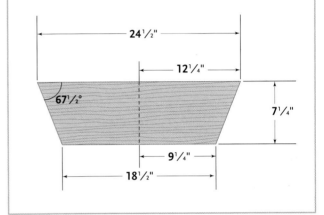

MAKING THE ARCHES

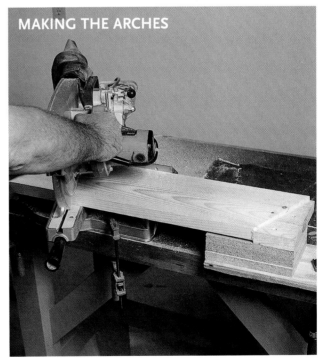

1 Cut the arch segments to size using a chop saw or a miter box. Screw (or clamp) a stop block to the table at one end of the saw to make cutting multiple boards easier. (continued on page 232)

231

(continued from page 231)

2 Stack the arch segments on top of each other as shown in the drawing at right. Each pair of segments in the second row meet at a layout line marked on the segments in the first row.

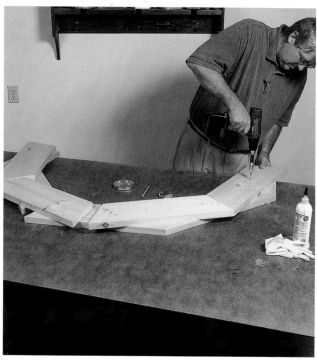

3 Once all the segments fit the lay out correctly, drill pilot holes for the temporary screws that hold the parts together. Then drive the screws tight to make sure the segments are aligned properly. Back out the screws and separate the boards.

4 Spread waterproof glue on the underside of each segment in the second row. Then turn over each segment and press it against the segments below, making sure each abuts its layout line. Redrive the screws in their holes.

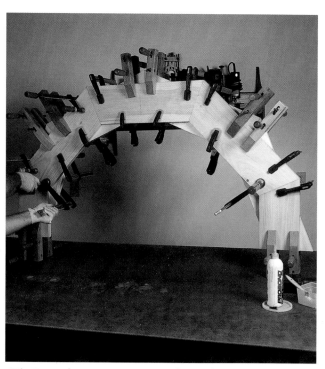

5 Once the parts are screwed together, clamp the assembly to get the strongest lamination. Try to place a clamp every 6 in. along the top and bottom arches. Use as many clamps as you can. *(continued on page 234)*

ARCH BLANK ASSEMBLY

Begin building each arch by joining two layers of precut wood segments together. Place the first layer on the table; apply glue; and attach the second layer with stainless-steel screws.

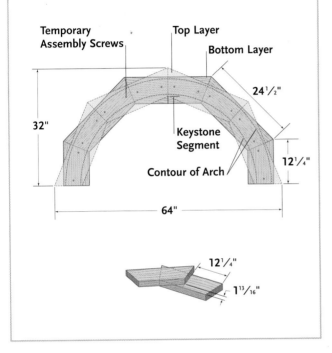

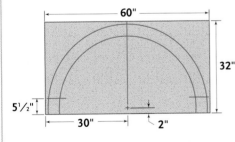

RUNG MORTISE JIG

The arbor rungs are joined to the arches with mortise joints. The arches are laid out so these mortises are spaced evenly along the span of each. You can cut these mortises to match the tenons on the ends of each rung with a sharp chisel and hammer. But this is time-consuming and often yields a poor joint unless you are experienced with hand joinery techniques. But these mortises can be cut easily with a router. All you need is the simple jig shown below.

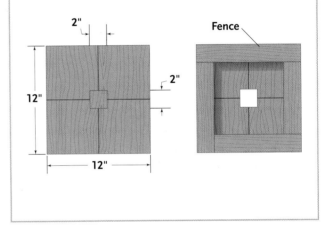

MAKING THE ARCH TEMPLATE

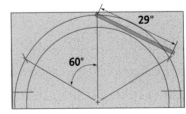

1. Lay out both sides of the arbor arch on a piece of plywood or medium density fiberboard (MDF).

2. Lay out the first rung mortises by marking a 29-in. radius from the centerline on both sides of the arch.

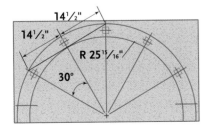

3. Bisect the arch between the centerline and the first rung position with two 14½" long radii.

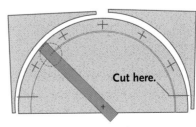

4. Cut the template with a router attached to a simple plywood trammel. Trim the template to size as shown.

(continued from page 232)

6 Use a simple, homemade trammel to mark the top and bottom curves on the arch template. Then, use the same trammel to mark off the first pair of rung mortises, one at each end of the arch.

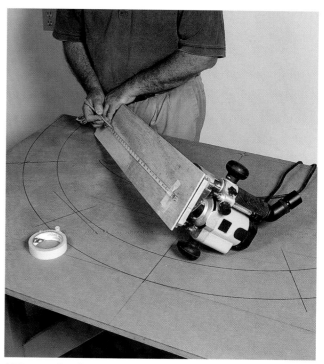

7 Attach a homemade plywood trammel to the router base with double-faced carpet tape. Then measure from the router bit to the pivot point that's drilled in the template and transfer this measurement to the bottom of the trammel. Drill a hole at this point.

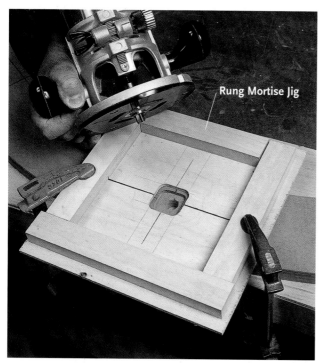

Rung Mortise Jig

9 Once the arch curves are cut, cut the rung mortise holes in the template. Build the router jig shown on page 233 to make these cuts. Then clamp the jig to the template, and cut the hole with a router and a straight bit.

10 Place the completed template on the side of one of the top arches. Then using a router and pattern bit, cut through the laminated arch in a series of $1/8$-in.-deep cuts. Work on the top curve first, followed by the bottom curve.

8 Loosely attach the trammel to the template with a screw. Then set the router bit depth to about ⅛ in. Cut the top arch of the template by swinging the router from one side to another in ⅛-in.-deep cuts. Cut the bottom arch.

11 When the arch curves are cut, cut the rung mortises in the sides of the arches with a router and straight bit. Remember that these mortises should be cut only 1¹⁄₁₆-in.-deep because the rung tenons are only 1 in. long. *(continued on page 236)*

(continued from page 231)

a router and the tenoning jig shown on page 236. Test fit the rungs in both arches. When you are satisfied with the fit, apply waterproof glue to both parts of each joint and pull the arches together with pipe clamps.

Posts And Beams

Next assemble the posts, and cut the mortises in their sides to receive the mounting blocks that support the railings on both sides. Use the drawings on page 236 as a guide to fabricating these posts and making a mortising jig for the mounting blocks. Once these posts are complete, build the box beams (also shown on page 236) that join the posts together. These two beams stabilize the whole arbor and provide a sturdy bases for attaching the top arches. These beams are joined to the posts with mounting blocks that are glued and screwed to the side of the posts and fit inside the ends of the beams. Slide the beams over these blocks and attach them with stainless-steel screws.

Railings

The side railings (rails) are assembled with a simple combination of top and bottom rails with pales (balusters) installed between them. To build these components, start by cutting the rails to size and notching the ends to receive the mounting blocks that hold the rails to the posts. Also cut the pale mortises in the rails using the mortising jig shown on page 236. Do a test run first using scrap material for the jig—cutting the mortise and squaring the mortise corners using a chisel or jigsaw. Make adjustments as necessary. When you have a template that works, cut the pales to size and shape; then slide these pales in the mortises in the bottom rail. Slide the top rail over the top of the mortises, and drive it into place with a soft-faced mallet to prevent denting the wood. Join the rails to the post-and-beam assembly, and carefully transport the arbor to the site. Install the arbor posts on extension posts in the ground following the directions given on page 239.

Arch Assembly

To install the arch assembly to the top of the arbor, first cut the mortises in the ends of the arches and the top of the arbor box beams. Then fabricate and install loose tenons, and lower the arch assembly in place. This assembly does not need to be attached because its weight will hold it down. *(continued on page 243)*

(continued from page 235)

TENONING JIG

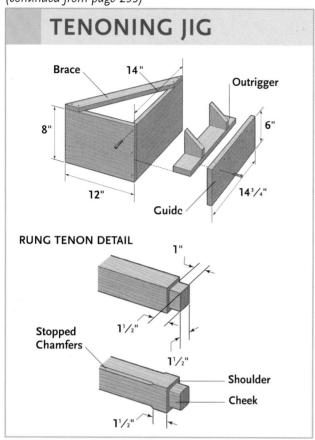

Brace

14"

Outrigger

8"

6"

12"

14³/₄"

Guide

RUNG TENON DETAIL

1"

1¹/₂"

1¹/₂"

Stopped
Chamfers

1¹/₂"

Shoulder

Cheek

1¹/₂"

12 Cut the rung tenons to size on a table saw (inset). Then round the corners of the tenons with sandpaper, and test fit each in its arch mortise. The joint should be tight, but not so tight that you can't push the rung into the mortise with hand pressure.

POST CONSTRUCTION

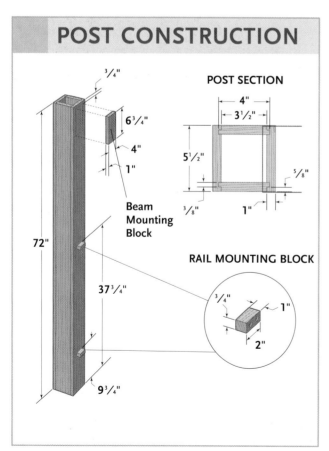

³/₄"

6³/₄"

4"

1"

Beam
Mounting
Block

72"

37³/₄"

9³/₄"

POST SECTION

4"

3¹/₂"

5¹/₂"

⁵/₈"

³/₈"

1"

RAIL MOUNTING BLOCK

³/₄"

1"

2"

BOX BEAM CONSTRUCTION

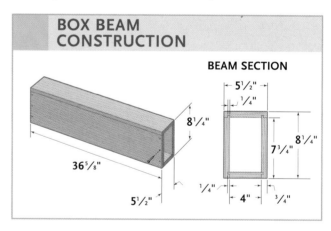

BEAM SECTION

5¹/₂"

¹/₄"

8¹/₄"

36⁵/₈"

7³/₄"

8¹/₄"

¹/₄"

4"

³/₄"

5¹/₂"

SIDE RAIL MORTISING JIG

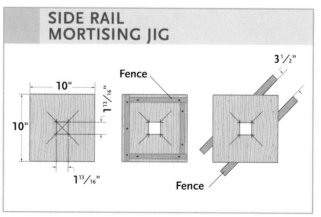

10"

10"

1¹³/₁₆"

Fence

3¹/₂"

1¹³/₁₆"

Fence

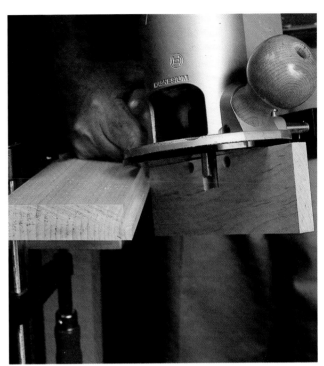

13 The arbor post boards are joined with a rabbet-and-groove joint that runs down each corner. Rout a 1/4-in.-deep groove down both ends of two opposing sides. Make the cuts in at least two passes, instead of one, to get the cleanest cuts.

14 Cut mating rabbets in the ends of the other post boards. Use a straight bit and an edge guide attached to the router base to control the cut.

MAKING THE SIDE ASSEMBLIES

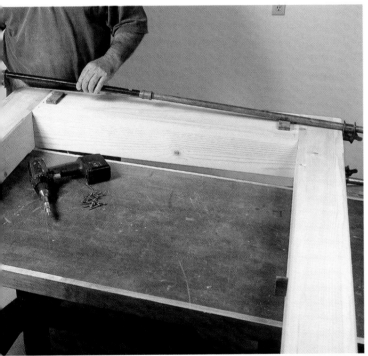

Side-Rail Mortising Jig

15 Assemble the posts, and attach the beam mounting blocks as shown at left. Build the box beam, and place it between the posts and over the mounting blocks. Tighten this assembly with a pipe clamp and attach the beam with screws driven into the blocks.

16 Cut the mortises for the railing pales in the top and bottom rails using a router and the mortising jig shown at left. Once all the holes are cut, square their corners with a sharp chisel so the pales will fit cleanly inside the mortises. (continued on page 238)

(continued from page 237)

17 Push the pales into the bottom rail, and stand this assembly on the floor. Then slide the top rail over the pales and push it down into place. Usually this fit is tight, but don't drive the rail with a hammer because it will dent the wood. Use a soft-faced mallet instead.

18 Install the rails between the arbor posts; then install the trim on the box beam and the posts, using the drawing below as a guide. Attach the pieces with galvanized finish nails. (continued on page 240)

RAIL-NOTCHING JIG

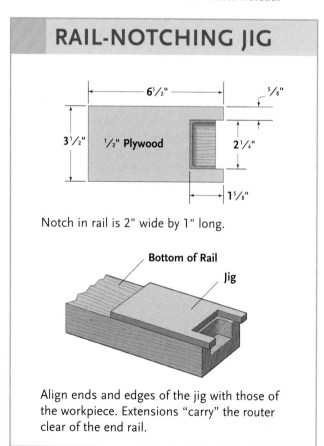

Notch in rail is 2" wide by 1" long.

Align ends and edges of the jig with those of the workpiece. Extensions "carry" the router clear of the end rail.

SIDE MOLDINGS

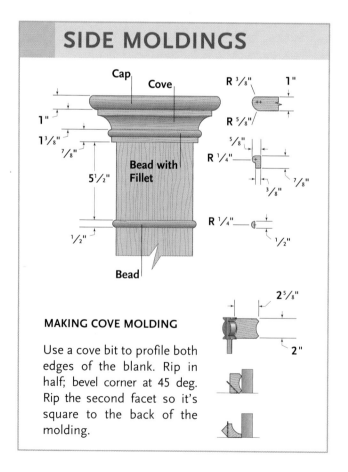

MAKING COVE MOLDING

Use a cove bit to profile both edges of the blank. Rip in half; bevel corner at 45 deg. Rip the second facet so it's square to the back of the molding.

● SETTING UP THE ARBOR

The first step in installing this arbor is to decide exactly where you want it. Then layout the ground in this location and dig 4 postholes using a manual posthole digger or a rented gas-powered auger. To determine how deep these holes should be, you need to know how deep the frostline is in your area. If you don't know, consult your local building department. By installing your arbor posts so they rest on ground below the frostline, you greatly reduce the chance of frost damage.

Once the holes are dug, pour 4 to 6 inches of gravel in the bottom on each hole. Then install 4x4 pressure-treated posts in the holes so they extend 3 feet above the ground surface. These extension posts will slide inside the arbor posts and support the whole arbor structure, without being damaged by moisture or insects. Plumb these posts in the holes; then backfill around them with excavated soil. Tamp the soil down tightly around the posts.

Before installing the first side, double-check the inside measurements of the arbor posts and the outside measurements of the extension posts. Because the first has to slide over the second, make sure the first is slightly bigger. If it's not, remove stock from the extension post with a hand plane or a belt sander. Then, install the first side by sliding the bottom of the arbor posts over the post extensions. Stop an inch or two above the ground so the posts don't sit directly in the soil and attach the sides of the arbor posts to the extension posts with stainless-steel screws. Level the assembly from side to side; then attach the other posts. Stabilize the first side by attaching a diagonal brace to the top of one post and to a stake driven into the ground, as shown at right.

Install the other side of the arbor using the techniques described for the first side. Establish how far off the ground the arbor posts should be by marking a level line from the bottom of the posts on the first side to the extension posts for the second side.

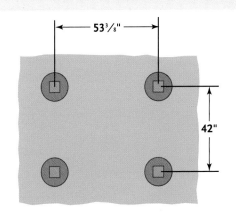

1. Begin installation by laying out the position of the postholes using the dimensions shown.

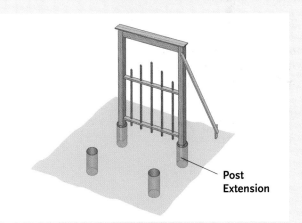

2. Lower one side onto the extension posts; plumb the side; and brace it to the ground.

3. Install the second side; plumb the posts; and attach braces between the two sides.

(continued from page 238)

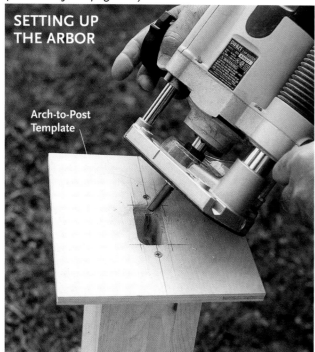

**SETTING UP
THE ARBOR**

Arch-to-Post
Template

19 The bottom ends of the arbor arches are attached to the top of the arbor posts with loose tenons. These tenons fit into mortises cut in the arches and posts. Use the template, shown below, and a router with a straight bit to do the job.

20 To locate the exact position of the mortises on the top of the posts, insert the tenons in the arches and lift the arches into place. Mark the perimeter of the tenons on the posts tops.

ARCH-TO-POST
MORTISING TEMPLATE

The arbor arches are joined to the side posts with loose tenons. These fit into matching mortises cut in the bottom of the arches and the top of the posts. To cut these mortises, build the router jig shown below.)

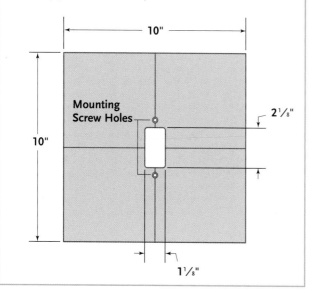

10"

10"

Mounting
Screw Holes

2¹⁄₈"

1¹⁄₈"

smart tip

THIS PROJECT FEATURES A NUMBER OF MORTISE-AND-TENON JOINTS THAT ARE FAMOUSLY STRONG AND ALSO SOMEWHAT DIFFICULT TO MAKE. THE RUNGS ARE JOINED TO THE ARCHES WITH THESE JOINTS, AS ARE THE ARCHES AND POSTS AND THE RAILS AND POSTS. A GOOD ALTERNATIVE TO THESE JOINTS IS THE SIMPLE DOWEL JOINT. HARDWOOD DOWELS ARE COMMONLY AVAILABLE IS LARGE SIZES, OFTEN IN DIAMETERS UP TO ³⁄₄ IN. TO INSTALL THEM, ALL THAT'S REQUIRED IS A DRILL BIT OF THE SAME DIAMETER AND AN ELECTRIC DRILL. TO MAKE A DOWEL JOINT, JUST DRILL MATCHING HOLES IN BOTH PARTS; CUT THE DOWEL OR DOWELS TO LENGTH; SPREAD GLUE ON ALL PARTS; AND PUSH THE PARTS TOGETHER.

MAKING THE GATE

21 Use the same template for cutting the post mortises as you used to cut the arch mortises. Center it on the lines you scribed around the tenon, and screw it in place. Cut the mortise with a router.

22 Cut the gate top rails to approximate size using a saber saw. Then clamp the rail stock onto a worktable, and cut the top and bottom curves using the same template you used for cutting the arbor arches. *(continued on page 242)*

CUTTING THE GATE TOP RAILS

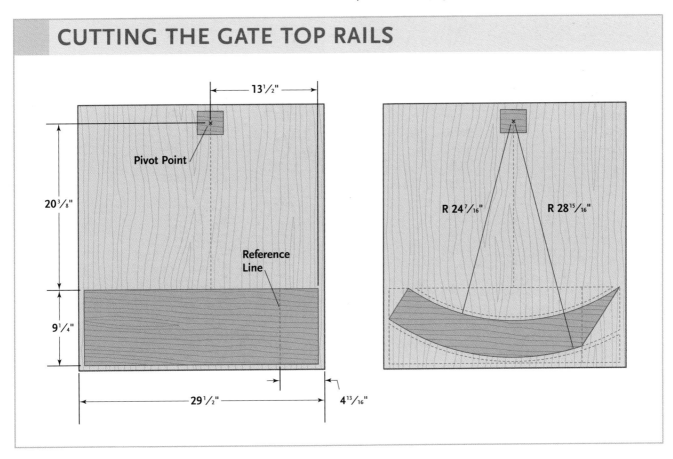

13 1/2"

Pivot Point

20 3/8"

Reference Line

9 1/4"

29 1/2"

4 13/16"

R 24 7/16"   R 28 15/16"

13 arbor projects

(continued from page 241)

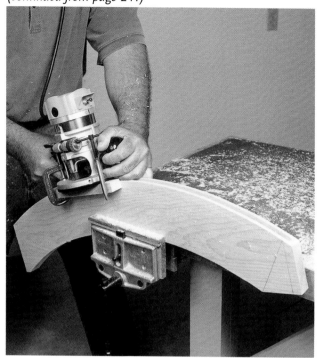

23 Cut the grooves that house the tenons on the end of the gate stiles and slats. Use a straight bit and an edge guide attached to the router base. Hold the rail in a vise or clamp it to the side of a worktable.

24 Place the gate stiles and slats on a worktable and slide spacers in between. Clamp all these pieces together, and clamp the arch template to the top. Use a router to cut the tenons on the top (and bottom) of these parts as shown in the drawings on the facing page.

25 Turn this gate assembly over and clamp the template on the other side. Cut the same tenons on this side with a router. Then, using a saber saw, cut through the waste that's left while the parts are still clamped together.

26 Use waterproof glue and clamps to join the gate parts together. Mount the clamps on the edge of the curved top rail using curved scrap blocks. When the glue is dry, remove the clamps and hang the gate panels on the arbor posts.

TENONING STILES AND SLATS

The gate stiles and slats are joined to the top and bottom rails of the gate with groove-and-tenon joints. The grooves are cut in the bottom edge of the top rail and the top edge of the bottom rail with a router and an edge guide. The tenons on the stiles and slats are also cut with a router, but require the use of the template shown below to yield clean, accurate cuts. You'll get good results if you make the template out of plywood or medium-density fiberboard (MDF).

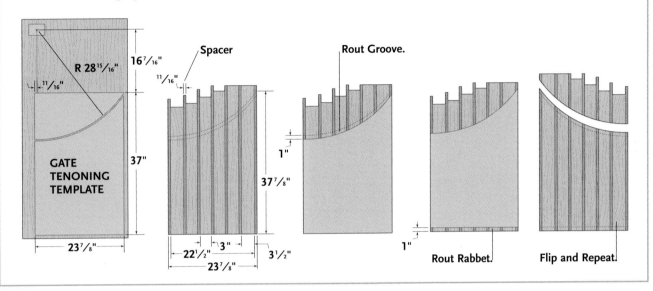

BASEBOARD DETAIL

The baseboard trim at the bottom of each arbor post is a classic treatment that is easy to make. Just cut a cove shape on the top edge of the trim stock; then miter the trim to fit on three sides of the posts. Attach the trim; and finish the open ends with short mitered returns glued in place.

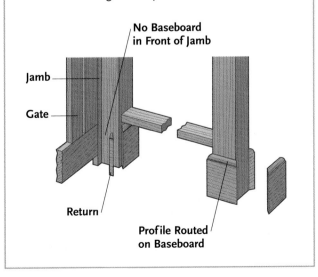

(continued from page 235)

Building the Gate

Cut all the gate parts to size and fabricate a router template for cutting the arch on the top rails and the top edge of the gate stiles and slats. Then cut the top gate rail to shape using a router and this template. Also cut a groove down the bottom edge of the top rails, and the top edge of the bottom rails using a router with a straight bit and edge guide.

Next, clamp the gate stiles and slats together on a worktable and clamp the router template on top of this assembly. Cut the tenons on the top of the stiles and slats with a router; then cut the waste off these boards with a saber saw. Also, cut the tenons on the bottom of the stiles and slats with a router and the same template.

Assemble the gate parts with glue and clamps and when these assemblies are dry, hang the gates in the arbor opening with hinges. Add the handles, the gate latch, and the remaining baseboard trim on the bottom of the gate posts. Finish up the project by coating the parts with 100 percent acrylic primer and two coats of 100 percent acrylic latex paint.

GRAPE ARBOR

A grape arbor, like the example shown here, is one of the great traditional garden structures. It's designed so it's strong enough to support heavy vines and all the fruit that comes with them in the summer. But it can also function as a covered walkway, similar to a colonnade, that connects a house to an outbuilding like a garage or barn. Grape arbors can also do double-duty as privacy screens, especially when the grape vines are mature, to block anyone's view of your yard or garden.

This substantial arbor is 12 feet long and will support a lot of grapes. But if you want a longer structure, just use this arbor as your first module and add more whole (and partial) modules until your arbor is complete.

Building this project is not difficult, once you get the posts installed in the ground. This "foundation" work does take some time and effort. But once you establish a system for digging the holes and supporting the posts, the rest of the job will progress quickly.

● CUTTING LIST (See "Tools & Materials," page 246.)

Part	Quantity	Thickness	Width	Length	SYP Stock
Posts	8	3½"	3½"	144"	4x4 12'
Rafters	4	1½"	5½"	67"	2x6 12'
Nailers	4	¾"	1½"	4"	1x2 8'
Roof interior strips	6	¾"	1½"	42½"*	1x2 8'
Roof cross strips	12	¾"	1½"	55"*	1x2 8'
Roof long strips	7	¾"	1½"	59⅛" **	1x2 8'
Roof long strips	7	¾"	1½"	85⅜" **	1x2 8'
Side horizontal strips	16	¾"	1½"	47¾" **	1x2 8'
Side horizontal strips	16	¾"	1½"	93¾" **	1x2 8'
Side vertical strips	24	¾"	1½"	77"*	1x2 8'

*Approximate finished lengths
**Approximate finished lengths. Sets of strips will be butted and then trimmed to produce strips to equal length of arbor.

EXPLODED VIEW

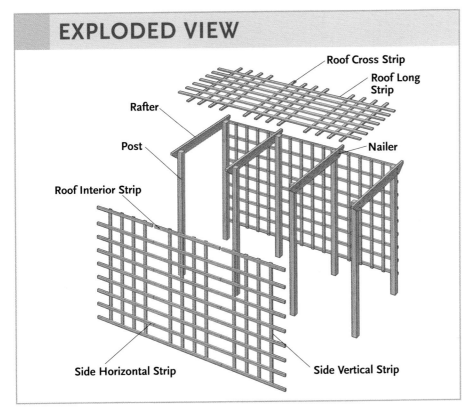

Roof Cross Strip

Roof Long Strip

Rafter

Post

Nailer

Roof Interior Strip

Side Horizontal Strip

Side Vertical Strip

FRONT AND SIDE VIEWS

67"

6½"

5½"

Center

8"

84"

36" Min.

144½"

7⅜"

84"

84"

8"

89½"

12½"

46"

46"

46"

141½"

builder's notes

Though large, this grape arbor is fairly simple to build. The trickiest part is setting the eight posts. Here, patient and methodical work pays off.

Materials

You can use any of a number of the woods that are durable outdoors. If you choose to use oak, cedar, or redwood, you need stainless-steel fasteners in order to avoid the black stains around every bolt and screw.

Tools and Techniques

A large part of this project involves layout and digging of holes for the eight posts. Use extra strips of the lattice material to construct batter boards, and then ran mason's string from one to another, thereby outlining the perimeter of the arbor.

When plumbing the posts, you will find it helpful to use both an 18-inch and a 4-foot level to plumb the posts and the vertical lattice, and to level the rafters and the horizontal lattice. When laying out the postholes, use a tiny line level designed to be suspended on a horizontal string.

Finish

When built with treated lumber, the grape arbor will last many years without a finish. Stain, however, works better and is easier to apply than paint on treated wood.

smart tip

DIGGING POSTHOLES WITH A CLAMSHELL POSTHOLE DIGGER CAN BE EASY WORK IF YOUR SOIL IS SANDY. BUT IF YOU HAVE ROCKY OR CLAY-FILLED SOIL, HAND DIGGING CAN BE A TERRIBLE JOB. ONE GOOD OPTION IS TO RENT A TWO-PERSON, GAS-POWERED AUGER. AND IF THE AUGER DOESN'T DO IT, HIRE SOMEONE WITH A SMALL BACKHOE TO COME IN AND DIG THE HOLES.

BUILDING A GRAPE ARBOR

project

Begin by laying out your lawn for the location of the postholes. The drawing at right shows how to do this. Then determine how deep the holes should be excavated to prevent frost damage. If you don't know how deep the frostline is in your area, contact your local building department.

Dig the holes accordingly and place the post in the holes. Then line up the posts using mason's string and diagonal braces that tie the posts to stakes driven in the ground. When all the posts are properly aligned and braced, backfill the postholes with concrete mixed in a wheelbarrow.

Join the top of the posts in pairs with the arbor rafters. These are attached to the sides of the posts with galvanized carriage bolts. Make sure that they are installed level from side to side and between rafters. Then cut and install lattice strips on the top of these rafters, followed by attaching lattice strips to the sides of the arbor. Keep in mind that this structure was designed as a module that can be easily duplicated if you wanted your arbor to be longer.

TOOLS & MATERIALS
■ Tape measure ■ Line level
■ Mason's string ■ Shovel and hoe
■ Clamshell posthole digger ■ Level
■ Wheelbarrow ■ Trowel
■ Chop saw ■ Power drill with bits
■ Framing square
■ Hammer
■ Bar and spring clamps
■ 8 pcs. 4x4 12-ft. treated southern yellow pine
■ 2 pcs. 2x6 12-ft. treated southern yellow pine
■ 75 pcs. 1x2 8-ft. treated southern yellow pine
■ 16 galvanized carriage bolts, nuts, and washers, $\frac{1}{4}$ x 5 in.
■ 1$\frac{5}{8}$-in. deck screws
■ 1-in. deck screws
■ 1$\frac{1}{4}$-in. stainless-steel brads
■ Concrete as needed

1 Begin the posthole layout by installing batter boards as shown in the drawing at right. Drive two stakes in the ground; then add a crosspiece between them near the top. Attach one end to the first stake; then level the other end and screw it to the other stake.

2 To install the opposite batter board, attach a string (with a line level in place) to the crosspiece on the first batter board, and hold this string on top of the second crosspiece. Move this crosspiece up or down until the string is level; then attach it to the stakes.

LAYING OUT POSTHOLES

This diagram shows the location of the postholes for our grape arbor project. To make sure the holes line up on the sides and are square at the corners, set up bat-ter boards and string as shown. The red numbers indi-cate the pairs of batter boards that support a single string: 1 and 2, 3 and 4, 5 and 6, and 7 and 8.

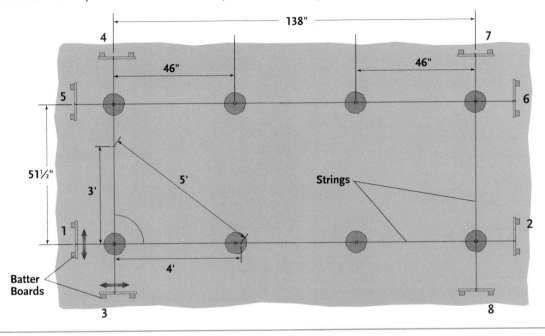

3 To establish that the layout is square, check the in-tersection of the side and end strings with a 3-4-5 triangle. If you measure from the 3-ft. point on one string to the 4-ft. point on the other the distance should be 5 ft. if the strings are square.

4 To establish the center of the arbor corner posts, lower a plumb bob to the ground below the intersec-tion point of the end and side strings. Drive a stake at this point. *(continued on page 248)*

(continued from page 247)

5 Once the holes are excavated, lower the posts into the holes and attach braces to adjacent sides. Drive stakes in the ground so the braces can reach from the top of the post to these stakes. Then plumb the post with a level, and attach the braces to the stakes so the post doesn't move.

6 Continue to install the rest of the posts in a similar fashion. Plumb and brace each post in place and make sure that the distance between the posts on one side of the arbor and those on the other side is 42$\frac{1}{2}$ in.

7 When all the posts are installed and braced in a plumb position, mix some concrete in a wheelbarrow and pour it around each post to backfill the holes. Smooth and taper the top of the concrete (so water will run off) using a mason's trowel.

8 Mark the finished post height on one of the corner posts. Then stretch a string with a line level in place between this post and others in the arbor. Mark a level line on each; then use a square to draw a cutline through the level line. Cut off the waste with a circular saw.

SETTING POSTS

After the postholes are excavated and the posts are lowered in the holes, reattach the layout strings to the batter boards to establish the exact locations of the posts. These strings have to move 1³⁄₄ inches out from their original location at the centerline of the posts. Now the reference line is on the outside surface of the posts.

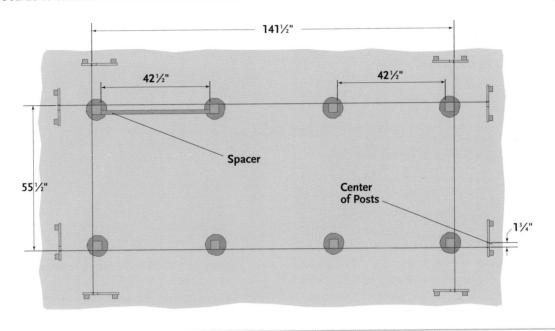

141½"

42½"

42½"

Spacer

Center of Posts

55½"

1³⁄₄"

RAFTER LAYOUT

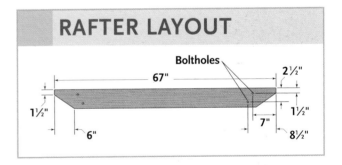

Boltholes

67"

2½"

1½"

1½"

6"

7"

8½"

9 Layout the size and shape of the arbor rafters with a framing square and tape measure. Place the rafters on sawhorses or a worktable, and make the cuts using a circular saw.

10 Clamp each rafter to the sides of the posts. Then lay out and drill the carriage bolt holes through both, using a spade bit. Slide the galvanized bolts into these holes and tighten them in place.

(continued on page 250)

(continued from page 249)

11 Install the nailer blocks on the side of the rafters to receive the interior roof strips. Then attach these strips between the rafters with galvanized screws. Be sure to drill pilot holes to avoid the risk of splitting the thin strip.

12 Cut the cross strips for the arbor roof lattice to size, and install them over the interior roof strips. Space these strips evenly using blocks made of scrap wood. Nail the strips together using stainless-steel brads.

TOP VIEW

This top view shows how the lattice strips fit on top of the arbor. First, the interior roof strips are installed between the rafters. Then the short roof strips are nailed to the interior strips, followed by the long roof strips that are joined to the short strips underneath with stainless-steel screws.

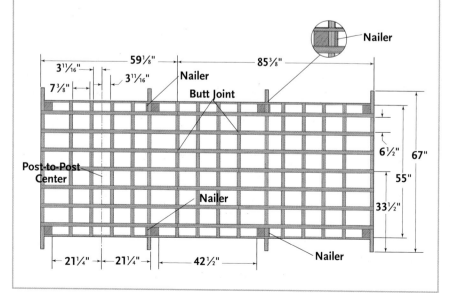

VERTICAL LATTICE

Once the lattice is done on the top of the arbor, install the strips on the side. Attach the horizontal ones to the outside of the posts and the verticals to the inside of the horizontals. Use stainless-steel screws to attach them and make sure all the strips, are spaced evenly.

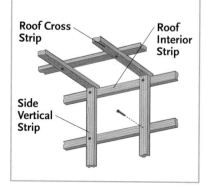

13 Once all of the roof cross strips are installed, lay the long roof strips over them and attach the two with galvanized screws. Use scrap blocks as spacers between the long strips, and be sure to drill pilot holes to prevent splitting.

14 Install the horizontal strips on the sides of the arbor posts using galvanized screws. To maintain even spacing, clamp uniform scrap blocks to the posts before sliding the next strip in place.

15 The vertical strips on the side are attached to the inside surface of the horizontal strips. Clamp each vertical strip in place so it aligns with the roof cross strip above. Then plumb the strip so its bottom aligns with where the top is clamped.

16 Attach the vertical strips to the horizontal ones underneath with galvanized screws. Drill pilot holes for these screws, and check for uniform spacing from side to side and top to bottom.

arbor designs

Arbors make great getaway spots for reading and relaxing, above, even if these places are confined to your backyard.

Pergolas with closely spaced roof members, left, can function as arbors and still create a substantial entryway.

A gate arbor, right, that's covered with climbing roses, makes a welcome entryway into any yard or garden.

Pre-built arbors, left, that mix structures like a deck bench and a pergola roof can still support climbing vines.

The elegant arbor, right, comes in kit form and is assembled with hidden fasteners to create a seamless look.

Large ready-made trellises and arbors, below, are usually delivered in sections and assembled on site.

more arbors

Arbor design can be as exuberant as you want, above, with different lattice panels appearing on the sides, gate, and adjacent fence sections.

A large deck is a perfect setting for a shade arbor, right, that can accommodate lots of outdoor furniture, from chaise longues to dining tables and chairs.

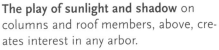

The play of sunlight and shadow on columns and roof members, above, creates interest in any arbor.

Once the plants or vines mature, above right, the structure of an arbor can practically disappear.

A simple backyard arbor, right, can immediately become a resting place with the addition of a bench.

14 plants for trellises and arbors

No matter how sophisticated the design of your trellis or arbor, the project isn't really complete until it includes a climbing plant of some kind. When selecting plants, take cues from the rest of your landscape. Pick specimens that either match or complement the color and texture of other plants in your yard. Discuss your selections with a knowledgeable person at the local garden center. They can tell you how quickly the plant will grow, the necessary soil conditions, and the size of your plant at maturity. You can begin your search for the perfect plants with the selections in this chapter. You'll find a variety of colorful vines as well as popular climbing roses.

SELECTING PLANTS

Typically, the plants used on trellises or arbors fall into one of two categories: vines and climbing or rambler roses. Within these groups there are many beautiful and interesting possibilities. But for success, choose a plant that is compatible with the style and physical characteristics of the structure, as well as the growing conditions that exist at the site of the structure.

Consider Style

Most plants have a style—that is, they evoke a certain atmosphere or feeling. A climbing nasturtium (*Tropaeolum majus*), for example, gives an informal, country feeling, while a well-trained and carefully pruned climbing rose (*Rosa* spp.) can look somewhat formal.

English ivy (*Hedera helix*) speaks of tradition and culture; bright, heavy trumpet vines are cheerful and generous; and balloon vines (*Cardiospermum halicacabum*) are softly whimsical. When you set about choosing a vine, picture it in your mind and see what associations it brings.

Structures also have particular styles, thanks to their design and materials. A wrought-iron arbor has a traditional feeling, while an arbor of the same shape but made from sleek, shiny tubing feels contemporary. A fan trellis made of wood lathing strips gives a decorative touch, while a rectangular latticework trellis made from the same material is a no-nonsense, practical structure.

The trick to developing a planting that will please you for years to come

is matching the structure to the style of your home and the plant to the style of each. For example, if your house is a formal Federal design, a hyacinth bean (*Lablab purpureus*) growing on a vine arbor at the front gate is going to look out of place; a thornless rose on a simple wrought-iron arbor would be far more appropriate. But don't think that you can never grow that hyacinth bean—it could add a bright, cheerful touch to your more informal backyard.

Match Physical Properties

Structures must also suit the plant in strength and the way in which the plant "climbs." Imagine that you've built a wooden arbor out of 6- by 6-inch posts to complement your substantial-looking log home. This structure would completely dwarf a honeysuckle vine

Multiple types of support are in place for this robust clematis. The fan trellis supported it when it was first planted, and now the lattice top of this board fence does, too.

Match the plant's climbing style to its support. Delicate vines, such as sweet peas and morning glories, can even climb on a simple arrangement of twine or wire.

(*Lonicera* spp.) with its delicate foliage and small red blooms. But a wisteria (*Wisteria* spp.) would be right at home on it. After a few years, the thick, twining wisteria trunks and the sturdy posts will be in such good proportion that you'll barely notice the posts, but unlike most supports, this one will be strong enough to carry the weight of a full-grown wisteria vine.

Accommodate Climbing Style

Vines climb in particular ways. As illustrated and explained below, some stems twine around their supports; some vines grow tendrils that grasp and curl around any slender support that they touch; some grow grasping aerial roots from their stems; and a few are fitted with "holdfasts," small suction-cup like structures at the ends of short stems. Scandent vines aren't equipped for any of these climbing strategies. Instead, they lean on their supports. Climbing roses are an example of a scandent vine; even though they have thorns that catch on nearby shrubs, trees, and poles, you must tie them to a support to keep them upright. (See page 273 in this chapter.)

For success, the climbing style of the plant must be appropriate to the characteristics of the support on which you want it to grow. Information about climbing styles of vines is given in the Vine Directory, pages 266 to 271, but you can also figure it out just by looking at the plant.

Plants with tendrils, such as sweet peas and gourds, must have a network of thin supports to climb. Strings, nylon or woven netting, chicken wire, chain-link fences, and trellises that are made from slender lathing strips are all appropriate.

Vines with twining stems must be able to encircle their support; wisteria can easily twine around a 6-inch-square post, while morning glory vines thrive on anything from a piece of nylon cord to a 4-inch-wide post.

Ivies and other plants with holdfasts and aerial roots need a fairly continuous and rough surface to climb. Stone or brick walls are ideal for them. They also climb well on most wooden walls, but because they can sometimes damage them by growing under a board and prying it loose, this is rarely a good idea. Wrapping and tying these vines around their supports is another choice.

CLIMBING STYLE

Twining stems simply wrap themselves around a support, even one as thin as twine or a metal wire.

Tendrils wrap tightly around their supports. Give them both vertical and horizontal structures to climb.

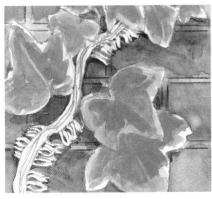

Aerial rootlets grow into crevices in a wall. They are strong enough to pry boards loose but don't hurt bricks.

Holdfasts can attach themselves to smooth surfaces because they secrete an adhesive substance.

● NORTH AMERICAN HARDINESS ZONE MAPS

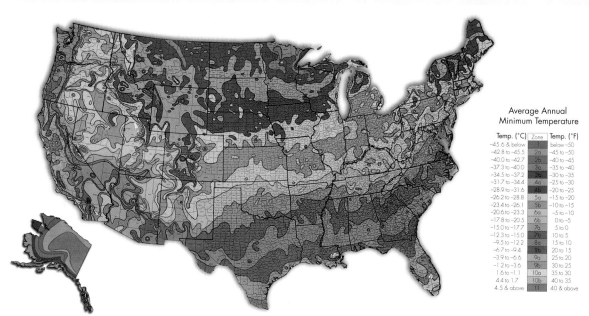

Average Annual
Minimum Temperature

Temp. (°C)	Zone	Temp. (°F)
−45.6 & below	1	below −50
−42.8 to −45.5	2a	−45 to −50
−40.0 to −42.7	2b	−40 to −45
−37.3 to −40.0	3a	−35 to −40
−34.5 to −37.2	3b	−30 to −35
−31.7 to −34.4	4a	−25 to −30
−28.9 to −31.6	4b	−20 to −25
−26.2 to −28.8	5a	−15 to −20
−23.4 to −26.1	5b	−10 to −15
−20.6 to −23.3	6a	−5 to −10
−17.8 to −20.5	6b	0 to −5
−15.0 to −17.7	7a	5 to 0
−12.3 to −15.0	7b	10 to 5
−9.5 to −12.2	8a	15 to 10
−6.7 to −9.4	8b	20 to 15
−3.9 to −6.6	9a	25 to 20
−1.2 to −3.6	9b	30 to 25
1.6 to −1.1	10a	35 to 30
4.4 to 1.7	10b	40 to 35
4.5 & above	11	40 & above

The USDA Hardiness Map divides North America into 11 zones according to average minimum winter temperatures. Hardiness zones are used to identify regions to which plants are suited based on their cold tolerance, which is what "hardiness" means. Many factors, such as elevation and moisture level, come into play when determining whether a plant is suitable for your region. Local climates may vary from what is shown on this map. Contact your local Cooperative Extension Service for recommendations for your area.

Plant Hardiness Zones

Canada's Plant Hardiness Zone Map outlines the different zones in Canada where various types of trees, shrubs, and flowers will most likely survive. It is based on the average climatic conditions of each area. The hardiness map is divided into nine major zones: the harshest is 0 and the mildest is 8. Relatively few plants are suited to zone 0. Subzones (e.g., 4a or 4b, 5a or 5b) are also noted in the map legend. These subzones are most familiar to Canadian gardeners. Some significant local factors, such as micro-topography, amount of shelter, and subtle local variations in snow cover, are too small to be captured on the map. Year-to-year variations in weather and gardening techniques can also have a significant impact on plant survival in any particular location.

Hardiness. Plants thrive in an environment that approximates their native habitat. For many years, plants have been labeled with their USDA (United States Department of Agriculture) hardiness zone rating, which indicates their tolerance to cold. There is a corresponding rating for Canada. When buying plants consider the rating it has been given. Although the USDA ratings are a good starting point, several factors can affect their accuracy. For example, city temperatures tend to be 5 to 10 degrees F warmer than those of the surrounding countryside, raising the hardiness rating of a city garden by a full zone. In addition, every garden has microclimates that may be warmer, cooler, drier, or more humid than another part of the property is. The longer you garden in one location, the more familiar you will be with its microclimates. If you choose a plant that is at the extremes of its stated zone rating, be prepared to give that plant more attention.

Wind. Few plants thrive in windy conditions. But a simple trick will allow you to grow climbing plants where winds are fairly constant. Grow them on a fence, screen, or trellis—not an arch, arbor, or pergola—placed with the long side parallel with the usual wind direction. When the wind blows, it will rush past the slender line of your plants rather than blowing against them.

Planting Vines

The first step in planting a climber is setting its supporting structure in place. Some supports, such as a tower trellis (pages 190–197), can be just placed where you want. Others, such as a fan trellis (pages 162–167), need to be staked into the ground and perhaps supported by a fence or tied into a wall. You might also want to add 10-inch-long spacers in between a trellis and a wall. This distance will allow air to circulate behind the plant, even a mature one, helping it to resist fungal diseases. Structures with posts are often set into the ground. For information on setting posts into the ground, refer to instructions within the project "Grape Arbor," pages 244–251.

A thick, lush grape vine can provide welcome shade during a hot summer's day, as well as a tasty and rewarding snack. Flowering hanging plants add more color to the setting.

Annuals

Annuals last for a single growing season and are easy to plant. Although you can start them from seed in the garden, they will grow to cover their support more quickly if you start some plants indoors or buy healthy seedlings. Guarantee success by choosing plants with lush green leaves but no open flowers.

After all chance of frost has passed, transplant the seedlings just to one side of your support. If you are growing them on a trellis that is accessible from both sides, you can plant on each side of it, leaving a distance of 8 to 12 inches between the facing plant rows. Add compost to the area, and dig it about 6 inches into the soil. If the fertility is low, add a fertilizer, too.

Perennials

Perennial plants live for three or more years and generally flower each year. You can buy perennial plants in containers or "bare root," that is, the plants have no soil around their roots. Container-grown plants can be planted at almost any time of year, as long as you keep them well watered while they are getting established. Bare-root plants are more delicate; you must plant them in early spring so that they can grow leaves and send roots into the surrounding soil before summer heat arrives.

To plant either type, start by digging a hole where you want the plant to grow. For a containerized plant, make the hole deep enough so that the soil in the container will be level with the ground around it. For bare-root plants, soak its roots overnight in water; then spread the roots over a mound of soil that will bring the crown of the plant even with the surface of the hole. (Some plants are exceptions to this rule; follow directions that accompany the plant.) Keep plants moist for a few weeks.

Experts once advised that the soil around your plant be amended with fertilizers and other soil conditioners. But research has shown that plants grow better over the long term if they are planted into unamended soil. Add organic mulches and slow-release, balanced fertilizers each year.

WINTER CARE

Most vines need only a little extra care to get them ready for winter. If they are herbaceous, meaning that their leaves and stems die back to the ground in fall, 6 inches of straw mulch or 2 to 3 inches of a dense material, such as bark chips, will protect the crown and roots during the winter.

Evergreen vines can require more care, particularly if they are planted in an unprotected spot where winter winds are fierce. The best protection is a winter wrapping of burlap. This material allows moisture to escape, so that it won't promote fungal diseases, but it still holds enough so that the plant won't become dehydrated. Mulch the crown of an evergreen vine in the same way as you would for a herbaceous one. Tie or secure the burlap in place if necessary.

PLANTING ANNUALS

Holding only the root ball, carefully lower the seedling into the planting hole. Fill in the hole, and press down gently to put the roots in contact with the soil. Water well.

BARE-ROOT PERENNIALS

Mound the soil, and gently spread the roots out over the mound. Work soil around the roots, and when it's half filled with soil, water and let drain. Then fill the hole with soil.

TRAINING AND PRUNING

Training and pruning requirements differ for various plants, even among species. For specific information, check with your supplier for pruning instructions for your particular plant. But no matter what plant you are growing, the following guidelines always hold true.

Training Techniques

Most climbing plants need at least a little training. If you are growing a morning glory on a chain-link fence, you won't have to do more than weave the stems through the bottom openings as soon as they can reach that far. However, if you are growing a vine, such as a clematis up and over an arbor, you'll probably have to tie it in

Planting a vine or climbing rose in a pot and pairing it with a trellis can be the ideal solution if you have only a deck or patio. If you have a sunroom, use a portable trellis and the plant can go indoors to flourish during the winter.

place to direct its growth. If you tie branches for the first month or so, their habit will quickly take over and they'll climb by themselves.

Time Your Pruning

The timing of major pruning is determined by the blooming style. If the plant blooms on "old wood," that is, growth that was formed the previous year, prune after the flowers have faded. But if the plant blooms on the current season's growth, you prune in the late winter or very early spring. In general, plants that bloom on old wood do so in spring and early summer, and those that bloom on current growth flower in midsummer, late summer, or early fall.

When a plant is damaged or diseased, break the timing rule. The minute you notice the damage, even if it is in the middle of the summer, it's best to cut out the affected branch right away. If the problem is a disease, cut well below the site of infection and disinfect your pruning tool before and after you make the cut.

Shape the Planting

You can affect the form that a plant takes by the way you prune it. The bud immediately below a cut will be the first to form a new branch. Because of this, it's usually best to cut above a bud that faces away from the center of the plant so that air can easily circulate through it. An alternative is to prune just above a bud that faces in the direction that you want the plant to grow.

Frequently, once you cut off the terminal growth, more than one of the remaining buds will develop into branches. Use this to your advantage: when you plant a new vine, cut the main stem back if you want it to become bushy. To encourage flowering plants to bloom more lavishly, always

cut back the branches by about one-third when you prune.

Many vines bloom more vigorously on horizontal rather than vertical growth. When you are pruning, pay attention to this factor. Leave as many branches that are growing horizontally as possible, just cutting them back to stimulate lots of blooms.

Branches cut in midsummer usually don't regrow as quickly as those that are pruned in late winter and early spring. Slow down faster than wanted growth cutting it back when the temperature is warm and the days are long. If you are working to cover a screen with a great deal of horizontal growth, cut off the vertical shoots in summer to minimize the formation of new ones. But don't cut in the fall; you'll stimulate new growth that won't have time to harden up before winter.

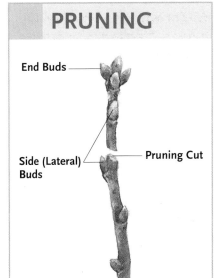

PRUNING

End Buds

Side (Lateral) Buds

Pruning Cut

Pruning growing tips stimulates lateral buds to develop. When cutting stems with alternate buds, prune at a 45-deg. angle just above the bud you want to stimulate. If buds are opposite, cut across the stem in a straight line.

VINE DIRECTORY

Explanation of Icons

Light Requirements: Yellow sun means full sun; half-yellow/half-black sun means partial shade; black sun repesents shade.

Water Needs: Full drop denotes high moisture requirements; half-full drop, moderate needs; low level (bottom third) means low water needs.

Growth Rate: 12:15 represents slow growing; 12:30 means moderate rate of growth; 12:45 means fast growing.

Fragrance: F means fragrant; F denotes that only some species or cultivars in the species are fragrant; F means the plant is not fragrant.

Care Level: Green spade means easy-care; yellow represents moderate care; red means difficult.

Actinidia deliciosa, A. arguta, A. kolomikta
Kiwifruit, Hardy Kiwifruit
A. deliciosa　　*A. arguta, A. kolomikta*

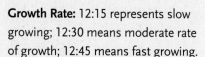

This perennial vine has cream-colored flowers that bloom in the spring. Both *A. deliciosa* and *A. arguta* have green leaves that are slightly reddish when young. Those of *A. kolomikta* are variegated in green, cream, and pink shades.
Climbing Style: Scandent; tie to supports
Soil Requirements: High fertility with high humus content.
Hardiness Zones: *A. deliciosa*, 7–10; *A. arguta, A. kolomikta*, 4–9

Actinidia deliciosa (Kiwifruit)

Campsis spp. (Trumpet Vine)

Ampelopsis brevipedunculata
(Porcelain Berry)

Cardiospermum halicacabum
(Balloon Vine)

Ampelopsis brevipedunculata
Porcelain Berry

The leaves of this perennial vine are triangular and lobed or toothed, and bright red and yellow in autumn. Blooms mid- to late summer. Its small, green flowers are followed by decorative berries.
Climbing Style: Tendrils
Soil Requirements: Fertile, well-drained
Hardiness Zones: 5–8

Campsis spp.
Trumpet Vine

 to

This woody perennial punctuates late-summer gardens with vivid orange, yellow, or red flower clusters. It needs a strong support. The vines cling to their vertical supports, but blooming branches extend for several feet in all directions.
Climbing Style: Aerial roots
Soil Requirements: Moderately fertile and well-drained
Hardiness Zones: 5–9

Cardiospermum halicacabum
Balloon Vine, Love-in-a-Puff

This tender perennial has delicate, deeply toothed leaves that can grow to about 8 inches long. It has small, white, summer-blooming flowers, but it's mostly grown for its balloonlike seedpods that start out a light green color, then turn brown as they age.
Climbing Style: Tendrils
Soil Requirements: Fertile, well-drained
Hardiness Zones: 10–11

Clematis 'Henryi'

Cobaea scandens (Cup and Saucer Vine)

Clematis 'Duchess of Albany'

Hedera helix (English Ivy)

Clematis
Clematis

 to

The appearance of a clematis varies radically depending on group and cultivar. Flowers range from cross-shaped with only four petals to large double blossoms to bell-shaped, tulip-shaped, and tubular blooms. Colors range from deep purple to pink, white, and yellow, with orange being the only color not represented. Clematis is a perennial. Depending on its group, it blooms early spring to late summer and fall. Some species are deciduous; others are evergreen.
Climbing Style: Twining leaf stalks
Soil Requirements: Fertile, high humus
Hardiness Zones: 4–9

Cobaea scandens
Cup and Saucer Vine, Cathedral Bells

 to

The common names for this fast-growing tender perennial refer to the shape of its flowers. It blooms summer into the fall. The flowers open as a creamy green color and age to purple, or in the case of *C. scandens* f. *alba,* white. It also makes a good sunroom plant.
Climbing Style: Tendrils, small hooks
Soil Requirements: Moderately fertile, or humus-rich potting soil
Hardiness Zones: 9–11

Hedera helix
English Ivy

Appearance varies depending on the cultivar, but ivies are grown for their leaves. In most species the leaves are triangular and lobed. Many species have variegated leaves, some have dark purplish leaves, and a few have leaves that are yellow. Ivies bloom late in the summer, and berries form on many cultivars. Because ivies do not twine, tie them to an openwork structure, or let the vine climb a tree or wall.
Climbing Style: Aerial roots
Soil Requirements: Moderately fertile
Hardiness Zones: 5–10

Ipomoea spp. (Moonflower)

Lablab purpureus (Hyacinth Bean)

Ipomoea spp. (Morning Glory)

Jasminum spp. (Jasmine)

Lagenaria siceraria (Bottle Gourd)

Ipomoea spp.
Morning Glory, Moonflower, Sweet Potato Vine, and others

The Ipomoea genus contains about 500 species classified as annuals and tender perennials. Most have showy colorful flowers that bloom mid- to late summer, but some, such as the Sweet Potato Vine, do not flower and are grown for their foliage. Moonflowers (*I. alba*) are large and so white that they seem to glow in the twilight conditions that stimulate buds to open.
Climbing Style: Twining stems
Soil Requirements: Moderately fertile
Hardiness Zones: 9–11

Jasminum spp.
Jasmine

to

Jasmines, which are perennials, are known for their fragrance, showy blossoms, and glossy, deep green leaves. Only *J. nudiflorum*, winter jasmine, and *J. humile*, yellow jasmine, tolerate freezing temperatures. Jasmine can be grown in heated sunrooms through the winter. Winter jasmine blooms in early spring, yellow jasmine in late spring to early autumn.
Climbing Style: *J. nudiflorum* and *J. humile* shoots are scandent; others have twining stems.
Soil Requirements: Fertile, well-drained
Hardiness Zones: 9–11

Lablab purpureus
(formerly *Dolichos lablab*)
Hyacinth Bean, Lablab, Egyptian Bean

This fast growing vine is a member of the pea family. Its pink flowers bloom from summer until autumn. The shiny, thick pods that follow them are a maroon-purple color.
Climbing Style: Twining
Soil Requirements: Fertile, high humus
Hardiness Zones: 10–11

Lagenaria siceraria
Bottle Gourd

This fast-growing annual vine with enormous (as large as a foot wide) heart-shaped leaves needs a strong support. Its white flowers bloom midsummer to late fall and have a crepe-paper quality. The gourds are pale green when mature but turn a cream color over the year or so that it takes for their skins to harden.
Climbing Style: Tendrils
Soil Requirements: Fertile, high humus

Lathyrus spp. (Sweet Pea)

Lycopersicon esculentum (Tomato)

Lonicera spp. (Honeysuckle)

Maurandella antirrhiniflora (Twining Snapdragon)

Lathyrus spp.
Everlasting Pea, Sweet Pea

Both everlasting peas (*L. latifolius,* a perennial) and sweet peas (*L. odoratus,* an annual) have ornamental leaves and lavish colorful blooms from midsummer to autumn. All 150 species of *Lathyrus* have flowers that look like those of edible peas. But, unlike the common garden pea, all parts of these plants are slightly poisonous.
Climbing Style: Twining tendrils
Soil Requirements: Fertile, high humus
Hardiness Zones: *L. latifolius,* 5–9

Lonicera spp.
Honeysuckle

There are about 180 honeysuckle species whose tubular to bell-shaped flowers vary in color: white, pink, yellow, bi-colored, red. They bloom from early to midsummer; the leaves turn red in the fall.
Climbing Style: Twining
Soil Requirements: Fertile
Hardiness Zones: 5 or 6–9

Lycopersicon esculentum
Tomato

These popular annual plants are grown for their fruit, not good looks. Some cultivars can grow to 8 feet high. Leaves are deeply toothed and somewhat hairy. Small, bright yellow flowers bloom from early summer to late fall.
Climbing Style: Scandent
Soil Requirements: Fertile, high humus

Maurandella antirrhiniflora
(formerly *Asarina antirrhiniflora*)
Twining Snapdragon

This plant grows vigorously enough to cover a trellis or screen by mid- to late summer in most regions. It is a tender perennial that is grown as an annual in most areas. The triangular, bright green leaves are decorative by themselves; the flowers add bright spots of color. Despite their name, the flowers are shaped more like trumpets than snapdragons. In warm regions this plant responds well to dappled shade during hot afternoons. It is a close relative to Chickabiddy (both were once considered members of the same genus), but differs in both size and color.
Climbing Style: Twining
Soil Requirements: Average fertility
Hardiness Zones: 9–12

Parthenocissus spp. (Virginia Creeper)

Rubus spp. (Red and Black Raspberries)

Rubus ursinus (Boysenberry)

Parthenocissus spp. (Boston Ivy)

Parthenocissus spp.
Virginia Creeper, Boston Ivy

  to

Virginia Creeper (*P. quinquefolia*) and Boston Ivy (*P. tricuspidata*) are the best known species of the ten in this genus. These perennial woody plants are admired for their foliage rather than the flowers. Leaves of these vines are green or reddish green in summer, but they turn various shades of brilliant red in autumn. Boston Ivy leaf blades often drop before their stalks do, giving the plant a skeletal, spidery look. Black berries sometimes follow the inconspicuous summer flowers.
Climbing Style: Sometimes tendrils twine around supports, but more often they cling with small suckers on the tips of the tendrils.
Soil Requirements: Fertile
Hardiness Zones: *P. quinquefolia*, 3–9; *P. tricuspidata*, 4–8

Rubus idaeus, R. occidentalis
Red Raspberry, Black Raspberry

  to

Leaves of these perennials are dark green with three leaflets; they turn dark red in autumn. The flowers are white or pink, and bloom from early to late summer. Fruits can be red, black, or yellow, and range in flavor from somewhat tart to very sweet.
Climbing Style: Scandent
Soil Requirements: Fertile
Hardiness Zones: 3–9

Rubus ursinus var. loganobaccus cv.
Boysenberry

 to

Similar to other perennial bramble bushes, boysenberries have dusky green leaves and pink or pinkish white, five-petaled flowers with prominent centers. Bloom time is in early summer. Bred from blackberry, loganberry, and raspberry, boysenberries seem to combine the best of each of their flavors. They are also more drought tolerant than other brambles although they can't fruit well if they are severely moisture-deficient.
Climbing Style: Scandent
Soil Requirements: Fertile; can tolerate very sandy soils.
Hardiness Zones: 6–10

Schizophragma hydrangeoides (Jap. Hydrangea)

Vitis labrusca (American Grape)

Vitis spp. (Hybrid Grape)

Tropaeolum majus (Nasturtium)

Wisteria spp. (Wisteria)

Schizophragma hydrangeoides
Japanese hydrangea

 to   to

Showy, dramatic flowerheads characterize this woody perennial in midsummer, but the plant is lovely at any time of year. It is particularly effective when grown against a wall or fence and is sometimes trained to grow up a large tree. Allow at least 2 feet between the stem of this plant and its support because it is extraordinarily vigorous.
Climbing Style: Aerial roots
Soil Requirements: Moderately fertile
Hardiness Zones: 6–9

Tropaeolum majus
Nasturtium

The brightly colored nasturtium flowers have a texture that is similar to crepe paper. Blooms of most cultivars are about 2 inches wide and spurred. Leaves are round with prominent veins fanning out from the center; edges can be lobed; and the color is a bright, clear green. Nasturtiums, which are edible, are annuals that bloom from early summer into autumn.
Climbing Style: Twining
Soil Requirements: Low to moderate nitrogen levels

Vitis labrusca
American Grape

The lobed leaves of these perennials are a dull, dark green with an almost quilted appearance. They turn yellow in autumn. Flowers form in small, green, inconspicuous clusters in spring; the grapes form in early summer and are harvested in late summer or fall.
Climbing Style: Scandent
Soil Requirements: Fertile, high humus
Hardiness Zones: 5–9

Vitis spp.
Hybrid Grapes

The dark green leaves of these perennials are lobed and about 6 to 8 inches long. In the autumn, they turn yellow rather than red. In the spring, the small green flowers are inconspicuous. Grapes begin developing in early summer and ripen in late summer or fall, depending on cultivar.
Climbing Style: Scandent
Soil Requirements: Fertile, high humus
Hardiness Zones: 7–9

Wisteria spp.
Wisteria

The blue, violet, pink, or white flowers are shaped like those of peas. Blooms of most species form in 6- to 12-inch-long clusters, but those of *W. floribunda* can be 2 to 3 feet long. The deciduous leaves of these perennial plants are decorative throughout the growing season; the sinuous, gray, rough-barked trunk and branches are dramatic during the winter months. Bloom time is spring or early summer; some *W. sinensis* plants bloom again in early autumn. Provide a very sturdy support for this vigorous plant because it will tear down anything that is insubstantial.
Climbing Style: Twining
Soil Requirements: Fertile, high humus
Hardiness Zones: *W. sinensis*, 5–8; all other species, 6–9

CLIMBING AND RAMBLER ROSES

No rose really climbs. Instead, they grow long canes that lean against supports. In the wild, they tend to weave themselves into trees and shrubs, but in the garden, they are tied to their supports.

The roses we refer to as "climbing roses" are divided into two categories: climbers and ramblers. Most ramblers bloom only once a season. Climbers, on the other hand, bloom more than once. Their canes are also stiffer and their flowers are generally larger than those of the ramblers. Despite this, ramblers can put on just as effective a show, even if it is for a shorter period of time. Many of them are so floriferous that the plants are literally covered with flowers for the two to four weeks that they bloom. By pairing them with another flowering climbing plant, such as a clematis that blooms from midsummer until fall, you can create a trellis that is covered with blooms from late spring until fall.

Choosing a Rose

If you have decided on a rose for your structure, you'll need to choose a cultivar that is well acclimated to your climatic conditions. If it is not, it is likely to suffer more than a fair share of problems with pests and diseases. For

Climbing and rambler roses, cascading over a trellis, arbor, fence, or other open structure, can be the crowning touch to any yard or garden.

example, if you live in a humid climate, you'll want to choose a cultivar that is resistant to the fungal diseases that thrive there. In a cold climate, you'll want to pick a rose that is winter hardy. Check the Rose Directory, pages 274 to 277, for information on the roses that you like, and ask advice at a nursery or garden club in your area.

You'll also want to be sure that the rose you pick suits the planned location. Does the color of the bloom complement the colors of the house or other nearby structures? Is there enough room so that the rose can grow wide as well as tall? Does the exposure match the plant's requirements? In general, you'll find that ramblers are more suited to arches, pergolas, and arbors because their canes are so flexible, while climbers are more suited to a trellis or fence.

Fences, especially those with an open design and situated in a sunny location, are well-suited to the growing needs of climbing roses.

Planting Your Rose

The most important factors are the depth of the bud union, or area where the rootstock was grafted to the top growth, the size of the planting hole, and sound contact between the roots and the soil. Many experts once advised planting a rose with the bud union an inch or so above the soil surface in warm, frost-free climates. In cold winter areas, they advised gardeners to place the bud union several inches below the soil surface. Today, however, almost everyone agrees that no matter where you live, it's best to bury the bud union a few inches below the ground.

If you are planting a bare-root rose, dig a hole at least 18 to 24 inches wide and 18 inches deep. Again, expert advice has changed. Gardeners used to mix the soil they removed from the hole and which they were going to put back around the roots with copious amounts of peat moss and compost. However, this isn't necessary if your soil is fertile and has a high humus content; amend only those soils that are not suitable for

Plant a rose so its bud union is at the prescribed depth, usually below-ground.

roses. See page 264 to learn how to handle a bare-root plant.

Bare-root roses must be planted in very early spring or, in Zones 6 and warmer, in autumn, about a month before the first frost. In contrast, you can plant a container-grown rose almost any time, as long as you keep the top growth shaded and the soil consistently moist while the plant is getting established.

Pruning and Training

For the first two years, simply tie the canes to their supports. Because horizontal growth flowers more than vertical growth, spread out the canes as much as possible. The only pruning you need to do is removing dead, diseased, or damaged growth.

In the second or third year, your roses will begin blooming. Deadhead any flowers that form up to a month before the first expected frost by cutting just above the first pair of five-leaflet leaves below the bloom. Then stop deadheading, and let the plant form hips.

The best blooms on climbing roses are produced on one-year-old wood; in early spring, cut back the canes that bloomed the year before to only 3 or 4 inches. New canes will grow to replace

Wire is used to hold the canes of this rose to the column of its support.

TRAINING ROSES

Tie roses to the support, in the manner shown here. Allow some slack, and use a figure-eight tie at fairly close intervals.

them. Roses in the wichuraiana group, such as 'New Dawn', are an exception to this. They are so free-blooming that you don't need to cut back two-year-old canes except when they crowd the plant.

Noisette roses are slow to produce new canes, so it's best to leave some of the canes that flowered the year before. Bend them to as far of a horizontal position as possible, and then tie them to the support to stimulate their blooming again the following year.

If your rose blooms only once, early in the season, cut back the flowering canes right after bloom. In addition to removing old canes, some climbers and ramblers need to be pruned to stay within bounds. Do this by cutting back the canes by several inches in late winter or early spring.

Care

It's important to choose a cultivar suited to your environment, care for its soil, and prune it enough to keep air circulation high. If all that is done, you probably won't have more trouble with your roses than you do with any other garden plant.

Natural beneficial insects are your best allies against many of the rose pests. To encourage these creatures, grow small flowered plants such as lavender, dill, garlic chives, and sweet alyssum under your roses and mulch with a well-made compost. The most common rose diseases are black spot and powdery mildew. Garlic chives are said to help protect against these fungus diseases, but a preventive spray made from 1 teaspoon baking soda, 1 teaspoon fine horticultural oil, and 1 teaspoon liquid kelp to each quart of water is also effective. Spray every week starting early in the season, and continue until frost.

Most roses need winter protection in frost areas. Some are hardy as far north as Zone 6b without protection. However, you must mulch the crown of the plant to protect it from freezing.

ROSE DIRECTORY

Explanation of Icons

Light Requirements: Yellow sun means full sun; half-yellow/half-black sun means partial shade; black sun represents shade.

Water Needs: Full drop denotes high moisture requirements; half-full drop, moderate needs; low level (bottom third) means low water needs.

Thorns: Full thorn represents very thorny; a half-thorn means somewhat thorny; a one-quarter thorn means a few thorns.

Hardiness: Full snowflake denotes very hardy; a half-flake means some temperature resistance; a quarter-flake means not reliably hardy.

F   **F**   **F**

Fragrance: F means fragrant; F denotes that only some species or cultivars in the species are fragrant; F means the plant is not fragrant.

'Altissimo'

 to   **F**

The single blossoms of 'Altissimo' are 4 to 5 inches wide, deep blood-red with golden stamens; the petals are cupped when first open but quickly become flat. Its foliage is dark green, serrated, and leathery. It blooms in the summer and repeats again in fall. The flowers have long stems, making them an excellent choice for a cut flower. When in full bloom, the plant is spectacular.
Type: Climbing floribunda
Comments: This easy-to-grow climber is resistant to powdery mildew but susceptible to black spot.

'Altissimo'

'America'

'America'

     F

The salmon pink blooms are 4 to 5 inches wide and shaped like hybrid tea flowers. They form in clusters. The semiglossy foliage is dark green. Plants bloom on new wood and flowers form until autumn.
Type: Large-flowered climber
Comments: 'America' received the AARS award in 1976, partially because it is such a beautiful plant and partially because it is so disease resistant and winter hardy. The fragrance is reminiscent of carnations. The plants are vigorous and cover arbors and trellises quickly.

'Blaze'

     F

The crimson red semidouble blossoms of this rose are 2 to 3 inches wide and have 18 to 24 petals. They grow in clusters and have a somewhat cupped form. Bloom time is midseason, with good repeat performance. The foliage of this rose is medium green and semiglossy.

'Blaze'

'Blush Noisette'

Type: Large-flowered climber, hybrid multiflora
Comments: Hardy to about Zone 7, this rose has excellent heat tolerance. It resists powdery mildew but is susceptible to black spot. The plant is a vigorous grower with strong, flexible canes that can be easily trained.

'Blush Noisette'

 to   **F**

The double flowers of this rose form in loose clusters and are mauve, deep pink, or blush pink. It has dark green, abundant leaves, and blooms almost continuously from midsummer until autumn.
Type: Chinensis, noisette
Comments: Introduced in 1814, this is the original noisette rose. The fragrance resembles that of cloves. It is resistant to most fungal diseases if it grows in full sun in a spot with good air circulation.

'Cherokee'

'Dr. Huey'

'Constance Spry'

'Golden Showers'

'Cherokee'

    F

The large single white flowers with prominent yellow stamens bloom late spring only—there are no repeat blooms. The leaves are bright green and large and are evergreen in mild climates.

Type: Rambler

Comments: This rose is a wild rose from China with origins so old that no one knows its parentage. Its thorns are a reddish, chocolate brown color and quite large. The fragrance is lovely. It does not tolerate frosts well and performs poorly in areas where winter frosts are common.

'Constance Spry'

 to   **F**

The flowers of this rose are large, clear pink, full, and globe-shaped; they bloom in early summer only. Its mid-green foliage is coarse.

Type: English rose

Comments: This is the first English rose that David Austin hybridized. It displays many of the qualities that make these cultivars so popular: vigor, hardiness, and disease resistance. It is very thorny and should be planted well away from paths and walkways or play and dining areas.

'Dr. Huey'

    F

The deep maroon semidouble flowers with golden stamens and 12 to 15 petals are saucer-shaped and about 3 inches wide. They form in clusters and bloom midseason only. Its foliage is dark green and glossy.

Type: Large-flowered climber

Comments: 'Dr. Huey' has been used as a rootstock for many years because it confers good hardiness to roses grafted onto it. However, the top growth sometimes dies anyway, leaving the rootstock to grow.

'Golden Showers'

   F

The cupped, canary yellow blooms of this rose average 4 inches across and are double with 20 to 35 petals. It has dark green, glossy foliage. This rose blooms continuously throughout the summer and fall, stopping with the first frost.

Type: Large-flowered, floribunda climber

Comments: This plant is known for its vigorous, bushy growth. Its canes are flexible and easy to train. 'Golden Showers' is ideal for covering a wall or fence with its abundant flowers and attractive foliage. The brilliant yellow blooms make a great backdrop to a garden of yellow, white, and soft blue flowers. Its soft fragrance makes it a good choice for patios and seating areas.

'Iceberg, Climbing'

'Mme Alfred Carrière'

'Lady Banks Yellow'

'Mlle Cécile Brunner, Climbing'

'Iceberg, Climbing'

The cupped, double 3-inch-wide blooms are white with high centers and grow in clusters. Its light green leaves are semiglossy. This rose blooms in the summer, with good repeat throughout the season.
Type: Climbing floribunda
Comments: 'Iceberg' is justifiably famous. Its blooms have a lovely form, and plants are extremely floriferous. While it is reliably winter hardy in most of the United States and southern Canada, it is susceptible to both black spot and powdery mildew.

'Lady Banks Yellow'

This rose has multiple clusters of from 5 to 10 1-inch-wide yellow double blooms with 30 to 50 petals. It blooms in late spring; its evergreen leaves are dark green, small, and elongated.

Type: Climber
Comments: This plant spreads for a distance of 8 to 12 feet, so give it a great deal of room when you plant it. Although it won't live through frosts, it's quite disease resistant. 'Lady Banks White' differs from 'Lady Banks Yellow' in that it has fragrance and blooms throughout the summer.

'Mme Alfred Carrière'

  to   **F**

Milky white, very fragrant double flowers, many of which are touched with a hint of pink, bloom from late spring with good repeat blooms until autumn. Its light green leaves are abundant.
Type: Chinensis climber
Comments: This rose is vigorous and will quickly climb any support it finds. It will grow to 20 feet or more and develop a trunk like a tree. 'Mme Alfred Carrière' can tolerate somewhat lean soils but grows better in good ones. Similarly, it

will grow in partial shade, although full sun promotes the best bloom.

'Mlle Cécile Brunner, Climbing'

  to   **F**

The 1-inch-wide light-pink double flowers are shaped like miniature hybrid tea roses and are abundant. This rose blooms late in the season, repeating until frost. Its small, bright green leaves grow densely.
Type: Polyantha climber
Comments: A vigorous, strong grower, 'Mlle Cécile Bunner, Climbing' can become almost as wide as it is tall (can grow to 25 feet high). It grows well on walls and trellises in partial shade. While not reliably hardy in severely cold climates, it will overwinter in Zones 6 and 7 with winter protection. It also has good disease resistance. Because it has few thorns, you can grow it near a path or outdoor recreation or dining area. It is only mildly fragrant, however.

'Maréchal Niel'

'New Dawn'

'Phyllis Bide'

'Souvenir de La Malmaison, Climbing'

'Zéphirine Drouhin'

'Maréchal Niel'

   F

Soft, buttery yellow flowers open from pointed buds. Bloom time is from late spring with good repeat performance throughout the summer. The full flowers droop from their slender stems; the foliage is dark, copper-green.
Type: Chinensis climber
Comments: The softness of the flower color in combination with the superb fragrance and the way the blooms droop make this a wonderful rose. Unfortunately, it is not winter hardy. In Zones 7 and 8, place it in a very sheltered location. In colder areas, think about growing it in a greenhouse.

'New Dawn'

to

Silvery pink blooms are wide, semidouble with 18 to 24 petals, and grow in clusters. When the flowers open, golden yellow sta-

mens complement the color of the petals. It flowers continuously from midseason until frost. The canes are upright; the medium green leaves are glossy; and the plant becomes bushy.
Type: Old-fashioned *R. wichuraiana* climber
Comments: This hardy plant resists most diseases, and grows well on cold, north-facing walls. It tolerates soils with low fertility.

'Phyllis Bide'

to

Clusters of dainty, double flowers in yellow, cream, pink, and red bloom summer until autumn and deepen in color as they age. Its foliage is light green in color.
Type: Polyantha climber
Comments: This plant tolerates partial shade and cool, north-facing walls.

'Souvenir de La Malmaison, Climbing'

   F

The double flowers of this rose are white with a pink blush, and they bloom in summer, reblooming in good environmental conditions. Its foliage is midgreen in color.
Type: Bourbon climber
Comments: This rose is extremely sensitive to wet soils and will languish in them. It thrives in warm weather but has difficulty in cold conditions.

'Zéphirine Drouhin'

 F

Large semidouble light-to-deep-pink flowers repeat over the summer amid midgreen, lush foliage.
Type: Chinensis climber
Comments: This hardy climbing rose can go without winter protection as far north as Zone 6b. Beyond that, the crown requires mulching. Because it is very susceptible to powdery mildew, it is best grown against a fence or up an arbor where air circulation is high.

This list of manufacturers and associations is meant to be a general guide to additional industry and product-related sources. It is not intended as a listing of products and manufacturers represented by the photographs in this book.

American Fence Association
800-822-4342
www.americanfenceassociation.com
An organization created to benefit both the fence industry and consumers.

American Hardware
Manufacturers Association
847-605-1025
www.ahma.org
A trade service organization that offers resources for the consumer hardware and home improvement marketplace.

Arch Wood Protection
1955 Lake Park Dr., Ste. 250
Smyrna, GA 30080
770-801-6600
www.wolmanizedwood.com
Manufactures pressure-treated wood for fences and other items.

AvalonGarden.com
200 Wildwood Rd.
Hendersonville, NC 28739
800-854-0880
www.avalongarden.com
Offers many home and garden products, including trellises and arbors.

Bosch Power Tools
4300 W. Peterson Ave.
Chicago, IL 60646
800-267-2499
www.boschtools.com
Manufactures tools and accessories for a number of trades.

Boundary Fence & Railing Systems
800-628-8928
www.boundary-fences.com
Manufactures and distributes a variety of fences, railings, gates, and hardware in a multitude of styles, including vinyl and chain-link.

California Redwood Association
405 Entrente Dr., Ste. 200
Novato, CA 94949
888-225-7339
www.calredwood.org
A nonprofit association that offers general assistance and information about redwood.

Carolina Vinyl Products
P.O. Box 1137
Grifton, NC 28530-1137
252-524-5000
www.carolinavp.com
Manufactures a line of PVC products, including fences and fence materials.

CertainTeed Corporation
750 East Swedesford Rd.
Valley Forge, PA 19482
800-233-8990
www.certainteed.com
Sells numerous types of building materials, including Bufftech fences.

Chain Link Manufacturers Institute
10015 Old Columbia Rd., Ste. B-215
Columbia, MD 21046
301-596-2583
www.chainlinkinfo.org
Offers a list of approved chain link retailers and chain-link information.

DeWalt Industrial Tools Company
626 Hanover Pike
Hampstead, MD 21074
800-433-9258
www.dewalt.com
Sells a wide selection of power tools.

Elyria Fence Inc.
230 Oberlin-Elyria Rd.
Elyria, OH 44035
800-779-7581
www.elyriafence.com
Provides custom fences, trellises, arbors, and decks all year round.

FenceLink
7040 Avenida Encinas, # 104286
Carlsbad, CA 92009
www.fencelink.com
A directory of fence manufacturers, distributors, and associations for all types and parts of fences.

The Flood Company
800-321-3444
www.floodco.com
Makes a variety of paint-related products, including penetrating stains, sealers, wood renewers, and cleansers.

Garden Artisans
P.O. Box 4393
Crofton, MD 21114
410-721-6185
www.gardenartisans.com
Sells decorative backyard structures such as garden art, trellises, arbors, and planters.

G.I. Designs
700 Colorado Blvd. #120
Denver, CO 80206
877-442-6773
www.gidesigns.net
Manufacturer of wooden and metal garden structures such as trellises, arbors, and gazebos.

Heritage Vinyl Products
1576 Magnolia Dr.
Macon, MS 39341
800-736-5143 ext. 2944
www.heritagevinyl.com
Maufactures fencing made from polyvinyl chloride.

Homeproductsnmore.com
800-690-0132
www.homeproductsnmore.com
An online source of various products for the home, including garden furnishings and structures, such as arbors and trellises.

Hoover Fence
5531 McClintocksburg Rd.
Newton Falls, OH 44444
330-358-2624
www.hooverfence.com
Sells metal, vinyl, chain-link, and specialty fences.

Hitachi Power Tools U.S.A.
3950 Steve Reynolds Blvd.
Norcross, GA 30093
800-829-4752
www.hitachi.com/powertools
Carries an extensive line of heavy-duty electric tools.

The Intimate Gardener
4215 N. Sheridan Rd.
Chicago, IL 60613
800-240-2771
www.theintimategardener.com
Carries garden furnishings and ornaments including trellises, arbors, and feeders.

Jepson Power Tools, a div. of Ko-shin Electric and Machinery Company
20333 S. Western Ave.
Torrance, CA 90501
800-456-8665
www.jepsonpowertools.com
Manufactures electric drills, saws, and other tools.

Kinsman Company
P.O. Box 428
Pipersville, PA 18947
800-733-4129
www.kinsmangarden.com
Offers an extensive selection of outdoor accessories such as elegant trellises, obelisks, and plant supports.

Kroy Building Products
P.O. Box 636
York, NE 68467
800-933-5769
www.kroybp.com
Manufactures vinyl fencing and deck materials and offers free technical advice.

Milwaukee Electric Tool Corp.
13135 W. Lisbon Rd.
Brookfield, WI 53005-2550
262-781-3600
www.mil-electric-tool.com
Sells portable power tools and accessories through authorized distributors.

National Ornamental & Miscellaneous Metals Association
532 Forest Pkwy., Ste. A
Forest Park, GA 30297
www.nomma.org
Connects you with ornamental metal manufacturers.

National Paint and Coatings Association (NPCA)
202-462-6272
www.paint.org

A voluntary nonprofit trade association that represents numerous paint companies.

Porter-Cable Corp.
4825 Hwy. 45 North
P.O. Box 2468
Jackson, TN 38302-2468
888-848-5175
www.porter-cable.com
Manufactures compressors, electric drills, and other professional power tools.

Ryobi North America
1424 Pearman Dairy Rd.
Anderson, SC 29625
800-525-2579
www.ryobitools.com
Produces portable and bench-top power tools for contractors and DIYers.

Southern Pine Council
504-443-4464
www.southernpine.com
A nonprofit trade organization that offers construction tips, complete project plans, and other helpful information on pine and its uses.

Stanco Incorporated
2780 SE 19th St.
Salem, OR 97302
800-443-7826
www.stanco-inc.com
Offers a full line of fences, including privacy, decorative, and ranch.

The Stanley Works
1000 Stanley Dr.
New Britain, CT 06053
860-225-5111
www.stanleyworks.com
Manufactures an extensive line of hand and power tools.

Sycamore Creek
P.O. Box 16
Ancram, NY 12502
518-398-6393
www.sycamorecreek.com
Specializes in copper garden furnishings such as arbors and trellises.

Trellis Structures, Inc.
P.O. Box 380
60 River St., rear
Beverly, MA 01915
888-285-4624
www.trellisstructures.com
Designs and manufactures western red cedar trellises and arbors, as well as other structures.

The Vinyl Institute
1300 Wilson Blvd., Ste. 800
Arlington, VA 22209
www.vinylinfo.org
A U.S. trade association that represents manufacturers and provides information about vinyl.

Actual dimensions The exact measurements of a piece of lumber after it has been cut, surfaced, and dried. For example, the actual dimensions of a 2x4 are $1\frac{1}{2}$ x $3\frac{1}{2}$ inches.

Alkyd paint Often referred to as oil-based, although the oil has been replaced with alkyd resins. It is more expensive, takes longer to dry, and must be cleaned with paint thinner. Alkyd paint is generally considered tougher than latex paint.

Arbor An open, overhead structure held up by posts and typically used to support climbing shrubs or vines and to provide shade.

Backfill Sand, dirt, gravel, or crushed stone used to fill-in the space around excavation.

Batter boards Horizontal boards set between stakes outside the excavation area used to support layout strings that mark the position of a fence at the start of construction.

Bevel An angled surface, typically cut into the edge of a piece of lumber.

Blank The piece of lumber from which you plan to cut a certain part, as in "the template blank."

Bowing Warping or bending of horizontal rails (or any lumber) that occurs due to weathering.

Bracing Wood member used to support a structure. In fence building, bracing is usually only temporary.

Building permit A document that may be required for some fence projects, which confirms municipal approval of the proposed construction.

Carriage bolt A bolt with a wide, rounded head, often used to create a finished appearance on the outer surface of joints.

Cauls Small pieces of scrap lumber used as pads between the jaws of a clamp and the workpiece to prevent damage to the workpiece.

Chip-out Wood fibers splitting off of the face of a board at the point where the router bit exits the wood. Because the bit is essentially cutting end grain as it exits the wood, the wood will chip out if not backed with another piece of wood.

Clear A grade of lumber that is largely free of knots and other structural and cosmetic defects. Clear wood is generally recommended for applications where the wood is visible.

Collet The chucklike device on the end of a router drive shaft that secures the router bits.

Come-along A hand-cranked winch attached to steel cables and hooks used for many purposes, including straightening fence posts and stretching chain-link fencing.

Counterbore Enlarging the top or bottom part of a drilled hole so that a screw, bolt head, or nut will set below the wood's surface.

Crosscut A cut across the grain of a piece of lumber at a 90-degree angle to the edge. For example, you shorten an 8-foot-long 2x4 to 6 feet by crosscutting it.

Dado A rectangular groove across the grain. On fence projects, large dadoes are sometimes cut in wooden posts so that rails can be recessed.

Dry rot Decay from fungi that causes wood to become brittle and crumble to powder.

Finial A decorative element at the top of a post. You can purchase posts with precut finials, cut your own, or purchase separate finials with a screw mount already fitted.

Frost line Depth above which the ground freezes, as recorded for your area by the local building department. Posts must be placed below this line to avoid heaving when the ground freezes.

Galvanized finish Mesh, nails, screws, or other metal materials that are coated with zinc and other chemicals to prevent rusting.

Half-lap A joint between intersecting members formed by removing half of the thickness of each piece so that the two mate with the surfaces flush.

Heartwood The harder, stronger, and usually more rot-resistant wood taken from the core of a tree.

Kerf The narrow slot a saw blade cuts in a piece of lumber, usually about $1/8$ inch thick.

Knot A dark spot on a board that is the base of a branch. The wood is very dense but often not connected to the wood around it.

Lag screws Large screws (usually with hex-shaped heads that you turn with a ratchet) used to join wooden fence sections.

Lap A joint in which the full dimension of one member is set into a recess—the lap—cut in the other piece.

Latex paint A water-based paint made up of acrylic and/or vinyl resins and pigments. It cleans up with water and provides adequate protection from the elements in most situations.

Lattice Thin strips of wood that are crossed at right angles or at 45-degree angles, available in pressure-treated wood and colored plastic.

Masonry anchor Galvanized metal fastener, typically with a U-shape and a mounting pin, that is used to hold wood posts on a masonry pier.

Miter A joint in which two boards are joined at angles to form a corner.

Mortise and tenon A type of wood joint in which a hole is cut in one piece of wood, the mortise, to specifically receive the protruding element on another piece of wood, the tenon.

Mounting brackets Metal brackets available in many shapes to fit around the ends of stock lumber. The brackets have predrilled flanges that make it easy to nail or screw wooden timbers to each other.

Nominal dimensions The identifying dimensions of a piece of lumber (e.g. 2x4) that are larger than the actual dimensions ($1\frac{1}{2}$ x $3\frac{1}{2}$ inches).

Overspray Paint expelled from a paint-sprayer that travels beyond pickets, posts, or other targets and can damage nearby grass and plants.

Pilot bearing A router bit's built-in steering mechanism. The bearing rides on the edge of the workpiece, limiting the cut and guiding the router.

Pilot hole A hole drilled to receive a screw. It eases the entry of the screw and prevents it from splitting the wood.

Plumb Vertically straight and perpendicular to a level reference line.

Plunge cut A cut that doesn't begin at the edge of a board but is made by plunging the cutter into the face of the board. Sometimes referred to as a pocket cut.

Posthole digger A double-handled tool with shovel-like sides that come together in a scissor-like action to dig post holes.

Prefabricated fence Fence made with posts and panels that are prefabricated of wood, metal, or PVC plastic and come ready to assemble.

Pressure-treated board Wood that has rot-resistant preservatives forced into it under pressure during the manufacturing process.

Privacy fence Fence with solid or almost solid boards used to lend privacy to whatever it encloses.

Rabbet A cut along the edge of a board that removes only part of the thickness of the board. Often made with a router, this cut leaves a small shelf that is useful in forming joints. Two shallow rabbet cuts on the top and bottom of an edge form a simple tenon.

Rebar Short for reinforcement bar. Metal bars that can be added to concrete piers for added strength.

Rip cut A cut made with the grain to reduce the width of a board. This type of cut is easiest to make on a table saw, but it can be done with a handheld saw, as well.

Strut A structural piece designed to resist pressure in the direction of its length.

Subrail A horizontal rail set between the main upper and lower rails that is used to separate fence sections in designs with more than one material, such as a fence with boards on the low section and lattice on the high section.

Tear-out Shavings lifted on a newly cut face but not trimmed off by the router bit. This is most likely to happen when you are routing with the grain, and the grain pattern twists and turns.

Tenon A tongue formed on the end of a board to fit into a mortise. See also Mortise.

Trellis A latticework used as a light screen or as a support for climbing plants.

Turnbuckle Hardware with an adjustable eye hook at each end, often set on the diagonal to provide extra support for gates.

Utility fencing Also called snow fencing because it reduces snow drifting, it consists of narrow wood slats held together with wire. It is sold in large rolls.

Wane A defect in lumber in which either bark is present or wood is lacking on an edge or corner for any reason.

Welded wire Woven wire mesh available in several grid sizes, often attached to fence posts to act as a trellis for climbing vines or to seal spaces between posts and rails and provide more security.

Sapwood The living wood near the outside of a tree trunk that carries sap. Sapwood is weaker and less stable than the heartwood.

Screw eye Often called an eyescrew, this fastener has the top portion of its shank bent into a circle. It is often used with S-hooks or other hardware to support hanging swings.

Slat A narrow strip of wood typically used in multiples to form a lattice.

Spacer board A board ripped to the width between pickets or other repeating components. It is used to make even spaces on a fence.

Stop block A scrap of wood that is attached to a tool's fence to limit the extent of the cut. For example, a stop block attached to the fence of a miter saw allows you to cut multiple parts to exactly the same length.

Stretcher A horizontal member that extends from post to post.

index

photo credits

Page 1: Charles Mann **pages 6–7:** Jerry Pavia **page 8:** *all* John Parsekian/CH **page 9:** Brian Vanden Brink **pages 10–13:** *all* John Parsekian/CH **page 14:** Mark Lohman **page 16:** *top* Olson Photographic, LLC **page 17:** Mark Lohman **page 20:** *all* John Parsekian/CH **page 21:** Brian Vanden Brink, design: Ron Forest Fences **page 22:** *both top* John Parsekian/CH; *bottom* Brian C. Nieves/CH **pages 23–24:** *all* John Parsekian/CH **page 25:** *all left* Brian C. Nieves/CH; *all right* John Parsekian/CH **pages 26–31:** *all* John Parsekian/CH **page 32:** *all left* Brian C. Nieves/CH; *top center & bottom center* courtesy of California Redwood Association; *both right* Stephen E. Munz **page 33:** *all* courtesy of California Redwood Association **page 34:** *all* Freeze Frame Studios/CH **page 35:** Brian Vanden Brink, design: Ron Forest Fences **pages 36–38:** *all* Freeze Frame Studios/CH **page 39:** *top* Mark Lohman; *bottom* John Parsekian/CH **page 41:** Freeze Frame Studios/CH **page 42:** *both left* Freeze Frame Studios/CH; *right* H. Armstrong Roberts **page 44:** *left* Brian C. Nieves/CH; *right* Mark Lohman **page 45:** *both* Freeze Frame Studios/CH **page 46:** *top* Freeze Frame Studios/CH; *center & bottom* Brian C. Nieves/CH **pages 47–48:** *both* Todd Caverly **page 49:** *all* Brian C. Nieves/CH **page 50–52:** *all* Freeze Frame Studios/CH **page 53:** Mark Lohman **pages 54-55:** *all but bottom right* Brian C. Nieves/CH; *bottom right* Tria Giovan **page 56:** *all* Freeze Frame Studios/CH **page 57:** *top left* Gillian Darley/Edifice Photo; *top right* Philippa Lewis/Edifice Photo; *all other* Brian C. Nieves/CH **page 58:** *all* Freeze Frame Studios/CH **page 59:** *left* courtesy of Vermont Fence; *right* Brian Vanden Brink, design: Ron Forest Fences **page 60:** Brian C. Nieves/CH **page 61:** *all top* Brian C. Nieves/CH; *bottom* Jerry Pavia **pages 62-63:** *all but bottom right* Brian C. Nieves/CH; *bottom right* Todd Caverly **page 64:** *top left* Mark Lohman; *bottom left* Olson Photographic, LLC; *right* Jerry Harpur, design: Bob Clark **pages 65-66:** *all* Freeze Frame Studios/CH **pages 67-71:** *all* Brian C. Nieves/CH **page 72:** *top* Freeze Frame Studios/CH; *center & bottom* Brian C. Nieves/CH **page 73:** Mark Lohman **pages 74-79:** *all* Freeze Frame Studios/CH **pages 80-81:** *all* Brian C. Nieves/CH **page 82:** Mark Lohman **page 83:** *all* Brian C. Nieves/CH **page 84:** *all* Freeze Frame Studios/CH **page 85:** Bufftech Fences, courtesy of Hoover Fence **page 86:** Tony Giammarino/Giammarino & Dworkin **page 87:** *all* Freeze Frame Studios/CH **page 88:** *top* Tony Giammarino/Giammarino & Dworkin; *bottom* courtesy of Stanco **page 89:** *all* Bufftech Fences, courtesy of Hoover Fence **pages 90-93:** *all* Freeze Frame Studios/CH **page 94:** *all* Brian C. Nieves/CH **page 95:** Jerry Pavia

page 96: *top* Jerry Pavia; *center* H. Armstrong Roberts; *bottom* Mike McClintock **page 97:** *top* Mark Lohman; *bottom* Jerry Pavia **pages 98-99:** *all* Freeze Frame Studios/CH **pages 100-103:** *all* Brian C. Nieves/CH **page 104:** *top & center* Brian C. Nieves/CH; *bottom* Freeze Frame Studios/CH **page 105:** Brian Vanden Brink, design: Ron Forest Fences **page 107:** Freeze Frame Studios/CH **page 108:** *top* John Parsekian/CH; *both bottom* Brian C. Nieves/CH **pages 109-114:** *all* Brian C. Nieves/CH **page 115:** *top left* Gillian Darley/Edifice Photo; *all others* Brian C. Nieves/CH **page 116:** *all left* John Parsekian/CH; *right* Brian C. Nieves/CH **page 117:** *bottom right both* Freeze Frame Studios/CH; *all others* Brian C. Nieves/CH **pages 118-119:** *all* Brian C. Nieves/CH **page 120:** *top & bottom* Freeze Frame Studios/CH; *center* Brian C. Nieves/CH **page 121:** Jerry Pavia **pages 122-123:** *bottom* Freeze Frame Studios/CH; *top* Mark Lohman **page 124:** *top* Jerry Pavia; *bottom* Brian C. Nieves/CH **page 125:** *both top* Freeze Frame Studios/CH; *center left* courtesy of Garden Iron; *center right* Jerry Harpur, design: Oehme Van Sweden; *bottom* Brian C. Nieves/CH **page 126:** John Parsekian/CH **page 127:** *top* Olson Photographic, LLC; *bottom* Freeze Frame Studios/CH **pages 128–129:** *all but Smart Tip* Freeze Frame Studios/CH; *Smart Tip* John Parsekian/CH **page 130:** *top* Freeze Frame Studios/CH; *center left* Dr. James Jarett, Mississippi State University, Dept. of Entomology; *center right* John Parsekian/CH; *bottom left & bottom right* Agricultural Research Service **page 131:** *all* Brian C. Nieves/CH **page 132-133:** *Smart Tip* Brian C. Nieves/CH; *all others* Freeze Frame Studios/CH **pages 134-135:** *Smart Tip* Brian C. Nieves/CH; *all others* Freeze Frame Studios/CH **page 136:** *top* Brian Vanden Brink; *center* Positive Images, design: Gay Bumgarner Design; *bottom* Richard Felber **page 137:** Walter Chandoha **page 138:** *left* Walter Chandoha; *top right* Jennifer Ramcke, garden by: Maggie & Frank Cefalu; *bottom right* Derek Fell **page 139:** Richard Felber **page 140:** Brian Vanden Brink, architect: Ron Forest Fences **page 141:** *top* Richard Felber; *bottom* Walter Chandoha **page 142:** *both* Brian Vanden Brink **page 143:** Richard Felber **page 144:** Brian Vanden Brink, architect: Dominic Mercadante **page 145:** *left* Positive Images, design: Gay Bumgarner Design; *bottom left* Jerry Pavia; *bottom right* Walter Chandoha **page 146:** *top* Tony Giammarino/Giammarino & Dworkin; *bottom* courtesy of California Redwood Association **page 147:** *top* Brian Vanden Brink; *bottom* Walter Chandoha **pages 148-149:** *top left* Richard Felber; *top right* Donna H. Chiarelli/CH; *bottom left* Philip Clayton-Thompson, garden by: Karen & Frank

Capillupo; *bottom right* Brian Vanden Brink, design: Weatherend Estate Furniture **page 150:** *top* Derek Fell; *bottom* Jerry Pavia, Butchart Gardens **page 151:** *left* Walter Chandoha; *right* Tony Giammarino/Giammarino & Dworkin **page 152:** *all* Donna H. Chiarelli/CH **page 153:** Mark Lohman **pages 154–213:** *all* Donna H. Chiarelli/CH **page 214:** *top* courtesy of Trellis Structures; *bottom* courtesy of Elyria Fence, Inc. **page 215:** *top* courtesy of Elyria Fence, Inc.; *bottom* courtesy of Trellis Structures **page 216:** *top* Jerry Howard/Positive Images; *bottom* Philip Clayton-Thompson, garden by: Bev Cooney **page 217:** Richard Felber **pages 218-251:** *all* Donna H. Chiarelli/CH **page 252:** *top* Richard Felber; *bottom* Walter Chandoha **page 253:** Richard Felber **page 254:** courtesy of Elyria Fence, Inc. **page 255:** *top* courtesy of Trellis Structures; *bottom* courtesy of Elyria Fence, Inc. **page 256:** *top* Anne Gordon Images; *bottom* Jerry Howard/Positive Images, design: Bernie Tatleis **page 257:** *left* Brian Vanden Brink, architect: Payette & Associates; *both right* Walter Chandoha **page 258:** *top* Anne Gordon Images; *center* David Cavagnaro; *bottom* Neil Soderstrom/Michael Cady **page 259:** Derek Fell **page 260:** *left* Anne Gordon Images; *right* Jerry Pavia **page 263:** Jerry Pavia **page 264:** David Cavagnaro **page 265:** Jerry Howard/Positive Images **page 266:** *top left* Jerry Pavia; *top right* John Glover; *inset* Jerry Pavia; *bottom left* John Bova/Photo Researchers; *bottom right* Derek Fell **page 267:** *top left* Walter Chandoha; *top right* Derek Fell; *bottom left* Anne Gordon Images; *bottom right* Alan & Linda Detrick **page 268:** *left* Walter Chandoha; *inset, top center & bottom center* Derek Fell; *top right* Jerry Pavia; *bottom right* Michael Gadomski/Photo Researchers **page 269:** *top left* Anne Gordon Images; *top right* Derek Fell; *bottom left* Jerry Pavia; *bottom right* Michael S. Thompson **page 270:** *top left & bottom left* Walter Chandoha; *center & right* David Cavagnaro **page 271:** *top left* John Glover; *top center* Walter Chandoha; *top right* Neil Holmes/Garden Picture Library; *bottom left* David Cavagnaro; *bottom right* Jerry Pavia **page 272:** *both* Derek Fell **page 273:** *top* Neil Soderstrom/ Michael Cady; *bottom* Derek Fell **page 274:** *top left* John Glover; *top right & bottom left* Derek Fell; *bottom right* Jerry Pavia **page 275:** *all* Derek Fell **page 276:** *top left* Derek Fell; *top right* Jerry Pavia; *bottom left & bottom right* Michael S. Thompson **page 277:** *all left* Derek Fell; *top right* Jerry Pavia; *bottom right* Derek Fell **page 279:** Jerry Pavia **page 280:** Brian Vanden Brink, architect: Payette & Associates **page 282:** courtesy of Trellis Structures **page 286:** Walter Chandoha

Have a home improvement, decorating, or gardening project? Look for these and other fine Creative Homeowner books wherever books are sold.

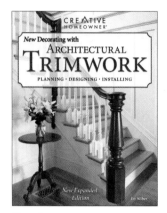

Transform a room with trimwork. Over 550 color photos and illustrations. 240 pp.; 8¹/₂" × 10⁷/₈"
BOOK #: 277500

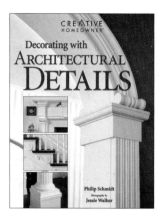

Covers design treatments such as moldings and window seats. 300+ color photos. 224 pp.; 8¹/₂" × 10⁷/₈"
BOOK #: 278225

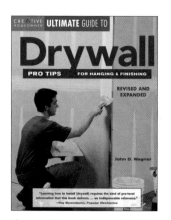

A complete guide covering all aspects of drywall. Over 450 color photos 160 pp.; 8¹/₂" × 10⁷/₈"
BOOK #: 278320

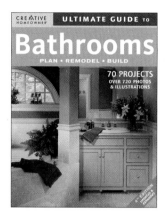

Includes step-by-step projects and over 630 photos.
272 pp.; 8¹/₂" × 10⁷/₈"
BOOK#: 278632

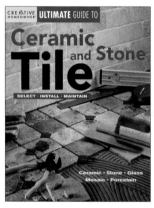

Complete DIY tile instruction. Over 550 color photos and illustrations. 224 pp.; 8¹/₂" × 10⁷/₈"
BOOK #: 27753

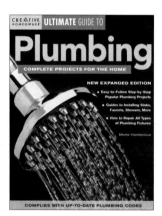

The complete manual for plumbing. Over 750 color photos and illustrations. 288 pp.; 8¹/₂" × 10⁷/₈"
BOOK#: 278200

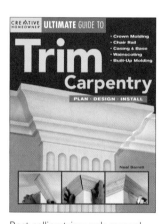

Best-selling trimwork manual. Over 500 color photos and illustrations. 208 pp.; 8¹/₂" × 10⁷/₈"
BOOK#: 277516

The ultimate home-improvement reference manual. Over 300 step-by-step projects. 608 pp.; 9" × 10⁷/₈"
BOOK#: 267870

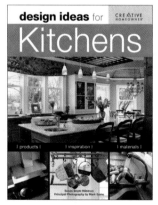

Design inspiration for creating a new kitchen. Over 500 color photographs. 224 pp.; 8¹/₂" ×10⁷/₈"
BOOK #: 279415

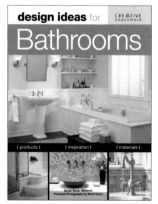

Design inspiration for creating a new bathroom. Over 500 color photos. 224 pp.; 8¹/₂" × 10⁷/₈"
BOOK #: 279268

An impressive guide to garden design and plant selection. 950 color photos and illustrations. 384 pp.; 9" × 10"
BOOK #: 274610

Lavishly illustrated, with descriptions of over 1,000 plants; more than 700 photos. 240 pp.; 9" × 10"
BOOK #: 274222